CONSTITUTIONALISM
IN AMERICA

VOLUME II

EL PLURIBUS UNUM

Constitutional Principles and the Institutions of Government

EDITED BY

SARAH BAUMGARTNER THUROW

University of Dallas

UNIVERSITY
PRESS OF
AMERICA

Lanham • New York • London

Library of Congress Cataloging-in-Publication Data

E pluribus unum.

(Constitutionalsim in America ; v. 2)
"First presented as papers at a conference at the University of Dallas in Irving, Texas,
on October 16, 17, and 18, 1986"—Pref.
Includes bibliographical references.
1. Separation of powers—United States—History—Congresses.
2. Federal government—United States—History—Congresses.
I. Thurow, Sarah Baumgartner, 1947–   . II. Series.
KF4541.A2C58   1988   vol. 2   87–31723 CIP
[KF4565]   342.73 s [342.73'04]
347.302 s [347.3024]

ISBN 0–8191–6778–9 (v. 2 : alk. paper)
ISBN 0–8191–6779–7 (pbk. : v. 2 : alk. paper)

Contents

4 The Judiciary: Supreme Interpreter of the Constitution?

5 Federalism and Freedom

Contributors   286

Preface

The essays in this volume were first presented as papers at a conference at the University of Dallas in Irving, Texas, on October 16, 17, and 18, 1986. The concluding essays were written by the panel moderators and are meant in part to preserve the best of the conference comment and debate as well as to suggest how each essay relates to the overall concerns of the conference.

Both the conference and publication of this volume were supported by a grant from the Bicentennial Office of the National Endowment for the Humanities. The University of Dallas Bicentennial Project has been recognized by The Commission on the Bicentennial of the United States Constitution. The opinions in this volume are those of the contributors and do not in any way reflect official policy of the National Endowment, the Commission on the Bicentennial, the United States Government, or the University of Dallas.

The participants in the conference were as follows. Panel 1: Anne M. Cohler, Dennis J. Mahoney, Michael P. Zuckert, Jeremy Rabkin, and Harold Hyman. Panel 2: Robert Scigliano, Jane Mansbridge, John Marini, and Morris Fiorina. Panel 3: Richard H. Cox, Larry Berman, Ken Masugi, Mackubin T. Owens, and Robert Krueger. Panel 4a: Grant B. Mindle, Gary L. McDowell, Jeffrey Wallin, and Clovis C. Morrisson. Panel 4b: Louis Fisher, Lino A. Graglia, Glen E. Thurow, and Neil Cogan. Panel 5: James L. Gibson, David Broyles, John Adams Wettergreen, M.E. Bradford, and Joshua Miller.

I wish to thank my husband, Glen, for his constant support and encouragement of this project as well as his invaluable advice in formulating the issues and structure of the conferences. Both Glen Thurow and Thomas West deserve credit for helping to select and invite such a well-balanced program of conference participants. Finally, I wish to thank those without whose help publication of this volume would not have been possible: Kate Hohlt, who cheerfully mastered the word-processing machine; Calan Thurow, who invented ingenious means for electronic copy editing; and especially Nicholas Janszen, who labored long hours beyond the call of duty to assist me in compiling, editing, and typesetting the book.

Sarah Baumgartner Thurow
Irving, Texas
August 5, 1987

Introduction

Constitutionalism in America

There is no time more appropriate than the Bicentennial of the Constitution for citizens and scholars to lift their eyes from immediate concerns to reflect on the principles, institutions, and way of life that characterize the United States. Our 200-year-old Constitution forms the center of our public and common life. It is the fount of all our political authority and constitutes us as a particular people guided by certain fundamental laws, institutions, and principles. What shape does the Constitution give—or ought it to give—to the lives and character of Americans? How may its influence be deepened or improved? What are the obstacles which may threaten the continuation of constitutional government, or the possibilities which may allow for its perfection? The aim of this series is to encourage both scholarly and public reflection upon these and other issues of constitutionalism in America.

There are three habits or opinions which hinder reflection on the fundamental principles of constitutional government and which these books are meant to combat. Chief among these is the habit of taking constitutional government for granted because it has endured for so long. What was a difficult task of construction for our forefathers has become an easy inheritance for us. We need to be reminded that such a familiar phenomenon as the rule of law is an achievement attained with difficulty and with difficulty maintained. In the first *Federalist*, Hamilton conveys the conviction shared by many of the founders that constitutional government is a momentous and unprecedented undertaking. A wrong step would destroy the possibility of "establishing good government from reflection and choice," and would not only condemn future generations of Americans to governments founded on "accident and force," but be "the general misfortune of mankind." One aim of these volumes, then, is to recapture this sense of the importance and fragility of constitutional government. Our intention is to reawaken the knowledge that constitutional government must be constantly examined, constantly attended to, constantly cared for.

Connected with this danger of an easy complacency is the danger that constitutional government may be fundamentally altered without our being aware of the change or what it may signify. Not only may circumstances such as the growth of technology or industry bring about new conditions requiring new applications of old principles, but our principles themselves may change without our being aware of it. We may speak the language of the founding, the language of equality and liberty, but mean something very different from what our forefathers meant by the same words. We may then fail to understand both our present situation and the original constitution. To reflect upon our constitutional principles thus requires Americans to confront the different understandings of such concepts as liberty, equality, and political rights evident in the writings and deeds of the founders as well as in our contemporary debate. This is not to say that where there are differences the advantage is always with the founders, but reflection on these differences is always necessary to make certain we have not unconsciously declined, to understand where we have been and where we are going, and to provoke reflection about what we are by reference to what we ought to be.

Thirdly, Tocqueville long ago noted that the chief danger to democracy in America was that it would decline unawares into a soft despotism. Liberty, that rallying cry of the Revolution, would come to be understood as the easy life of private gratification. The life formed by such a conception would be that of "an innumerable multitude of men, alike and equal, constantly circling around in pursuit of the petty and banal pleasures with which they glut their souls." Such people are suited for tyranny, not for the arduous life of self-governing men and women. By liberty the founders seem to have understood, first and decisively, the activity of republican government, an activity characterized by public-mindedness, rigorous control of one's private desires for gratification or self-expression, and ceaseless devotion to the common good. The founders equated freedom with living under the law and contributing to the making of law. Perhaps the most essential activity for a free people, therefore, was the habit of continually reflecting upon the fundamental principles of government by constitution. Without such reflection public discourse was all too likely to become immired in partisan and legalistic concerns and to lose all sense of common purpose.

The three volume series, *Constitutionalism in America*, addresses the American experience of government by constitution, first, by examining the distinctive principles which went into the framing of our Constitution; second, by considering how those principles were incorporated into the structures, institutions, and practices of government; and third, by re-examining constitutionalism itself both as a theory of politics and as a mode of political order.

The chapters in each volume are composed of one essay examining the founders' understanding of the issue, one examining today's views, and a concluding essay intended to recreate a sense of lively controversy, both with respect to what exactly the founders meant to do—or did without meaning to do—and with respect to what we today ought to think and do.

Volume II: *E Pluribus Unum: Constitutional Principles and the Institutions of Government*

The American Revolution has often been distinguished from the French by the fact that it resulted in a set of lasting constitutional institutions. The complexity of these institutions is as striking as their endurance. To understand them is to receive an education in the practical application of the principles of free government. Their endurance and complexity, however, have too often led observers to focus on particular questions of partisan or operational concern. This narrow perspective has led to the decay of a comprehensive understanding of these institutions and their place in the constitutional whole.

The aim of this volume is to raise again for both scholars and public the possibility of viewing our major institutions in a constitutional perspective. The essay topics have been chosen to include the two great structural principles of American government—separation of powers and federalism—and an examination of each of the three branches. Each chapter contains one essay examining the founders' views and one examining today's views in order to provide a breadth of perspective seldom given to institutional issues in contemporary political science. The authors represent the disciplines of political science, history, and law, as well as a variety of partisan and institutional perspectives.

In *Federalist #47*, Madison pronounces the accumulation of all powers, legislative, executive, and judiciary in the same hands" to be "the very definition of tyranny." The founders believed that their goal of limited government was achievable only by the principle of the separation of powers. But is the separation of powers the best way to secure limited government or does it create a "deadlock of democracy"? In Chapter One Anne Cohler argues that what the founders had in mind was less a *limited* government—as we have come to think of it today—than a *moderate* government, as Montesquieu understood that term. She offers an original and remarkable reading of *The Federalist* and the founding as reflecting less the principles of Locke than those of Montesquieu, attributing much of our present dissatisfaction with the constitutional separation of powers to our failure to understand the character of moderate government.

Dennis Mahoney traces the origin of today's misunderstanding of—and consequent opposition to—separated power in the political science which emerged out of the Progressive and New Deal eras. The founders' separated *political* powers have been replaced by a separation of politics from "administration," both in theory and in practice. Mahoney attributes the failure of the founders' system to work despite our misunderstanding of it to two factors: a change in the motives of the men in the legislative branch—a subject taken up in Chapter Two—and the acceptance of "judicial supremacy"—which is discussed in Chapter Four.

In any regime the character of the laws is of primary importance. In a liberal democracy the laws must reflect the popular will, and they seek prudently to secure the common good. How is Congress as an institution designed to reconcile these two potentially antagonistic goals? Have changes in Congress, such as the transformation of its staff into a major bureaucracy, worked to increase or diminish its capacity for deliberation? In Chapter Two Robert Scigliano provides an historical account of the development of the role of Congress in American government during the first half-century, showing especially that disputes between the executive and legislative branches over their respective powers in administration and foreign policy are nothing new. He traces the origin of standing commitees in Congress to the effort to prevent members of the executive branch from "deliberating" in Congress and, ironically, in the efforts of the executive to do just that. Jane Mansbridge examines the movement of deliberation from the floor of Congress to the committees, to the staffs, and "out the door" to parties, interest groups, and academic conferences. She concludes that the central deliberative role of Congress today seems to be "to aggregate and operationalize the deliberation of others," although she does not agree with Mahoney that our representatives no longer have ambition for more than reelection.

In claiming the right even to violate a law in order to carry out his duties, Lincoln asked, "are all the laws, but one, to go unexecuted, and the government itself to go to pieces, lest that one be violated?" Now that the President is the head of government for a superpower in a nuclear age, how far should his authority extend beyond the mere execution of the laws? Chapter Three begins with Richard Cox's detailed analysis of the philosophic considerations involved in constructing the executive in a republican constitution. He traces the problem of executive prerogative as both the major threat to human freedom and a necessity for good government from Hamilton's treatment of it back to Locke and Aristotle. Larry Berman, on the other hand, calls for greater executive-legislative unity for the sake of effective governance, without however, sacrificing republican safety. This is possible, he argues, because "checks and balances are not necessarily synonymous with separation of powers"—as many European governments demonstrate—and because a properly formed "government" increases the accountability of the executive.

In *Cooper v. Aaron* (1958) the Supreme Court declared that its interpretations of the Constitution are "the supreme law of the land," thus claiming for itself the same authority as the Constitution. Is this a fulfillment of the nature of constitutional government which secures the supremacy of the law and the protection of minority rights against partisanship and majority tyranny? Or does it undermine the constitutional government by placing one of its institutions above the Constitution itself? In order to reflect the extent of the current controversy over this issue we have included four essays in Chapter Four. Lino Graglia argues that the power of the Supreme Court has gone so far that it no longer makes sense to say that the American people in any way govern themselves: our constitution is no longer that of a republic—if, indeed, it ever was, given the potential for judicial review—but that of an almost monarchical oligarchy. Gary McDowell, too, views the Court as overstepping the bounds of a republican institution. He notes this especially vividly in the fact that the debate over the interpretation of the Constitution no longer turns on the question of strict versus broad interpretation, but on the question of whether to refer to the Constitution at all. Grant Mindle and Louis Fisher, on the other hand, see the Court's role as that of a power above the partisan fray capable of defending republican freedom against the tyrannies of minority or majority. In his detailed analysis of the judiciary debate of 1802, Mindle argues that what has appeared at times to be outrageous partisanship designed to thwart the democratic will may also manifest itself as an admirable independence for the purpose of guarding the rule of law. And Fisher argues that the Court's power over the Consitution is greatly exaggerated, that the truly authoritative interpretive process takes place elsewhere as well, in the other branches and in public debate.

Tocqueville wrote: "Local institutions are to liberty what primary schools are to science; they put it within the people's reach." Is local autonomy, as Tocqueville thought, necessary for the development of a citizenry suitable for free, democratic government, or are freedom and equality threatened by local prejudice and the states? In the final chapter James Gibson sets out to prove by empirical data that federalism, far from decreasing political repression and majority tyranny, actually increases it within the states. He argues that small, homogeneous communities are inherently intolerant, and therefore, to the extent that the federal system allows such communities to persist and to govern themselves it fosters majority tyranny and political repression. David Broyles notes that both the partisans of the left and those of the right today—particularly in academe—are essentially "antifederalists" in their desire for a government which does not judge the merit of differing groups and individuals, but seeks only to guarantee them their "right" to self-expression. He sees in such a government the victory of "the Hobbesian war on politics" and the elimination of statesmanship.

Chapter One

Separation of Powers and Limited Government

*In **Federalist** #47, Madison pronounces "the accumulation of all powers, legislative, executive, and judiciary in the same hands" to be "the very definition of tyranny." The founders believed that their goal of limited government was achievable only by the principle of the separation of powers. But is the separation of powers the best way to secure limited government or does it create a "deadlock of democracy"?*

Moderate and Free Government:
The Division of Powers

Anne M. Cohler

In considering and writing the Constitution in 1787 the question for the founders was to assure a moderate rather than a despotic government, not to assure a limited rather than an absolute government. To put the matter another way, the problem was not to limit sovereignty, but to shape its use. Rule was to be exercised in a particular way, according to a law. This point of view is close to that of Montesquieu's in *The Spirit of the Laws*. Here we are going to take a look at the U.S. Constitution, as it was first devised and written, from the point of view of the first half of the eighteenth century in France, rather than, as is more commonplace, the seventeenth century in England.

In 1766, Louis XV stood before the Parlement of Paris and gave a speech that expresses eloquently the despot's view of rule. The Parlement of Paris was a court which claimed powers analogous to those of our Supreme Court by asserting that it could refuse to inscribe, and thus then to enforce, the king's laws if they were not congruent with past laws and with the way things were done, with the constitution. However, the king could appear in person and require that the laws be inscribed. The king said, in part:

> To try to make principles of such pernicious novelties is to injure the magistracy, to deny its institutional position, to betray its interests and to disregard the fundamental laws of the state; as if anyone could forget that the sovereign power resides in my person only, that sovereign power of which the natural characteristics are the spirit of consultation, justice, and reason; that my courts derive their existence and their authority from me alone; that the plenitude of that authority, which they only exercise in my name, always remains with me, and that it can never be employed against me; that to me alone belongs legislative power without subordination and undivided; that it is by my authority alone that the officers of my courts proceed, not to the formation, but to the registration, the publication, the execution of the law, and that it is permitted for them to remonstrate only within the limits of the duty of good and useful councilors; that public order in its entirety emanates from me, and that the rights and interests of the nation, which some

dare to regard as a separate body from the monarch, are necessarily
united with my rights and interest, and repose only in my hands.[1]

One can well imagine a democratic people speaking, in effect, in Louis
XV's voice. The danger in despotic rule is rule through fear, through fear
of the capricious, unpredictable, unreliable will of the powerful despot,
who is subject only to his own passions. If we listen to Madison's description of the passions of the people, we can hear more than an echo of
Montesquieu's fear of such a despot.

Despotism in a democracy is due to the tendency of the passions of the
people to move the whole, or a substantial majority. The size of the group
is critical: the passions cannot move easily across a vast country, or within
a small group.

> The truth is, that in all cases a certain number at least seems to be
> necessary to secure the benefits of free consultation and discussion and
> to guard against too easy a combination for improper purposes: As on
> the other hand, the number ought at most to be kept within a certain
> limit, in order to avoid the confusion and intemperance of a multitude.
> In all very numerous assemblies, of whatever characters composed,
> passion never fails to wrest the scepter from reason. Had every Athen-
> ian citizen been a Socrates; every Athenian assembly would still have
> been a mob.[2]

Passions affect groups of men in the same way. Their danger is in their
making groups with identical views, in their sweeping across a democratic
assembly.

The passions tend toward unanimity; it is reason that divides men.

> When men exercise their reason coolly and freely, on a variety of
> distinct questions, they inevitably fall into different opinions, on some
> of them. When they are governed by a common passion, their opinions
> if they are so to be called, will be the same.[3]

This view of the relation between passion and reason in politics runs quite
counter to the most frequently seen enlightenment view, in which it is the
private interests and passions which divide men, who would be unified
and even unanimous if their prejudices did not obscure the reasonable
view, which was assumed to be singular. Reason in the Federalist does not
seem to be an abstract truth to which everyone should aspire, but the

---

1. "Excerpts from the Official Transcript of the 'Session of the Scourging,' " 3 March 1766
   in *History of Western Civilization*, Topic VIII *The Ancient Regime and the French Revolution*,
   Selected Readings by the College History Staff (Chicago: The University of Chicago
   Press, 1982), p. 84.
2. *Federalist* 55, see also 62, 63, 78.
3. *Federalist* 50.

varying results of applying thought to the variety of goods pursued in political life. Thus, division checks the passions and can encourage reason.

Moderate governments are those in which the rulers obey the law, in which there is some rule other than the momentary will of the ruler. Free governments are a kind of moderate government, one within which there is some space for political action and choice "formed by a certain distribution of the three powers" and, for the citizen, "security or one's opinion of one's security" formed by the disposition of the laws, received examples, and certain civil laws.[4] It is in this context that one can understand the purposes of the division of power in the American Constitution, the claim that tyranny is, as the "celebrated Montesquieu" said, the consequence of the accumulation of legislative, executive, and judicial powers in the same hands and liberty the consequence of separate powers.[5]

First, we must understand what the meaning of moderate government would be to Montesquieu in a context like that of America in the eighteenth century. Montesquieu says that moderate governments are those with some principle of action, and therefore some regularity, other than the will of the ruler. Rule whose only guide is the will of the ruler is despotic. The activities of moderate governments, then, are necessarily limited by whatever the rulers—whoever they are—are to pursue. In this sense, moderate government is limited government. Although Montesquieu calls aristocracies in which the nobles restrain themselves from taking advantage of others and democratic republics with a virtuous citizenry which obeys its own laws moderate, this kind of moderation, which is a result of the education and character of a citizenry, is not the issue here. Such moderation was—as he, *The Federalist*, and the Anti-Federalists agreed—only possible in small, intensely regulated and ordered countries. Rather, the issue is the moderation that is intrinsic to Montesquieu's monarchies, to his English example, and conceivably to a new, large democratic republic. That moderation is the result of something within, or about, the government that acts upon and influences all its activities and the activities of all those who take part in it.

A moderate government in this last sense has a life, a spirit, a spring of its own. Early in his book, in the first discussion of moderation in the sense of its being intrinsic to some governments just as despotism is to others, Montesquieu remarks:

---

4. Montesquieu, *The Spirit of the Laws* 12.1 (The translations are from: Montesquieu, *The Spirit of the Laws*, tr. by Anne M. Cohler, Basia M. Gulati, and Harold Stone).

5. *Federalist* 47.

A moderate government can, as much as it wants and without peril, relax its springs. It maintains itself by its laws and even by its force.[6]

In monarchical and moderate states, power is limited by that which is its spring; I mean honor, which reigns like a monarch over the prince and the people.[7]

Moderate governments have both some strength apart from the power of the rulers and some spring that acts upon the rulers. The limits on their actions come, therefore, not externally, but internally. That is, they are limited not because they ought not do certain things—whether by precept or fear, even fear of the wrath of the people—but because doing such things is not in the nature of the government; they could not imagine doing them and would be unable to carry them out.

Montesquieu offers two examples of such a government. The first is his monarchy. There, the king is sovereign but he must rule through the nobility. The great offices of the kingdom are filled by the old warrior nobility and the judicial offices by the newer judicial nobility. As the old nobility expends itself and its wealth in service to the monarchy, its membership can gradually be replaced from the judicial nobility. The members of these great families, including that of the king, think well of themselves, think they deserve such distinction: they have a sense of honor. That sense of honor makes it difficult for the king to ask, or for the nobility to perform, dishonorable acts—whether as executive or as judicial officers of the kingdom. But the limits of monarchical moderation are marked by the fact that nobles indeed do dishonorable things at the king's behest and that the will of the king can be inscribed as law whether or not the proposal is consistent with what might have been called constitutional practice when he appears in person before the parlement. The king in these instances acts as a willful sovereign, outside of the established channels, rather than as a member of the nobility.

In the English example, Montesquieu takes up the institutions of the English government, explaining how their interaction leads to both moderation and liberty. The House of Commons is immediately recognizable as a representative institution. Montesquieu, like *The Federalist*, assumes the need for such an institution in a government claiming to be free, saying: "As in a free state, every man, considered to have a free soul, should be governed by himself, the people as a body should have legisla-

---

6. Montesquieu, *The Spirit of the Laws* 3.9.
7. Montesquieu, *The Spirit of the Laws* 3.10.

tive power; but, as this is impossible in large states and is subject to many drawbacks in small ones, the people must have their representatives do all that they themselves cannot do."[8] It is essential to a free government that each man think he could have been the legislators or the judges (jurors). It is in this sense that a free government is also a democracy. Like the king in the monarchy, the people in a republic rule, but they rule through others formed into institutions. Here the institutions are more carefully crafted into an intricate balance of power that will maintain itself without being identified with any order or rank. Montesquieu's England does still have a House of Lords and an inherited monarchy. One is to be a check on the aspirations of the popular branch toward despotic leveling and the other to be the executor of the laws of others. To the extent to which the nobility and the king of England were content to perform offices England was truly a republic under the forms of an absolute government.[9]

To move on to the American case, one need only imagine a situation in which the demand is that the government be altogether free, democratic, republican, that there be no other source for the rulers than the people, who are not differentiated by inheritance into political categories. But also, such a government is to be moderate in the sense that it obeys the law and to be free in the sense that decisions are a result of deliberation, not of the force of the passions of the majority. To be moderate such a government must somehow be given an orderly life of its own. That order must be reflected sufficiently in the population that it too obeys the law and does not force its erratic will upon the government. To be free, that orderly life must somehow encourage, even require, the deliberation characteristic of free men governing themselves. In this essay, I shall examine the thinking of those at the Constitutional Convention and in *The Federalist* and suggest that this structure of thought characterizes the way they went about devising and defending the new Constitution. First, I shall take up some evidence that they thought of the government as moderate and not limited, that it was defined by its own purposes not those arising directly from its source, the people. Second, I shall take up the question of the structure that gave life to those purposes—the separation and balance of powers.

---

8. Montesquieu, *The Spirit of the Laws* 11.6.
9. Montesquieu, *The Spirit of the Laws* 19.27.

Moderation

The propositions "that the means ought to be proportioned to the end; that every power ought to be commensurate with its object; that there ought to be no limitation of a power destined to effect a purpose, which is itself incapable of limitations,"[10] run throughout the first thirty-six *Federalist* papers. In these papers, it is the need to provide for the common defense that brings along an array of powers to the federal government, particularly the power to raise and maintain an army and the power to tax directly. Given the limitless possibilities for actions that the government might need to take, its powers must be as limitless. But this proposition is coupled with the argument that adherence to this principle will encourage adherence to the law:

> that nations pay little regard to rules and maxims calculated in their very nature to run counter to the necessities of society. Wise politicians will be cautious about fettering the government with restrictions that cannot be observed; because they know that every breach of the fundamental laws, though dictated by necessity, impairs that sacred reverence, which ought to be maintained in the breasts of rulers towards the constitution of a country, and forms a precedent for other breaches, where the same plea of necessity does not exist at all, or is less urgent and palpable.[11]

No disjunction is envisioned between a governmental power without formal limits and one which observes the law. That is, *The Federalist* sought a government that was moderate in Montesquieu's sense, a government that follows the laws, that stays within the bounds implied by its purposes as it deals with the circumstances that affect it.

Let us turn briefly to the Lockian prerogative to make clear the distinction between this moderate government and that limited government. "This power to act according to discretion for the public, without the prescriptions of the law and sometimes against it, is that which is called 'prerogative' . . . ."[12] Locke goes on to say that in the infancy of governments almost all of government was prerogative. The law, then, is a kind of codification from experience of the judgments about the proper applications of natural right in the circumstances of a particular country. The best rulers present the greatest dangers to the law, and Locke offers no remedy other than the appeal to heaven, the sense of the majority that

---

10. *Federalist* 31.
11. *Federalist* 25.
12. John Locke, *Second Treatise of Government.* 160

they are weary of such rule.[13] There is no suggestion here, as there was in *The Federalist*, that the law could somehow contain the responses to extraordinary circumstances. For the law to be able to contain, and even shape, the responses to these unforeseen events, it must hold within itself some principles of action other than, even beyond, executing the natural right in a given circumstance.

In this moderate government, the character of the government is primarily thought to be a result of the government itself, not of the character of the underlying population. In the American founding there were primarily two contexts in which the character of the people who were to make up this new government was raised. First, there was an attempt to describe the structure of the population of Americans. Second, although characteristics of the citizenry, of the voting public, were touched upon, it remained peripheral to the discussion of the shape of the American government. This concern for the underlying shape of the population, lack of direct concern with a citizenry, and ultimately an interest in the effect of the government back on the population characterize Montesquieu's approach to moderate government.

The assessment that the new government had to be republican was based on an analysis of the character or genius of the people, upon which there was little disagreement. Madison simply remarked that, "It is evident that no other form would be reconcilable with the genius of the people of America; with the fundamental principles of the revolution, or with that honorable determination which animates every votary of freedom, to rest all our political experiments on the capacity of mankind for self-government."[14] Madison, like other Americans, assumes that the government is to be republican. There is no other choice because the population has no shape that can be used to give shape to a government: it has neither king, nobility, nor commons. In arguments over the suitability of England's use as a model during the Constitutional Convention, it was often said that England was of limited use as an example because it was a mixed government based on ranks and orders that had existed for a long time.[15] Even if monarchical, aristocratic, or democratic tendencies existed within the state, or always in all government, they had not taken a form

---

13. John Locke, *Second Treatise of Government* 160. See also discussion in *Federalist* 49 of Jefferson's suggestion of an appeal to the people.
14. *Federalist* 39.
15. *The Records of the Federal Convention of 1787*, 4 vols., ed. Max Farrand, vol. 1 (New Haven, Conn., 1937), Pinckeny, pp. 397-404; Madison, p. 421-423; Hamilton, p. 424-425.

that offered sufficient shape to the population to make mixing possible.[16] In addition, to point out that a proposal might lead to the development of a nobility and a people as distinct bodies was a criticism. Thus, more than one office could not be held by one person;[17] and sumptuary laws designed to keep the appearance of equality were admired,[18] but left aside with little conversation. A nobility, and thus a monarch, were prohibited.[19] The consequence of ending British rule, forbidding the development of a nobility and a monarchy, and not encouraging the development of an egalitarian democratic citizenry, was to leave the population formless.

In *Federalist 10*, Madison defends this very formlessness as the condition of republican politics, arguing that the very size of the United States would encourage its continuation by making difficult the most likely formation, that of democratic majorities. But Madison's remarks in the Constitutional Convention make it clear that he saw the distinction between Northern and Southern States—between societies based on slavery and those based on the work of free men—as central to the country at the time of the Constitution. In a late effort to establish representation in proportion to the population, he says: "It seemed now to be pretty well understood that the real difference of interests lay, not between the large & small but between the N. & South. States. The institution of slavery & and its consequences formed the line of discrimination."[20] Slavery produces an inherited, stable distinction between people. Thus there was a setted distinction between societies with and those without slaves that was quite contrary to the assumption that there were no permanent distinctions in the underlying population upon which this moderate republic was to be built. One is led to wonder whether Madison thought the union and its size could overcome the distinction caused by slavery.

The discussions of citizenship, of the suffrage, in a government based on the people take place only indirectly.[21] The census which establishes the population for the proportional representation in the House of Representatives; the criteria for voting for members of the House of Representatives, whose membership alone was to be directly elected; and the

---

16. *Records of the Federal Convention*, vol. 1, Franklin, pp. 82-83.
17. *Records of the Federal Convention*, vol. 2, pp. 284-287.
18. *Records of the Federal Convention*, vol. 2, p. 344, pp. 606-607.
19. Article 1, Section 9.
20. *Records of the Federal Convention*, vol. 2, p. 10. See also vol. 1, p. 476, p. 486 and vol. 2, pp. 370-374 for an illustration of the ease with which a discussion of this issue could begin.
21. In *Federalist 52*, the criteria are for the representatives, not for those who were to select them.

addition of new states all raised the issue of who was to be considered a citizen. The question of the census was considered in the context of a discussion of whether to apportion representation by some measure of wealth or of population. The agreement to count "other persons" as three-fifths of ordinary persons was interpreted by some as a compromise with the view that wealth was to be included in the criteria for establishing the ground for representation.[22] A brief discussion of the possibility of limiting the suffrage for the House of Representatives to freeholders raised sore issues—including that of counting the slaves as three-fifths— late in the Convention when these issues seemed settled.[23] Finally, an objection to admitting new states on equal grounds with the old in unlimited numbers was met with the observation that their inhabitants would be "our children and our grand Children" and not revived.[24]

The shape of political life, its moderation and its purpose, were not thought to be a direct consequence of things external to the political organization itself: neither the principle that governments are properly limited to certain activities, nor the character and principles of the citizenry. Rather, the Constitution seemed to have been based on an assertion that limits engender distrust for the law and that care must be taken to see to it that the population acquire no set shape or characteristics that would lead to or require expression in the political life. In a country like America where the basis for government is assumed to be democratic, representation makes it possible for political life to assume a shape.

"The distinction between these [ancients] and the American Governments lies *in the total exclusion of the people in their collective capacity* from any share in the *latter*, and not in the *total exclusion of representatives of the people*, from the administration of the former . . . ."[25] Montesquieu had written similarly that "the ancients did not at all know the government founded on a body of nobility and even less the government founded on a legislative body formed of the representatives of a nation."[26] Here representation must bear the entire burden of giving moderation and shape to the government. The intermediate powers of the monarchy have altogether disappeared. The sovereignty of the monarch was exercised through those intermediate powers—in England the representatives of the people

---

22. *Records of the Federal Convention*, vol. 1, p. 201, pp. 579-582.
23. *Records of the Federal Convention*, vol. 2, pp. 201-224.
24. *Records of the Federal Convention*, vol. 2, p. 3.
25. *Federalist* 63.
25. *Spirit of the Laws* 11.8.

were limited by the remaining nobles and "grands"—but in America the sovereignty of the people was to be exercised only through its representatives. The government was to be purely republican. Here we shall first look at the possibilities that were envisioned for the space between the people and their representatives created by representation: its size and its capacity for encouraging reason rather than passion in political life.

A look at the way the most famous disagreement during the Constitutional Convention—that between the big and small states over whether the states should be represented equally or in proportion to their population—was resolved will help make clear the extent to which the government formed by the representatives was thought to be a consequence of the particular scheme of representation adopted.

The dangers envisioned—foreign intervention, foreign alliances, smaller confederacies, wars among the states, the destruction of commerce—would be a result of the failure of the convention to come up with an adequate plan for union and of a union that relied upon the enforcement of general laws upon recalcitrant state governments. Such enforcement would amount to war, and thus lead to all the evils following from the end of the union. Somehow enforcement, both executive and judicial, had to be localized and individualized, either by creating federal enforcement institutions capable of acting on individuals and federal courts with jurisdiction over offenses against that administration of the laws, or by using state administrations and state courts, or by using both methods.

The great awkwardness of a union based on individuals, or upon representation from each state in proportion to its population, was in the establishment of an upper house, a Senate.[27] The view that such a body was necessary to check the passions of the electorate as they swept uniformly over the body politic and to restore the diversity of genuine political debate did not indicate a way to create such an institution in a society without a nobility and with no intention of encouraging the development of one.[28] The Virginia Plan, the first proposal before the Convention, resolved this difficulty by suggesting that the second branch should be elected by the first from nominations by the state legislatures. That proposal does not seem to have been seriously considered by the convention. One suspects that this was because the layering removed the second house too far from the people they were to represent and because

---

27. See also Gordon Wood, *The Creation of the American Republic, 1776-1787* (Chapel Hill, N.C.: University of North Carolina Press, 1969).

28. *Federalist* 50.

the arrangement violated the view that separation of powers could only be achieved when each power had an independent ground or source for that power. But, if the second chamber was to be elected by the state legislatures, it became difficult to imagine how they could produce a smaller deliberative body than the House. Constant juggling of figures at the Constitutional Convention indicated how difficult it would be to produce a smaller body in which each state had at least one member and the number of members from each state was proportional to its population.

All these awkwardnesses paved the way for compromise, but no compromise would have been possible if the view that the character of the government is a direct consequence of the way representation is organized dominated the convention. Patterson of New Jersey, who presented the New Jersey Plan settling representation equally among the states, used a notion of representation early in the Convention that suggest the understanding on which compromise could be reached. According to Madison's notes, he said:

> It has been said that if a National Government is to be formed so as to operate on the people and not only the states the representative ought to be drawn from the people. But why so? May not a legislature filled by the State legislatures operate on the people who chuse the state legislatures? or may not a practicable coercion be found.[29]

Patterson's own notes for his speech put the matter this way:

> Will the Operation of the natl. Govt. depend upon the Mode of Representation.—No—it depends upon the Quantum of Power lodged in the leg. ex. and judy. Departments—it will operate individually in the one Case as well as the other.[30]

Although Patterson's is the clearest expression of the opinion that the way the new national government can be expected to operate is an altogether different question from the way it is related to the people, some implicit opinion of this sort must underlie the compromise that made the new government possible.

In his introduction to the discussion of the institutions of the new government, Madison differentiated the institutions essential for the requisite stability and energy in a government from those due to liberty and to the republican form.[31] He limits the name republican to the government that "derives all its powers directly or indirectly from the great body of the people; and is administered by persons holding their offices during

---

29. *Records of the Federal Convention*, vol. 1, p. 179.
30. *Records of the Federal Convention*, vol. 1, p. 187.
31. *Federalist* 37.

pleasure, for a limited period, or during good behavior."[32] The particular method of derivation—through the states, individual votes, or appointment by representatives of the people—does not matter. Adherence to republican form does not seem necessarily to increase, or decrease, the possibility of stable and energetic government. Then he can go on to call the proposed government partly national and partly federal, the result of a compromise, without compromising, so to speak, the energy and stability of the resulting national government.[33]

There is, then, little indication that the government was to be limited or shaped by things external to it—whether it be by an opinion as to the things a government ought and ought not do or by the character of the sovereign people. Rather the moderation of the government, as well as its liberty, was to be a result of the distance of representative institutions from those they represent and the shape of those institutions. The government is protected against the passions that sweep across the people by its very distance from them. But the question remains of the shape of the institutions, of the character of the rule that was to order the government.

Liberty

The division of powers was intended both to break up the unanimity of the democratic passions and to be the mechanism that gave the government a character and spirit. In breaking up the passions the division of powers serves, as did size and representation, to curb the virtually random wills or desires that pass through a democratic populace, making it as much a despot as a single man when he imposes his momentary whims on a people. In this sense it ensures moderation. But *The Federalist* did not stop with this moderation; the government was further designed to promote good government. The question remains of the content of that government and its relation to the liberty of free men who rule themselves prudently.

The structure of the division of power that was proposed in the Constitutional Convention was not and could not be based on a division of the people into ranks and orders. A division of power which does not rely

---

32. *Federalist* 39.
33. In *Federalist* 44, the states are actually referred to as "intermediate powers." See also *Records of the Federal Convention*, vol. 1, Dickenson, p. 87, p. 157 and Forrest McDonald, *Novus Ordo Seclorum* (Lawrence, Kansas: University Press of Kansas, 1985), pp. 228-232.

upon a division in the people is characteristic of republican rather than monarchical moderation. But the manner in which republican power is divided points toward the particular kind of republican government. In order to understand the purpose those who wrote the Constitution had for their republican government, we should, following Montesquieu, inquire into the shape of the division of power—the sources of division, the grounds for attachment to the government or a part of it, and the effect of the division itself.

The first, most evident way of separating the branches of the government was for them to have different origins. The executive and the two branches of the legislature had different modes of origin in the people. Only the judiciary was to be ensured more by the conditions of its existence than those of its appointment. It is hard to understand how these different modes of election from a formless population could produce representatives peculiarly interested in or able to perform their tasks. There is no reason to believe that they would rest even somewhat content with the portion of governing they were elected to do. To the extent they considered themselves the representatives of the people, they would tend toward expanding their realm to the whole of ruling. This pre-disposition of the representatives of the people to think of themselves as the whole of government is one of the grounds for the expectation that the branches will compete with each other for influence over governmental activities. Republican government requires something more than different sources in the people to produce a government of divided and balanced power rather than one of competing democracies.

An altogether different notion of separate powers shaped the Virginia Plan. There all of the other offices of the government derived directly or indirectly from a House of Representatives whose membership was to be proportional to the population and elected directly by the people. George Washington's one public remark at the convention was, on the last day, to speak for a motion to decrease the maximum size of a district of the House of Representatives.[34] This concern for the House of Representatives as the popular body was shared by Hamilton,[35] and also by Madison, who often remarked in *The Federalist* that the legislature was potentially the most influential branch and whose first office was in the House. This could be an effort to increase the influence of the large states or to establish greater democracy. It could also be that this was the result of a

---

34. *Records of the Federal Convention*, vol. 2, p. 644.
35. *Records of the Federal Convention*, vol. 2, pp. 553-4.

lingering view that the House was *the* elected body, which survived the formation of a Constitution in which the President, the Senate, and the House were separated by their varied sources of election from the people as well as by their tasks. This suggests that these men kept a view of the Constitution which had its source in their understanding of the Virginia Plan. The structure required for separate powers there did not depend upon separate sources in the people, but rather upon the internal shape of the powers of the government themselves.

A look at the proposal in the Virginia Plan that there be a Council of Revision, a council made of members of the executive branch and the judicial branch that was to have a veto on legislation, will shed some light on their view of how the powers could be kept separate. Madison brought up this suggestion a number of times during the Convention, in spite of its never having been given serious consideration. Madison's argument was that executive and judicial activities are similar in respects that make it important that that similarity be recognized institutionally so that they can be effectively separated from each other. Both the executive and judicial branches are to enforce the laws, whether generally upon the people as a whole or upon specific offenders. Neither are likely to enforce laws they disagree with unless they know that those laws have substantial support in the other branches of the government. These possibilities can all be weighed, tried out, in a Council of Revision.[36] In this view, the branches of government are kept separate by acknowledging and giving an appropriate shape to the points at which they overlap. These conjunctions are ordinarily called "balances."

The separation of power must be maintained through sharing in parts of ruling and through the tension that results from that sharing. Madison wrote, "I shall undertake in the next place to shew that unless these departments be so far connected and blended, as to give to each a constitutional control over the others, the degree of separation which the maxim requires as essential to a free government, can never in practice, be duly maintained."[37] In sum, in the American republic the separation of powers has to be maintained through the different powers' controls over each other, through the aspects of governing they share.

We are accustomed to speak of the "checks and balances" of our Constitution, but it is useful to consider the possibility of distinguishing between the two. Checking at the Constitutional Convention seems to

---

36. See Hamilton on Council of Revision, *Federalist* 73.
37. *Federalist* 48.

refer to relations between the two chambers of the legislature, between the more immediate representatives of the people. This does seem to be the customary usage at the Convention, but Hamilton remarked that "a democratic assembly is to be checked by a democratic senate and both these by a democratic chief magistrate."[38] These checks are related to those popular passions that are opposed to the reasonable views of political action. They are designed to check those passions both as they move from the people to the legislature or the executive and as they act within the legislative bodies themselves.[39] Hamilton said that "gentlemen differ in their opinions concerning the necessary checks from the different estimates they form of the human passions."[40] These checks, then, serve to stop the passions of the public or of the legislatures when they act as democratic publics. They are those aspects of this government of checks and balances which produce a stalemate, although perhaps a stalemate between the democratic passions is enough to give some room for the development of reasoned opinions and political actions.

To examine this last possibility we need to return specifically to the understanding of the way the officers in the government will act within the structure of the government. Security for the balance of powers, for the separation of powers, "consists in giving to those who administer each department, the necessary constitutional means and personal motives, to resist encroachments of the others . . . . Ambition must be made to counteract ambition. The interest of the man must be connected with the constitutional rights of the place."[41] For ambition to counteract ambition and defend the separation of power, the ambition of the man must be attached to, identified with the power and status of the branch of government in which he holds office. Hamilton's argument that the officers of the new national government would not bother with the things that were in the province of state governments makes clear his view that the powers of the new government were required to attract the ambitious men to its working and its defense.

> The regulation of the mere domestic police of a State appears to me to hold out slender allurements to ambition. Commerce, finance, negotiation and war seem to comprehend all the objects, which have charms for minds governed by that passion; and all the powers necessary to these objects ought in the first instance to be lodged in the national deposi-

---

38. *Records of the Federal Convention*, vol. 1, p. 310.
39. *Records of the Federal Convention*, vol. 1, p. 421 (Madison on private passions).
40. *Records of the Federal Convention* , vol. 1, p. 289.
41. *Federalist 51*.

tory. The administration of private justice between the citizens of the same State, the supervision of agriculture and of other concerns of a similar nature, all those things in short which are proper to be provided for by local legislation, can never be desirable cares of a general jurisdiction. It is therefore improbable that there should exist a disposition in the Federal councils to usurp the powers with which they are connected; because the attempt to exercise those powers would be as troublesome as it would be nugatory; and the possession of them, for that reason, would contribute nothing to the dignity, to the importance, or to the splendour of the national government.[42]

There is, of course, no guarantee that in other times ambition will not become attached to these objects as well. But the point is that it is the purposes and powers of government itself that attract the ambitious.

Ambition, once attracted, is schooled by the institution that attracted it and that it serves, as with the honor of the nobility in a monarchy. Both ambition here and honor in Montesquieu imply an impulse to think very well of oneself, and be thought very well of, that is virtually without content. Ambition in a monarchy is transformed into honor as men demand recognition of the preferences and distinctions to which they are born.[43] Here Hamilton seems to presume that ambition attaches itself most easily, naturally, to political action and to political action that involves the evident use of power. Montesquieu said honor's shape was a consequence of the education that began as one entered the world.[44] The ranks of the nobility taught the noblemen and their followers how they ought to value themselves, taught them an array of rules about proper behavior which could even lead them to disobey the prince to defend their honor. In England, according to Montesquieu, the legislative and executive offered no shape or direction to those who adhered to them, so that the government's end was liberty in the sense of the government's offering no shape for men's lives; the men were uneasy, uncertain about their place and character. In the American republic, the government itself, and particularly its branches, attract the ambitious men and give shape to their ambition. Thus, even the general form of the government rested in some measure on "that honorable determination, which animates every votary of freedom, to rest all our political experiments on the capacity of mankind for self-government."[45]

---

42. *Federalist* 17.
43. Montesquieu, *The Spirit of the Laws* 3.7.
44. Montesquieu, *The Spirit of the Laws* 4.2.
45. *Federalist* 39.

The American division of power is explicitly functional: it is based upon the different processes that are a part of any rule—making a rule, enforcing that rule, and judging the offenders. What Locke called the federative power and Montesquieu called the execution of the law of nations here has been absorbed altogether into the national government. The explicit separation of judging from executing and then the investing of that judging in a body of judges, a judiciary, distinguishes this division of power from first Locke and then Montesquieu. Once the division of powers is seen as the separating out of parts of a single function, then each branch of government can be shaped from the point of view of performing its function well, can be held responsible for its part in prudential government, and the whole can be seen not as a result of competing parts, but as the whole of rule. In *The Federalist*, the ends of this government are said to be both justice and the common good—justice understood as the protection of the minority and the common good understood as something like what we have called "good government" or the capacity to act on the genuine interests of the whole.[46] However, these ends are to be brought about for Americans by their own actions; Americans are to learn to act and to act within a government that constrains them to provide these ends for themselves. That lesson, and that practice, are embedded in the division of powers.[47] Here we shall take a brief look at the three branches of government from this point of view.

The House of Representatives as the most numerous and directly elected branch is the most subject to the democratic passions. It can either participate in the passions sweeping the nation, or those passions can be generated within the microcosm of democracy that is any assembly.[48] The House must, therefore, be checked by the Senate, kept a reasonable size itself, and provided an internal structure that can make of the representatives legislators. "No man can be a competent legislator who does not add to an upright intention and a sound judgment, a certain degree of knowledge of the subjects on which he is to legislate."[49] So, the members must be elected for more than one year, two here, and to be eligible for re-election. "A few of the members, as happens in all such assemblies, will possess

---

46. See David Epstein, *The Political Theory of* The Federalist (Chicago: The University of Chicago Press, 1984) for a good discussion of these notions.
47. They are found to a much lesser extent, if at all, in Montesquieu's division of powers which is much more of a machine, affecting the direction of the passions of the men within it.
48. *Federalist* 55.
49. *Federalist* 53.

superior talents, will by frequent re-elections, become members of long standing; will be thoroughly masters of the public business, and perhaps not unwilling to avail themselves of those advantages."[50] The knowledge of local interests and circumstances need extend no further than the extent to which those are related to the national government,[51] and each representative will have to acquire much information about all the other states.[52] It seems likely that one who is distinguished as a representative will be distinguished in other ways as well, and "his pride and vanity attach him to a form of government which favors his pretensions, and gives him a share in its honors and distinctions."[53] Republican government presupposes not only depravity, but also the "other qualities in human nature, which justify a certain portion of esteem and confidence."[54] In the House it seems that provisions are made to check the most egregious democratic passions, to give a reason for proud and ambitious men to think themselves appreciated in this government, and then to provide the space required for good legislation. The notion seems to be that the men, once started by their vanity or pride, will move into these positions and take up the aspect of rule available to them, learning to use it, if need be.

The Senate was conceived as a step further along this same path. It moved further in the direction of supporting those aspects of deliberation over legislation which require a greater extent of information and stability of character,[55] wisdom, knowledge of the means by which that object can be obtained,[56] permance,[57] the order and stability that makes a government truly respectable,[58] and a due sense of the national character,[59] in defence of the people against their own temporary delusions.[60] These are to be encouraged by the criteria of age and length of citizenship, by the duration in office and rotation of election, and by the smaller size of the body itself, as well as by the relation to the executive in foreign affairs and appointments. The Senate's power to try cases of impeachment is grounded in this greater capacity for serious deliberation. "The necessity

---

50. *Federalist* 53.
51. *Federalist* 56.
52. *Federalist* 56.
53. *Federalist* 57.
54. *Federalist* 55.
55. *Federalist* 62.
56. *Federalist* 62.
57. *Federalist* 62.
58. *Federalist* 62.

of a numerous court for the trial of impeachments is equally dictated by the nature of the proceeding. This can never be tied down by such strict rules, either in the delineation of the offence by the prosecutors, or in the construction of it by the Judges, as in common cases serve to limit the discretion of courts in favor of personal security."[61] There is remarkably little attention to the role of their election by the state in their capacity, or incapacity, to legislate. Here the things that made the House work as a deliberative body are intensified, producing a space for genuine respectability to take hold, while the Senate is defended against its worst tendencies. There is, again, the notion that there are men with the character to move into the space, either as a result of their prior education, or of the education that comes from trying to act within a political space that gives them a chance to learn to deliberate by doing so, by trying out the avenues opened, and by coming against those that are closed.

It is helpful in thinking of the Presidency to remember that executing the law is closer to judging than to legislating. Both executive and judicial functions enforce the law set out by the legislature. Their proper interest in the law is in the consequences of its enforcement, on the country or on the law itself. This perspective helps explain the demand at the Convention for both democratic election and independence from direct electoral constraints. Thus Hamilton could suggest at the convention an executive elected for life and in *The Federalist* defend a process in which the "sense of the people" is filtered through the men most capable of analyzing the qualities adapted to the station.[62] He goes on to say:

> Talents for low intrigue and the little arts of popularity may alone suffice to elevate a man to the first honors in a single state; but it will require other talents and a different kind of merit to establish him in the esteem and confidence of the whole union, or of so considerable a portion of it as would be necessary to make him a successful candidate for the distinguished office of President of the United States. It will not be too strong to say, that there will be a constant probability of seeing the station filled by characters pre-eminent for ability and virtue.[63]

The independence assures, as for judges, that the President will be remote from the democratic passions, but "the best security for the fidelity of mankind is to make their interest coincide with their duty," and this is also true of the "love of fame, the ruling passion of the noblest minds."[64]

---

61. *Federalist* 65.
62. *Federalist* 68.
63. *Federalist* 68.
64. *Federalist* 72.

If men are not given the space to finish what they have begun, "the most to be expected from the generality of men in such a situation is the negative merit of not doing harm instead of the positive merit of doing good."[65] The total of unity, duration, adequate provision for support, and competent powers is conducive to energy in the executive, "a leading character in the definition of good government."[66] The executive will act, move energetically, if space is made for him to act. The pre-eminent men who are chosen are to be given the scope their ambition requires, or their best cannot be expected and their worst may well be feared.

A judiciary of judges who hold the office for some time is made necessary by the existence of a constitution. Once a constitution exists which is distinguished from ordinary laws passed by the legislature, the possibility of a conflict between the two kinds of laws emerges. "If there should happen to be an irreconcilable variance between the two, that which has the superior obligation and validity ought of course to be preferred; or in other words, the Constitution ought to be preferred to the statute, the intention of the people to the intention of their agents."[67] The interpretation of the laws is the province of the judges, not juries, so the judges become an important part of the constitutional balance here, although they were not in Montesquieu's England. To get men with the courage and knowledge required to perform these functions, the independence of the judiciary must be assured by tenure for good behavior. The check on the judiciary's misuse of this virtually unlimited charge is that they have no force or will, merely judgments, that they depend upon the executive and the legislature for enforcement.[68] In the cases of both the executive and the judiciary there seems to be an idea that the space for political action will itself be attractive to the ambitious, and even to those with the ambition appropriate to the job, and that the checks will protect the country from the ambition of bad, or even of incompetent, men.

If the American Constitution was designed to make it possible for some men to deliberate as free men and govern moderately, in accordance with the law, one might well ask about everyone else. Besides the possibility of joining that government or of voting for it, the citizen is only free if he is safe, or thinks he is safe, according to Montesquieu.[69] The issue here is the

---

65. *Federalist* 72.
66. *Federalist* 77.
67. *Federalist* 78.
68. *Federalist* 78.
69. Montesquieu, *The Spirit of the Laws* 12.1.

security of the citizens, the danger that the legislature or the executive will go beyond its proper bounds in pursuit of its ends. Only the judiciary can serve to protect the citizens from this over-reaching. The issues here are, first, those of habeas corpus, bills of attainder, the definition of treason, jury trials in criminal cases—all in the original Constitution before the Bill of Rights was added. In *Federalist* 84, Hamilton argues that enforcement of these provisions is the task of the judiciary and that they are enough of a bill of rights; the addition of an extensive bill of rights would, in his view, increase the scope of the judiciary. In Montesquieu, freedom to write, to speak, to think, were extensions of this first line of protection. The most dangerous crimes, those against the country itself or religion, raise the possibility of infinite prosecutions unless the prosecutions for political acts are defined carefully as for acts and not thoughts, and those for religion are left to the religions themselves. One cannot go in search of hidden offenses without endangering the security of the citizenry. From this point of view the Bill of Rights is an amplification of the rights already in the Constitution and could be read back into them as circumstances required. The judiciary can be seen, from this point of view, to have two functions, one in the constitutional balance supporting the moderation and liberty of the Constitution, and second in respect to the liberty, security, of the citizenry.

In action this balance of power has two aspects. First, each branch of government offers a claim to the whole of rule. The Congress can expand its law-making and surveillance to control the executive and the scope of the judiciary. The President can expand the importance of the capacity to act in a specific situation—international and even domestic—at the expense of general law-making and judicial enforcement. The courts can expand their adjudication of disputes to the statement of general principles and to the administration of their solutions. All of this is easily recognizable as the claims and denunciations in our discussions of the balance of power. But, in the partisan debate the second aspect of the balance of power is forgotten. The claims of each branch stem from a point of view about the nature of rule itself influenced by the function that predominates—no one of which is the whole. The deliberation that is the rule of free men over each other contains all these aspects, and for our government to deliberate it must balance its powers.

The Separation of Powers: A Constitutional Principle in Contemporary Perspective

Dennis J. Mahoney

Publius (Madison) conceded in *The Federalist* #47 that the proposed Constitution would be the subject of "universal reprobation" if it did not provide for the effective separation of the powers of government. The primary consideration in favor of such separation, of course, was the fear of that tyranny of which "the accumulation of all powers, legislative, executive, and judiciary," might justly be called the very definition. But this was not the whole story; the doctrine of separated powers was not, in its American genesis, a merely negative doctrine, nor were deadlock and frustration its aims. As has been most correctly observed, "In the view of the leading Federalists, it was not enough to provide a check upon the powers of government; it was also necessary to provide for energetic government."[1]

Contemporary writing about the separation of powers, with only a few notable exceptions, concentrates not upon the doctrine of separated powers itself, but upon the corollary doctrine of mutual checks and balances.[2] But, while checks and balances are probably necessary for the preservation of the separation of powers in a regime where all the powers of government are republican (that is, representatively democratic),[3] yet the two principles are distinct. Checks and balances are desirable for the preservation of the separation of powers, and not vice versa. This fundamental error of understanding has characterized writing about separation of powers, especially by political scientists, for the last hundred years.

---

1. Edward J. Erler, "The Constitution and the Separation of Powers," in Leonard W. Levy et al., *The Constitution: A History of Its Framing and Ratification* (New York: Macmillan, 1987), p. 151.
2. Publius, of course, uses the phrase "check[s] and balance[s]" only in reference to the relationship between the Senate and the House of Representatives. But the mutual checking of the legislative, executive, and judiciary branches is customarily so designated, and the custom has the additional sanction of time. It is in this sense that the phrase will be used throughout the present paper.
3. On why this should be so see Erler.

In fact, there are two distinct, but related, errors regarding the original intention of the framers with regard to separation of powers. First, most contemporary writers assume that it was a part of the purpose of the Framers to keep the government of the United States weak. This assumption should amaze anyone familiar with the Anti-Federalist arguments against the Constitution. Actually, the Framers wanted to make the United States government as strong as possible within the sphere of authority assigned to it. The word used by the Framers was "energy"— they wanted to energize the government.

The second error, that is, the supposition that the Framers invented separation of powers in order to make possible checks and balances, rather than, as was actually the case, the other way around, is a corrolary to the first. That this also mistakes the purpose of mutual balances and checks, and indeed the purpose of resorting to any or all of the "auxilliary precautions," need not concern us at this point or in this discussion.

For the Framers and for Publius, the separation of powers meant, in the first place, the separation of the executive power from the legislative. This was not necessary to frustrate the legislative will, or the will of the majority as reflected in the legislature. Separation of the executive from the legislative power was necessary in order to make it possible to attract to executive office the kind of men whose ambition directed them toward doing great things well. We might say that it made it possible to attract to the executive offices those persons of the noblest cast of mind whose ruling passion was the love of fame.

In the second place, the separation of powers meant the separation of the judiciary from both the legislative and the executive powers. Again, the independence of this branch from the others was necessary in order to attract to judicial office those men particulary suited to the exercise of the judicial function. In the regime of separated powers, properly arranged, the opportunties offered in each of the separated branches would be those most likely to attract to them the persons most likely to defend and to extend the prerogatives associated with them severally.

Today's views (that is, the views that are more or less authoritative in our own time) are generally hostile to the doctrine of separated powers. To a very large degree, this hostility rests on their proponent's misunderstanding of what that doctrine is and what the separation of powers was meant to accomplish. Today's views concerning separation of powers are essentialy those of American political science as it has existed for the last one hundred years, and which have been most influential during the Progressive era and the New Deal era. Those views, and that discipline,

have their origin in a decisive break from the tradition of political philosophy and from the teachings of the Founders of this republic. For while
both classical political philsophy and the American Founders (albeit in
very different ways) took their bearings from nature—from the laws of
nature and of nature's God that prescribed the ends of man and of
government—the new American political science took, and takes, its
bearings from History—from the interaction of impersonal forces, and
from the denial that any immutable end of man or state is possible.

The founders of the new American political science, Woodrow Wilson
and Frank Goodnow, introduced two new principles of government: the
combination of legislative and executive powers according to the Westminster model and the separation of administration from politics. These
principles of the new political science were then combined with an attack
on the motives of the Founding Fathers by such lights of Progressivism as
Charles A. Beard and J. Allen Smith.

The last one hundred years, then, is the period that we must have in
mind as we examine "today's views" of the separation of powers, because
the views that are important today were shaped during the Progressive
era. Both the theory and the practice of the separation of powers as we
know them today originated in the writings of the founders of modern
academic political science.

The year 1987 will be the bicentennial year of the Constitution of the
United States. The year 1986 is, in a sense, the centennial year of American academic political science.[4] It is scarcely too much to say that the
American academic discipline of political science was founded, in part, in
opposition to the notion of the separation of powers.

To the extent that one can identify "today's views" of the doctrine of
separated powers, those views are decisively shaped by the political
science of the progressive era. Progressive political science was founded in
keeping with the idea that the separation of governmental power into
legislative, executive, and judicial departments was an obsolete attempt to
make political reality conform to Whig theory. In its place, the new
political scientists proposed a separation of politics from administration.
In this regard, the most influential writers during the Progressive era were

---

4. The first graduate department of political science in the United States was founded at
   Columbia University in 1885. The first organization of political scientists (the Academy
   of Political Science) and the first political science journal (*Political Science Quarterly*) were
   founded in 1886. Woodrow Wilson's influential essay on the study of administration
   was originally published in 1887.

Frank J. Goodnow (the founder and first president of the American Political Science Association: APSA) and Woodrow Wilson (the APSA's sixth president). How this new separation was to be worked out was a matter of some difference of opinion, but its general desirability was conceded on all sides.

Woodrow Wilson regarded the doctrine of separated powers—and of checks and balances, as he did not view the two things as separable—as a failed attempt to put the Whig theory of government into practice. But, in the twentieth century, he argued, it was time to put that theory behind us. The question before the country, Wilson wrote, was: "Have we had enough of the literal translation of Whig theory into practice, into constitutions?"[5] If so, then "we must think less of checks and balances and more of coordinated power, less of separation of functions and more of the synthesis of action."[6]

Wilson especially admired the operation of the British government, not as it was revealed in real life, but as it was described in the writing of Walter Bagehot.[7] He argued that an executive collectively responsible to the legislature and capable of providing leadership to the legislature was the key to energetic government. But he also seems to have supposed that such a system would foster robust debate on public issues and real deliberation within the legislative assembly. He did not foresee a legislature subordinate to the executive that was to provide its guidance.

Curiously, executive leadership and legislative deliberation were not the principal concerns of Wilson's political science. Rather, according to Wilson, the most important contribution of poltical science in modern times was the study of administration. Political science was over 2,200 years old, he wrote, but the science of administration "is a birth of our own century, almost of our own generation."[8] In Wilson's opinion, the science of administration offered a way out of the paradox that while democracy is the most desirable form of government, democratic politics is a barrier to reform and progress.

---

5. *Constitutional Government in the United States* (New York: Columbia University Press, 1911), p. 221.

6. *Constitutional Government in the United States*, p. 221.

7. Indeed, Wilson's first published essay on politics was entitled "Cabinet Government in the United States," and was a plea for collectively responsible executive leadership of and in Congress.

8. "The Study of Administration," in *College and State: Educational, Literary and Political Papers (1875-1913)*, ed. R.S. Baker and W.E. Dodd (New York: Harper & Brothers, 1925), vol. I, p. 131.

The most important fact about administration, according to Wilson, was that "administration lies outside the proper sphere of *politics*. Administrative questions are not political questions."[9] Instead, administration was to be regarded as "part of political life . . . only as machinery is part of the manufactured product."[10]

Goodnow went even further than Wilson in his advocacy of the new separation of political from administrative power. He wrote that "there are two distinct functions of government," and he described the relationship between them: "Politics has to do with policies or expressions of the state will. Administration has to do with the execution of these policies."[11] Administration in a complex, modern society required, according to Goodnow, "establishment, preservation, and development of [a] vast force of officers and authorities" for the purpose of "insuring the most efficient execution of [the state] will after it has been expressed."[12]

At the same time that Wilson and Goodnow were writing about the necessity of securing the autonomy of public administration from politics, another branch of American political science was attacking the separation of powers on historical grounds. J. Allen Smith[13] and Charles A. Beard[14] both believed that the doctrine of separated powers was a part of a coherent scheme of wealthy conservatives to build into the American constitutional structure devices to frustrate the popular majorities that would otherwise use the national government to the disadvantage of the wealthy in general (Smith) or of the class of speculators in government bonds (Beard).

Smith, at least, had not lost sight of the fact that the principle purpose for framing the Constitution in 1787 was not to weaken, but to strengthen, the government of the Union. But the then-popular "notion that [the] Convention, in framing the Constitution, was actuated solely by a desire to impart more vigor and efficiency to the general government [was] but part of the truth."[15] The rest of the truth, as Smith understood it, was to keep the people—that is, the majority who were poor—from exercising an

---

9. "The Study of Administration," p. 145.

10. "The Study of Administration," p. 144.

11. *Politics and Administration* (1900 rpt. New York: Russell & Russell, 1967), p. 18.

12. *Politics and Administration*, p. 77.

13. *The Spririt of American Government* (1907; rpt. Cambridge, Mass.: Harvard University Press, 1965).

14. *An Economic Interpretation of the Constitution of the United States* (1913; rpt. New York: Macmillan, 1937).

15. *The Spirit of American Government*, p. 36.

effective share in the government. Whether or not Smith was right about the rest of the truth, he had not lost sight, as politicial science seems to have done subsequently, of the truth that invigorating and energizing the government was the main goal of the framers of the Constitution.

The government established by the Constitution, however, according to Smith's account, was to be vigorous and energetic only in a negative sense.[16] Smith's complaint was not that the system of checks and balances (within which he included the principle of separated powers) produced deadlock and stagnation, but that it biased the direction in which the vigor and energy of government were to be applied. According to Smith, the framers "believed in the theory of checks and balances in so far as the system implied the limitation of the right of popular control."[17]

The notion that separation of powers was consciously designed to bring about deadlock and to prevent governmental activity pervades the writings of Beard. For both Smith and Beard, active government (or what James Madison might have called "energetic" government) meant redistributionist government. Hence there is no discussion of the government's actively pursuing foreign policy goals, or actively defending individual rights (including property rights).

What are the views of today's political science? The most visible change in the form of American government since the Progressive era is that the Wilson-Goodnow prescription has effectively been enacted into law. The New Deal and the Great Society put in place the kind of autonomous administrative structure that Wilson and Goodnow advocated. When contemporary political scientists write about the independence of the regulatory agencies, they are defending the status quo.

This has not always been evident, however. As late as 1953, the growth of the administrative power could still be seen as the aggrandizement of the executive branch. New Jersey Chief Justice Arthur T. Vanderbilt, for example, wrote: "The overwhelming growth in size and power of the executive branch of the federal government in comparison with the other two great departments has been the outstanding American political phenomenon of the twentieth century."[18] To say as much, however, was to assume the continued vitality in practice of Publius's (Hamilton's) account of administration: "The administration of government . . . in its

---

16. *The Spirit of American Government*, p. 128.
17. *The Spirit of American Government*, p. 125.
18. *The Doctrine of the Separation of Powers and Its Present Day Significance* (1953; rpt. Lincoln, Neb.: University of Nebraska Press, 1963).

most precise signification ... is limited to executive details and falls within the province of the executive department."[19] If this be so, of course, then the persons "to whose immediate management these different matters are committed, ought to be considered as the assistants or deputies of the chief magistrate."[20] But both in political theory and in law, that account of relationship of the bureaucracy to the Presidency has been superseded by an account akin to the Wilson-Goodnow prescription.

In both political science and law, the bureaucracy is treated as an autonomous branch of government. Its functions are described as "quasi-legislative" (rule-making) and "quasijudicial" (adjudication).[21] Indeed, one might peruse the Administrative Procedures Act in vain looking for any function of the bureaucracy described as "quasiexecutive."

One of the most influential books in contemporary political science is James MacGregor Burns's *Deadlock of Democracy*. Burns's account of the working of the separation of powers is virtually identical to Woodrow Wilson's. Wilson wrote that "coordinate and coequal powers such as the framers of the Constitution had set up ... might at their will pull in opposite directions and hold the government at a deadlock ...."[22] Burns wrote of "the establishment within the national government of a 'balance of checks' that prevented the government ... from wielding too much power."[23] Nor have Burns's views altered significantly in the two decades since the publication of *Deadlock of Democracy*.[24]

Today, as in the Progressive era, the doctrine of separated powers is confounded with the system of checks and balances. Today, as in the Progressive era, the primary function of separated powers—enabling the government to act decisively by liberating the men who exercised each of the powers to pursue their ambitions and to prove their abilities—is ignored. Instead the emphasis, almost whenever the separation of powers is discussed, is on the possibility of mutual checking and frustration, and not on the independence of the branches from one another.

A peculiarly contemporary formulation serves to destroy whatever might otherwise survive of the distinction between separation of powers and checks and balances. That formulation, as it appears in one recent

---

19. *The Federalist* #72, first paragraph (J. Cooke ed., p. 486).

20. *The Federalist* #72, (J. Cooke ed., p. 487).

21. See, for example, the Federal Administrative Procedure Act, 5 U.S. Code secs. 551-557.

22. *Constitutional Government*, p. 200.

23. *Deadlock of Democracy*, p. 16.

24. See his *The Power to Lead: The Crisis of the American Presidency* (New York: Simon and Schuster, 1984), passim, especially pp. 106-119.

text is: "separate institutions, shared powers."[25] This formulation, which appears in many contemporary textbooks, takes the mixing of powers as the norm, rather than as the deviations from the norm necessary to preserve a prudent separation. Thus the doctrine of separated powers, so crucial in the founding period, is made irrelevant to the discussion of policy formation in the federal government. The powers of government are shared among separate institutions—no institution of the government is distinctively legislative or executive, no power is distinctively legislative or executive, there is only a "policy process" in which different institutional actors play roles.

The hostility of political science to the doctrine of separated powers persists in the seemingly endless proposals that academics put forward for revising the structure of the Constitution. A recent book by James L. Sundquist catalogues numerous proposals for constitutional reform.[26] Virtually all of the schemes he describes involved attempts to make the American government more nearly approximate the Westminster model. Sundquist himself understands the separation of powers as an instrument of deadlock and frustration, diminishing rather than enhancing the prospect of energetic government. According to Sundquist, while the framers "sought 'vigor' and 'dispatch' and 'strength' and 'efficacy' . . . they also were determined to erect safeguards to protect the citizenry from abuse of power."[27] Sundquist then confounds the doctrines of separation of powers and checks and balances by asserting that to protect the citizenry the framers believed that "power would have to be dispersed among branches of government capable of checking and controlling one another."[28]

Now that the fear of tyranny no longer haunts us as it did the Founding Fathers, Americans can consider "reforming" the political system. What reforms are necessary? What is wrong with the system the Founding Fathers created? Sundquist quotes the "reformers": according to former Secretary of the Treasury Douglas Dillon, "The division of powers between the President and the Congress makes 'stalemate' inevitable. . . . The country cannot speak with 'one clear voice.' "[29] With this critique,

---

25. Randall B. Ripley and Grace A. Franklin, *Congress, the Bureaucracy, and Public Policy*, 3rd ed. (Homewood, Ill.: Dorsey Press, 1984), p. 15.
26. *Constitutional Reform and Effective Government* (Washington, D.C.: Brookings Institution, 1986).
27. *Constitutional Reform and Effective Government*, p. 18.
28. *Constitutional Reform and Effective Government*, p. 18.
29. *Constitutional Reform and Effective Government*, p. 9.

Sundquist himself clearly agrees: "When government is divided, then, the normal and healthy partisan confrontation that occurs during debates in every democratic legislature spills over into confrontation between the branches of government, which may render it immobile."[30]

Sundquist, of course, is sympathetic to the cause of the institutional "reformers." Toward the end of his book, he lists the nine reforms that he regards as "ideal. Four of these would tend toward the abolition of the separation of powers: a Presidential-Congressional "team ticket," Congressional terms corresponding to Presidential terms, special elections to "reconstitute a failed government," and elimination of the prohibition on dual officeholding. Three others would alter the lines of separation: the item veto, the legislative veto, and constitutionalization of the War Powers Resolution of 1973. And his final proposal is for a national referendum to break deadlocks.[31]

But the hostility of professional political science would not be significant if the persons holding office in the various branches of the government behaved as Publius (Madison) had predicted that they would. The personal motives of the members of Congress, for example, should form a barrier to the aggrandizement of the administrative bureaucracy. And yet, this does not seem to be the case. More and more, Congress is a collaborator in the process of breaking down both the separation of powers as such and the legislative power of Congress in particular.

The phenomenon seems to be explained by Morris P. Fiorina's notion of a "Washington Establishment" with Congress as its keystone.[32] Publius's argument for the doctrine of separated powers had relied on associating not only the ambition and jealousy of politicians with the power of the offices they held, but also their particular interests, talents, and abilities. Hence, legislative office would be sought by those who particularly desired to take part in the making of the laws. But the personal motives of contemporary legislators are, by the look of things, somewhat different.

Members of Congress seem now to be motivated primarily by the "electoral connection." Congress has become "a place where members wish to stay once they get there . . . an assembly of professional politicians

---

30. *Constitutional Reform and Effective Government*, p. 75.

31. *Constitutional Reform and Effective Government*, pp. 240-241. Sundquist lists his proposals in order of importance, exactly in the order given in the text. His eighth proposal is to associate the House of Representatives with the Senate in the ratification of treaties.

32. Morris P. Fiorina, *Congress: Keystone of the Wasington Establishment* (New Haven, Conn.: Yale University Press, 1977).

spinning out political careers."[33] To the extent that Congressmen can be studied and discussed collectively, their common motivation is the desire to stay in office, rather than to do anything in particular while in office. Far from being interested in making public policy (the impulse that Madison counted on), contemporary members of Congress are willing to have others bear the onus of making policy that is potentially alienating to some bloc or other of the electorate.

Typically, Congress enacts general goals of a more or less noncontroversial nature, and then leaves another part of the government to devise the policy by which the goals are to be achieved. Most often, the policy-making body is the administrative bureaucracy. At the policymaking level, the views of interested bureaucrats, legislative committees, and private parties are considered in relation to the weight of their interests, and not by deliberation concerning the relationship of the policy to the general good. This is the phenomenon known as the "subgovernment" or the "iron triangle."

The Congressman can satisfy his personal motives by acting as an ombudsman for his constituents, that is, by intevening on their behalf with the bureaucracy. This is at least a partial explanation of the phenomenon captured in one political scientist's question: "If . . . Congress is the 'broken branch,' why do we love our Congressmen so much?"[34] At least to some extent, the decline of the doctrine of separated powers is attributable to a shift in the personal motives of the men who populate the legislative branch.

Another deviation of contemporary practice from the separation of powers envisioned by the Founding Fathers is the emergence of the doctrine of judicial supremacy. Separation of powers presumes that the branches of government are coordinate and coequal; yet there is general acceptance, even in Congress, of the idea that the federal courts, and the Supreme Court in particular, have a competence in constitutional matters that is of a different order from that possessed by the other two "political" branches.

The explanation of this phenomenon lies largely in the fact that the courts, like the bureaucracy, are perceived as nonpolitical, even in the most political function, judicial review of legislative and executive acts. The claim made on behalf of the courts is the same claim that Wilson and

---

33. David R. Mayhew, *Congress: The Electoral Connection* (New Haven, Conn.: Yale University Press, 1974), pp. 13-15.
34. The question forms the title of an article by Richard F. Fenno Jr.

Goodnow made on behalf of the bureaucracy—possession of a special technical competence. The decisionmaking that takes place in the judicial branch (like the decisionmaking of the administrative agencies) is perceived as applying a technique to raw input data in order to produce an output, and not as involving deliberation, judgment, and choice.

The one segment of American political life that preserves an attachment to the doctrine of separated powers is the electorate, the people themselves as citizens and voters. While political scientists and professional politicians treat the doctrine as anachronistic or irrelevant, the citizen body still acts as if the doctrine were essential. This is conceded even by James Sundquist, who has written that "there has been no powerful popular, or even elitist, movement on behalf of fundamental alteration in the governmental structure at any time in two hundred years."[35]

---

35. Sundquist, p. 239.

Toward an Agenda for the Third Century: Concluding Essay

Michael P. Zuckert

Heracleitus, the Greek philosopher of flux, concluded that one can never step into the same river twice. Events like the Bicentennial pose the question of whether one can step out of the same river even once. For such anniversaries invite us to stand above the flow which usually carries us along, and attempt to discern the shape of the bank and the direction in which we are headed. The essayists and their commentators have attempted just such an assessment of the separation of powers in the Constitution.

They have succeeded remarkably well in stepping out of the river, for if they do not provide the complete assay for which one might wish, they do provide us with much of the materials for our two hundred year assessment. Even more, they help us appreciate how complex, how difficult is that effort to step out of the river. Reflection on their achievement demonstrates that the task of assessment has at least two phases: one must first recover the political science of the Founders, and one must then look at the separation of powers with an eye informed by that political science.

Different as the two essays are, they agree in one major conclusion: the separation of powers is woefully misunderstood by contemporary political science (both academic and political), in that the Constitutional frame is almost universally understood to aim at securing limited government through establishing checks and balances. But, both Anne Cohler and Dennis Mahoney argue, this is a far too narrow and limited grasp of the original aim and potential achievement of the separation of powers. In order to assess the institutions properly, one must thus first recover the breadth of intentions behind them, and only when so armed is one in a position to assess intelligently today's constitutional order.

The two essays' most striking achievement then concerns not the separation of powers itself, but the implicit call for a political science adequate to come to terms with it. Dennis Mahoney's essay sketches the windings of political science during the Constitution's second century, windings which in the end produced a political science which not only largely rejected, but mostly forgot the political understanding originally animating the constitutional order. Only in the later moments of that second century has a counter-movement, of which Cohler and Mahoney are both part, arisen to embark on the very difficult task of recovery.

Professor Mahoney traces the process of rejection and forgetting to the Progressive movement, out of which, he argues, emerged the main outline of the political understanding which dominates today. He makes the truly striking observation that in Progressive political science the separation of politics and administration replaced the classical separation of powers. He only hints at the cause and significance of this substitution. The Progressive movement, as its very name implies, oriented itself around history, around the direction in which history was purported to be going. The political task came to be seen as fitting society to move progressively with the dominant forces of history. At about this time the label "liberal" in American politics ceased designating the party of liberty and began to identify the party of change. As Professor Mahoney says, not nature, which had guided the Founders' political science, but history provided the new standards.

The Founders' emphasis on the separation of powers stemmed from their orientation by nature, for they thought they knew rather clearly what the various political desiderata were. The Declaration of Independence stated the principles of politics and the ends of governance in a way that the entire founding generation could accept as authoritative. In a word, those ends were "to secure these rights" to "life, liberty, and the pursuit of happiness." Jeremy Rabkin, in his comments on the two papers at the conference, made the point very well: "We must always remember that the first thing the separation of powers rests on is personal rights."

That conception of the natural ends of politics translated into two more specific tasks—to provide a free polity and a free society. On the one hand, government could itself become a major threat to rights since government was the agency which could marshall the coercive powers of society, and the Founders knew (even before James Buchanan) political rulers can't always be counted on to act for the public good. Great pains had to be taken then to insure that government did not become such a threat. Americans devised institutions such as the checks and balances, the electoral control of the government, and the freedom of speech and press as ways to guarantee a free polity.

On the other hand, there was an even more pressing task: government must insure the conditions in which individuals can "pursue happiness" in their own ways. Government must supply a secure and stable environment for individual or societal action in pursuit of individual or societal purposes. All of that translated in turn, as James Madison outlined it in

Federalist 37, into a complex of political requirements which no simple set of institutions or practices could fulfill. Madison mentioned, as examples, the needs to combine safety (i.e., what we have called above the conditions for a free polity) with energy (i.e., strength and decision in government, the ability to act), and stability (i.e., the principled persistence in a course of action or policy, the provision of a legal environment with enough predictability that individuals could act accordingly). The genius of the separation of powers in the political science of the Founders was that the various institutions provided by that system could severally be designed to satisfy one or another of these political "desiderata." Not all of these desiderata could be supplied by any one sort of institutional structure because the different means conduced to different requirements. Thus the House of Representatives, a large body, frequently subject to popular review, tended to respond to the need for safety. The Senate, on the other hand, a small body, much less frequently exposed to the vagaries of popular opinion could supply stability.

Anne Cohler's extraordinary essay adds another dimension to our understanding of the subleties of the separation of powers as originally designed. Her analysis of the great French philosopher, Montesquieu, the man more than any other looked to as an authority by the authors of the *Federalist*, once again shows how inadequate is the view which sees limited government as the end of the separation of powers. Not so much limited, but moderate government was the goal, and her essay is a model for marking out the various and subtle ways in which institutions may be shaped to produce such delicate effects as moderation in the Montesquiean sense.

Jeremy Rabkin's comments at the conference developed the original understanding in a somewhat different, yet still remarkably Montesquiean direction, with his emphasis on due process of law. The institutions of the separation of powers were meant as one large set of devices for securing due process, a commitment the Americans inherited from their English progenitors and one which ran back centuries in English legal and political practice. Professor Rabkin detailed the logic of due process in a way which surely captured much of the Framers' viewpoint on the issue. Due process, and the antecedent rights which due process is to protect, means that no citizen may be acted against by government unless government has a sufficient warrant under law; no person may be deprived of that to which he or she has a right unless that person has been given a fair warning as to what kind of actions will produce such a deprivation. Properly spun out, this set of requirements points to the need for a legislature operating through general and proscriptive laws. Due process also means that any citizen accused of violating such a law has a right to a defense, a defense before someone who can impartially judge the adequacy of the defense. That implies, in turn, that neither the people who make the general rules, nor those trusted to enforce the general rules ought to be judges of the application of the rules to individuals. Thus separate structures to make, enforce, and adjudicate the laws flow from the logic of due process itself.

Thus Mahoney, Cohler and Rabkin are all correct in emphasizing the narrowness of most thinking about the separation of powers since the Progressives, thinking which, in effect collapses a very complex whole into the one single, although very important, goal of safety. But my real point here is this: the framers treated the separation of powers as they did because they understood the tasks of politics as naturally structured so as to be spoken to by the separated and differentiated institutions they established. But with the new Progressive orientation by history rather than nature, a new emphasis on change, or on action *per se* emerged. Professor Mahoney aptly quotes Woodrow Wilson, in a passage that summarizes the entire movement: "we must think less of checks and balances, and more of coordinated power, less of separation of functions and more of the synthesis of action." "Coordinated power and the synthesis of action"—these were now central because the tasks to be done were no longer known, even in outline, in advance, and the structure of political needs could no longer be specified. Rather, the long and the short of it is: government must be fit to act—a formula with which the Founders could agree only if one could specify what the action was for and how it was to be done.

Professor Mahoney correctly sees much continuity between these Progressive views and more recent assessments of political order. An example, from a very well known essay by a very well-known contemporary political scientist: "It seems not wildly unrealistic to hope that in the epoch ahead, human consciousness will change profoundly, and that what we might now consider as enlightened understanding, and the best ways to reach it, will be seen by our successors in a vastly different perspective."

Yet the discussion following the presentations of the papers brought out another dimension of current views which cannot simply be traced to the Progressive concern with history. Even though he was not at the conference we may again quote from Professor Robert Dahl: the American political order is wanting, says Dahl, because it is ill-suited to overcoming the "great differences in wealth, income, social esteem, eduction, occupational skills, and ethnic status" which exist in the United States. These differences render impossible the fulfillment of the dream of equal political power for all citizens, and are in themselves an affront to justice. This new emphasis leads to somewhat different assessments of the separation of powers than those typically made by the Progressives. Two examples make this clear: contemporary liberals respond far more favorably to the Supreme Court than the Progressives did, and contemporaries are quite skeptical about the politics-administration dichotomy, both as description and as prescription. Both changes relate to post-Progressive doubts about democratic governance, doubts based on the redistributionist agenda. The middle class majority, which can be expected to control the government under the majoritarian models favored by the Progressives, can hardly be expected to impose on itself policies adverse to its pocketbook interests and contrary to its moral sensibilities and prejudices. Thus independent political power for liberal elites is necessary to carry forward a perceived democratic mission independent of or even contrary to the democratic process. A full-scale treatment of the separation of powers today would thus have to note the irony of the liberal return to certain aspects of the Founders' views, but on the basis of a very different substantive conception of the justice to be sought in politics.

Present assessments of the separation of powers, therefore, do not take their character entirely from their ignorance of the original and full meaning of the institutions. That does not mean that the effort towards recovery of these fuller views is irrelevant, but it does mean it is not sufficient of itself. There is a genuinely different understanding of the ends to be served between, say, Madison and Dahl or James Sundquist. The assessment of the separation of powers thus becomes very quickly a debate over justice, an issue, of course, on which the Founders also have much to say from which modern political science and modern political practice could learn.

But even if, somehow, agreement could be won to Madison's understanding of justice and of the standards in terms of which the separation of powers should be viewed, we would need more. We need not merely the political science of the Founders, but to be political scientists like the Founders. They never stopped with any merely theoretical scheme, no matter how rich, but fastened their considerably astute collective eyes on the actual, not merely posited, operation of political institutions. It is not clear, for example, that merely to know it (the separation of powers) is to love it—even to know it as the Founders knew it and intended it. It is not self-evidently clear that the Founders' institutions are performing so as to produce the qualities the Founders expected from them (as Dennis Mahoney notes). Some political scientists speak, for example, of "performance failures" of the political system, the cause for which is, arguably at least, the separation of powers. Without going through the usual litany beginning with endemic deficits and concluding with anemic elections, it is difficult to see the present situation as marked by that desirable stability under which laws would stay in effect a long time before they were changed. And, one now wonders, given the breakdown of the post-war bipartisan consensus, whether the separation of powers system is capable of sustaining an adequate foreign and defense policy.

Moreover, Jeremy Rabkin raised the important corollary issue: to what extent does the logic behind the separation of powers—whether his logic of due process, or Madison's logic of conflicting desiderata of healthy politics, or Anne Cohler's of deliberation and moderate government—to what extent does that logic require any particular system of separated powers? For example, to what extent does it require what has come to be called the Presidential system as opposed to the Parliamentary system prevalent in some European nations? The members of the panel disagreed sharply on that question, Anne Cohler seeming to accept the implications of Rabkin's point and Dennis Mahoney rejecting them.

I certainly do not mean to attempt to settle this question here: still less do I mean to join the ranks of the detractors of the separation of powers. Rather I mean to decry the situation which seems to characterize the present state of political analysis in America. On the one hand, we have the armies of political scientists who examine the workings of our institutions—in great detail and often with great imagination and insight—but mostly uninformed by the depths of the political science which formed and remains crucial to understanding the American Constitutional order.

On the other hand, we have the smaller army of those who have moved forward to the task of recovery, who have uncovered for us all a more or less authentic version of the older and still necessary political science. Each group proceeds more or less independently, or rather in deliberate disregard of the other. In our third century we need to work to join together what a whole variety of causes has put asunder. If we would reach a happy Tricentennial, we must become again the "complete political scientists" that the Founders, whose deeds we celebrate this year, were.

Chapter Two

Congress: Representation and Deliberation

In any regime the character of the laws is of primary importance. In a liberal democracy the laws must reflect the popular will, and they seek prudently to secure the common good. How is Congress as an institution designed to reconcile these two potentially antagonistic goals? Have changes in Congress, such as the transformation of its staff into a major bureaucracy, worked to increase or diminish its capacity for deliberation?

The Framer's Congress

Robert Scigliano

Introduction

This essay will consider the framers' Congress in its relations to the other branches of government, especially the Presidency, and to the American people. To illumine its constitutional features, I will draw upon comments of its supporters and critics during the campaign for the ratification of the Constitution and upon government practice in the early decades of the republic. I might add that in dealing with issues of the past, I have not been unmindful of those of the present.

Congress and the Other Branches

In arranging the Constitution's articles, the framers accorded Congress precedence over the other branches of government, and in the legislative article they gave the House of Representatives precedence over the Senate. This seems fitting in that Congress represents the people in government and the House, as its name signifies, is the special depository of the popular will. The Senate was also considered to be a representative body but less emphatically, for it was to represent the people indirectly and the states directly, and its small size and its members' long incumbency removed it further from the people than the House. Occasionally—not often—the framers referred to the President as a representative of the people, but never, to my knowledge, did they describe judges this way.[1]

The power of the people is expressed through legislation, and the

---

1. On the President as a representative, see, e.g., Alexander Hamilton, "New York Ratifying Convention," First Speech of June 21, 1788 (Child's version), in *The Papers of Alexander Hamilton*, ed. Harold C. Syrett et al. (New York: Columbia University Press, 1962), vol. V, p. 38; Thomas Hartley, *History of Congress*, 1st Cong., 1st Sess., 1780, House of Representatives, June 17, 1789, col. 500; Abraham Lincoln, "Speech in House of Representatives," July 27, 1848, in *The Collected Works of Abraham Lincoln*, ed. Roy P. Basler (New Brunswick, N.J.: Rutgers University Press, 1953), vol. I, p. 504.

legislative power, as Alexander Hamilton tells us, is "the most compre-hensive and potent" of the powers of government. He defines it in *The Federalist* as prescribing the rules which govern society. By contrast, the executive power carries out the laws and uses the people's strength and the judicial power decides cases.[2]

We should not conclude from these comments that the framers made Congress the dominant *branch* of American government. This would miss the importance they attached to the principle of separation of powers, which declares the three branches not only to be separate from each other but also independent and coordinate. If the framers had wanted the other branches to be subordinate to Congress, they would not have placed the powers of those branches in the Constitution, nor have protected their officers' salaries from Congressional interference, nor have provided as they did for the election of the President and the tenure of judges. It is remarkable that only one delegate to the Convention, Roger Sherman, spoke in favor of making the executive ("absolutely") dependent on Con-gress, for its election, its powers, and even for the number of members, and that he abandoned his position later in the Convention.[3]

The framers wanted to separate the powers of government mainly to protect the people from the oppressions of government. They had learned from Montesquieu that "there can be no liberty where the legisla-tive and executive powers are united in the same person, or body of magistrates" or "if the power of judging be not separated from the legisla-tive and executive powers." The legislative power presented the biggest problem, for it "necessarily predominates in republican government," and the framers' solution was to "arm" the other branches with means of "self-defense"—to insert a series of "*legislative* balances and checks" in the Constitution in ways that have become familiar.[4]

When *The Federalist* considers the danger that Congress poses to separa-

---

2. Alexander Hamilton, "The Examination," No. XIV, Mar. 2. 1802, in *Papers* (1969), vol. XIV, p. 500; also "The Examination," No. III, Dec. 24, 1801, (1977), vol. XXV, p. 467. *Federalist* No. 75, in Alexander Hamilton, James Madison, and John Jay, *The Federalist*, ed. Jacob E. Cooke (Middletown, Conn.: Wesleyan University Press, 1961), p. 504. *Federalist* No. 78, pp. 522-23.

3. Compare Roger Sherman on June 1 and Sept. 4, 1787, *The Records of the Federal Conven-tion of 1787*, rev. ed., ed. Max Farrand (New Haven, Conn.: Yale University Press, 1937), vol. I, p. 65 and vol.II, p. 499. Unless otherwise indicated, all citations from this source are to Madison's notes.

4. Montesquieu, *The Spirit of Laws* I, xi, 6, as cited in *Federalist* No. 47, pp. 325, 326. *Federalist* No. 51, p. 350; *Federalist* No. 9, p. 51 (emphasis added).

tion of powers, it seems usually to refer to the House of Representatives. In a republic such as the Constitution created, it informs us, "the legislative power is [mainly?] exercised by an assembly which is inspired by a supposed influence over the people, with an intrepid confidence in its own strength"; that assembly "is sufficiently numerous to feel all the passions which actuate a multitude, yet not so numerous as to be incapable of pursuing the objects of its passions by means which reason prescribes"; thus "it is against the enterprising ambition of this department that the people ought to indulge all their jealousy and exhaust all their precautions." To check the House of Representatives, the framers drew the Senate toward the President by giving it a share in his appointments and treaties. Publius depends on the Senate to use its legislative veto to keep the House from engaging in "schemes of usurpation or perfidy," just as he depends on the President to use his veto to help prevent "the representatives of the people in a popular assembly" from exerting "an imperious control over the other departments." The judges, too, we brought into the arrangement.[5]

Checks and balances intricately modify the principle of separation of powers in order to preserve it. Each part of government is armed against every other part; the executive and judiciary are linked in an informal alliance against Congress, and the executive, judiciary, and Senate are linked in a similar alliance against the House of Representatives.

Montesquieu had convinced the Antifederalists, too, that liberty depended on placing government powers in different hands. But more doctrinaire than the Federalists, and more attached to the legislative power and fearful of the executive power (which amounted to pretty much the same thing), the Antifederalists disliked the ways in which the framers had mixed and blended powers. Frequently citing Montesquieu, they wanted governmental powers to be separated "as much as may be" or to be kept "entirely" distinct. They accepted a single executive elected indirectly by the people, but they wanted him to be restrained by a council and limited in his eligibility to hold office. They were emphatic in their dislike of the fact that "the Constitution [had] married the President and the Senate" and that the Senate, sharing in the executive powers of appointments and treaties and empowered to try impeachments, had become so formidable in its own right. Some Antifederalists criticized the judiciary's power to interpret the Constitution on grounds that such a

---

5. *Federalist* No. 48, pp. 334. *Federalist* No. 51, p. 350. *Federalist* No. 62, p. 418; *Federalist* No. 71, pp. 483-84. See also *Federalist* No. 78, pp. 522, 527.

power raised concerns of judicial supremacy over Congress. Others proposed locating the Supreme Court's appellate jurisdiction within the legislative branch.[6]

The dispute over separation of powers went on after the Constitution was adopted. The Federalists continued "to support the executive power against the encroachments, the ambition, and the superior strength of the popular branch," as one of their leaders avowed in 1801; and their opponents continued to take the side of the legislative power. Now, however, Republicans replaced Antifederalisats and the two parties fought largely over the boundaries of power between Congress and the executive branch, and the priority of contacts across those boundaries.[7]

A major dispute over boundaries concerned the scope of the President's executive power. In 1789, in establishing the Department of Foreign Affairs, the House of Representatives had to decide who had the power to remove its secretary. Nascent Republicans (the new parties had not yet taken form) argued that the Senate had to consent to his removal, as implied by its participation in his appointment, or that Congress could place the power of removal where it wished. Federalists, led by James Madison, maintained that the President had the power, implied in the vesting clause of Article II—"The executive power shall be vested in a President of the United States"—which Madison interpreted as a general grant of power limited by the need for the Senate's consent to appointments (but not removals). At stake was control over executive administration: the need for Senate consent to appointments, for example, would have made that body the arbiter of disputes between the President and his subordinates.[8]

The argument over the scope of the President's war power came up again in 1793, when Washington proclaimed it the "duty," "interest," and

---

6. "Essays of Brutus," No. XVI, Apr. 10, 1788, in *The Complete Anti-Federalist*, ed. Herbert J. Storing (Chicago: University of Chicago Press, 1981), vol. II, p. 442; "Letters from a Countryman from Duchess County," Jan. 22, 1788, No. V, vol. VI, p. 62. See also "Letters from The Federal Farmer," No. VI, Dec. 25, 1787, vol. II, p. 262; Richard Henry Lee, "To Gov. Edmund Randolph," Oct. 16, 1787, vol. V, p. 113; and James Monroe, "Some Observations on the Constitution, 1788," vol. V, pp. 393-94. George Mason, "Virginia Ratifying Convention," June 11, 1788, in *The Debates in the Several State Conventions on the Adoption of the Federal Constitution*, 2nd ed., ed. Jonathan Elliot (Washington: Jonathan Elliot, 1836), vol. III, p. 493. *Federalist* No. 81, p. 542. *The Federalist* contains an extensive list of Antifederalist objections to the Constitution.

7. Robert Goodloe Harper, *To His Constituents, March 5, 1801* (William Hilliard, 1801), p. 8.

8. *Annals of Congress*, 1st Cong., 1st Sess., 1789, House of Representatives, May 19, June 16-19, 22, 24, 1789, cols. 368-84, 455-585, 590-92.

"disposition" of the United States to remain neutral in the war that had erupted between France, on one side, and Great Britain and its continental allies, on the other. In effect, he interpreted the defensive treaty between the United States and France as not requiring the United States to enter hostilities on the side of France, that is, he assumed the right to determine whether or not a treaty obligated Congress to declare war. Republicans challenged the President's right to issue the proclamation, and Federalists, Hamilton most prominently among them, defended it. Larger issues were again at stake. As Madison had done in the removal debate, Hamilton argued that Article II's vesting clause gave the President a general grant of executive power; but, unlike Madison, Hamilton interpreted that grant to encompass foreign affairs, friendly or otherwise, limited only by the need of the Senate's consent for treaties and Congress' consent for going to war. If Hamilton was correct, the President might suspend treaties (the Senate being concerned only with their making), might engage the country in war started by another country (what then is there for Congress to declare?), might use the armed forces in hostilities short of war, and might recognize foreign governments—to set down an incomplete list. Now a Republican, Madison, writing as Helvidius, claimed for Congress what Hamilton had given to the President, insisting that the executive power essentially comprised executing the laws and appointing subordinates.[9]

The President and Senate were aligned against the House of Representatives in the case of the Jay Treaty with Great Britain. The Federalists held that the House was obligated to vote money to implement the treaty, and the Republicans, that the House could freely decide the question— that it had, in short, a right to defeat a treaty by refusing to implement it. Otherwise, as Albert Gallatin maintained in House debate on the issue, "the legislative power in fact resides in the President and Senate." Thus this dispute, too, had broad implications.[10]

The Federalists saw nothing wrong with executive officers mixing in certain legislative affairs. Their Presidents annually delivered an address before Congress that was answered by a delegation from each chamber, and once Washington went before the Senate to ask its advice on treaty

---

9. See Hamilton, Pacificus, No. I, and Madison, Helvidius, Nos. I-V, in Alexander Hamilton and James Madison, *Letters of Pacificus and Helvidius on the Proclamation of 1793* (Washington: Gideon, 1845), pp. 5-15, 53-102.

10. See Hamilton, "The Defence," No. XXXVIII, Jan. 6, 1796, in *Papers* (1974), vol. XX, p. 21. Albert Gallatin, *Annals of Congress*, 4th Cong., 1st Sess., 1796, col. 467.

negotiations. Most executive relations with Congress during the 1790s involved subordinate officers, however, above all Hamilton while he was Treasury secretary. By the act creating his department, which he is said to have drafted, Hamilton was to report to either house, "in person or in writing (as he may be required), respecting all matters referred to him, or which shall pertain to his office." As the House originated tax and spending measures, and was generally the more active of the chambers (the Senate sat behind closed doors for its first five years), it was there that Hamilton conducted most of his business. The House frequently referred important matters to him, and occasionally to Jefferson and Henry Knox, the secretaries of state and war. For example, Hamilton prepared his famous reports for funding the Confederation's debts and assuming the state ones, for establishing a bank, and for encouraging manufactures at its request. He also prepared plans on his own initiative and sometimes drafted legislation, in addition to working informally with his supporters in Congress.[11]

For twelve years the Republicans objected to what they considered executive trespasses on Congressional domain. They could do nothing about the President's annual "speech from the throne," as Jefferson called it, but they could try to keep Congress from referring legislative business to Hamilton and stop him from reporting on his own initiative, and rely instead on Congressional committees. Led by Madison (who was guided on the outside by Jefferson—a case of executive interference!), the Republicans in the House attracted enough Federalist votes to prevent Hamilton and Knox from appearing before that chamber in 1792 to discuss a military defeat at the hands of the Indians. That set the precedent that department secretaries not be allowed "to deliberate" (Jefferson's words) in Congress. And in 1794, with the Republicans in control of the House, Madison (and, from the outside, Jefferson) persuaded that body to deny Hamilton permission to report on a plan for raising revenue and to turn to its own committee instead. That year, Congress began to create standing (permanent) committees to consider legislation in place of the select

---

11. My account of early government practice owes much to Joseph Cooper, *The Origins of the Standing Committees and the Development of the Modern House*, Rice University Studies, vol. LVI, no. 3 (Houston: Summer, 1970); Ralph V. Harlow, *The History of Legislative Methods in the Period before 1825* (New Haven: Yale University Press, 1917); Robert Luce, *Legislative Assemblies* (Boston: Houghton Mifflin, 1924); and Leonard D. White, *The Federalists; A Study in Administrative History* (New York: Macmillan, 1948), and *The Republicans: A Study in Administrative History, 1801-1829* (New York: Macmillan, 1951). Albert Gallatin, cited in White, *The Federalists* p. 329. See Harlow, *Legislative Methods*, pp. 131-34.

(ad hoc) ones it had been relying on. The House Committee on Ways and Means was established in 1795, intended by its originator, Albert Gallatin, to replace the Treasury secretary as a source of financial reports. In 1797 Fisher Ames, a Federalist member of the House, wrote to Hamilton, who had resigned from office at the start of 1795, that in the House "committees are already ministers"—apparently not very effective ones, to judge from Ames's remark that the Ways and Means Committee had not written a page of its own in two years, but depended on information it collected from the Treasury Department.[12]

As the Republicans began their long reign in the executive and legislative branches in 1801, John Marshall expressed the common Federalist fear that Jefferson would weaken the Presidency while increasing his personal power by "embodying" himself in the House of Representatives. But Hamilton disagreed. On the basis of his service with Jefferson in Washington's cabinet, he denied that Jefferson was "an enemy to the power of the executive" or for "confounding all powers" in the House. Both men were right. As Secretary of State, Jefferson had often supported executive claims against Congress. Moreover, as President he acted on important occasions as Hamilton supposed he would. But he did so under a veil. One of Jefferson's first acts was to send a naval squadron to the Mediterranean Sea, without Congressional authority, to make war on any of the Barbary powers found to have declared war on the United States or engaged in hostilities on American shipping. But in reporting the matter to Congress, in December 1801, he transformed an attack by an American naval vessel upon a Tripolitan one into a defensive measure; and, "unauthorized by the Constitution, without the sanction of Congress" to go beyond defense, he asked the legislators if they wished to give him offensive power as well. He had planned to tell them on that same occasion that he believed the President could deem legislative acts unconstitutional and treat them accordingly (something Hamilton never claimed for the President), but at the last moment he omitted this issue from his message.

---

12. Jefferson, "To Martin Van Buren," June 29, 1824, in Jefferson, *The Writings of Thomas Jefferson*, ed. Andrew A. Lipscomb and Albert E. Bergh (Washington: Thomas Jefferson Memorial Assn., 1904), vol. XVI, p. 59. Jefferson, "To Thomas Pickney, Dec. 3, 1792, vol. VVIII, p. 443. Fisher Ames, "To Hamilton," Jan. 26, 1797, in Hamilton, *Papers*, vol. XX, pp. 486-87.

Jefferson exercised formidable powers in enforcing the embargo, but they were nearly all given to him by Congress—at his instigation.[13]

Thus Marshall too was right, for in veiling and redefining his executive power, Jefferson diminished the Presidential office. And, as Marshall predicted, he embodied himself with the House of Representatives and to a lesser extent with the Senate, governing Congress from within until nearly the end of his two terms. The practice of referring matters to the executive departments for opinions, greatly reduced in the late 1790s, was revived. More important, though, were the informal activities of cabinet secretaries—above all Gallatin, now Treasury secretary—with Republican members of Congress. They drafted bills, participated in caucuses and other informal gatherings, and attended meetings of legislative committees. The Republican floor leader in the House owed his appointment to Jefferson and served as his lieutenant, and Jefferson is said to have presided over some meetings of the Republican caucus there. Executive influence flowed much more heavily into the legislative branch during Jefferson's Presidency than ever it had in Hamilton's heyday.[14]

Thus the Republicans seemed to acknowledge the Federalist view that separation of powers allowed executive participation in the legislative business of Congress; at least, they acknowledged the indispensability of such participation. By depending on the President's influence rather than on his authority, they opened the way for influence to run from Congress to the executive after Jefferson's departure. Moreover, Congress strengthened the entities it had been gestating, including standing committees, which would gradually supplant select ones. In the Third Congress (1793-95), for example, there were 350 select committees; in the Thirteenth Congress (1813-15), only 70, as permanent committees were given more and more legislation. For its first twenty years, Congress discussed the

---

13. John Marshall, "To Hamilton," Dec. 21, 1800, in Hamilton, *Papers* (1977), vol. XXV, p. 290; Hamilton, "To James Bayard," Jan. 16, 1801, pp. 319-20. Compare Acting Sec. of the Navy Samuel Smith, "To Capt. Richard Dale," May 20, 1801, in U.S. Navy Dept., Office of Naval Records and Library, *Naval Documents related to the United States Naval Wars with the Barbary Powers* (Washington: Government Printing Office, 1944), vol. I, pp. 465-68, and Lt. Andrew Sterrett, "To Capt. Richard Dale," Aug. 6, 1801, p. 537, with Jefferson, "First Annual Message to Congress," Dec. 8, 1801, in *Messages and Papers of the Presidents, 1789-1897*, ed. James D. Richardson (Washington: Government Printing Office, 1896), vol. I, pp. 326-27. See "The Paragraph Omitted from the Final Draft of Jefferson's Message to Congress," Dec. 8, 1801, in Albert J. Beveridge, *The Life of John Marshall* (Boston: Houghton Mifflin, 1919), vol. III, pp. 605-606; Jefferson, "First Annual Message," in *Messages and Papers*, vol. I, p. 326.
14. See works cited in footnote 11.

policy of nearly all important legislation before turning it over to commit-tees to form into bills; in Madison's Presidency, the committees became the initiators of legislative policy and obtained the right to report bills without permission of the House. The speaker at this time, Henry Clay, also took prominence over the floor leader and the executive as the guiding force of the Republican caucus and of the whole House. Under his leadership, the caucus, in effect, replaced the electoral college, for it nominated the Republican Presidential and Vice-Presidential candidates. (Federalist electors were too few in number to matter.)[15]

In short, after Jefferson, the House of Representatives, through its own "executive" (the speaker) and "department secretaries" (chairmen of its standing committees) seized the party machinery that Jefferson had nur-tured. As John Randolph remarked of Madison in 1811: "He is President *de jure* only."[16]

Congress and the People

Congress represents the people in government as a substitute for their presenting themselves in an assembly. We often think of representation as a necessity, imposed on the framers by the extent of America in 1787, and some framers did speak of it that way. But if that was the case, why did the Constitution not bring representatives as close to the people as possible? Why did it not provide for the direct election of Senators as well as Representatives, for both to be elected to short terms, for far greater numbers of both, and for their rotation in office? Such talk came almost entirely from the Antifederalists, many of whom accepted representation with seeming reluctance. However, few among the Antifederalists regret-ted being represented in the state legislatures, and not many favored several confederations, which would have brought government closer to the people, over an extensive republic. To my knowledge, no one pre-ferred completely independent states or the selection of state or national representatives from among the people by lot, as New Jersey had done for a time in the preceding century.[17]

---

15. Luce, *Legislative Assemblies*, p. 99.
16. John Randolph, cited in Harlow, *Legislative Methods*, p. 197.
17. See, e.g. James Wilson, Constitutional Convention, June 6, 1789, in *Records of Federal Convention*, vol. I, pp. 132-33. See, e.g. "Letters from a Federal Farmer," No. VII, Dec. 31, 1787, in *Complete Anti-Federalist*, ed. Storing, vol. II, p. 265; Melanchton Smith, "New York Ratifying Convention," June 20, 1788, vol. VI, p. 153. Storing, "What the Anti-Federalists Were *For*," vol. I, p. 43, says that, "In the main, the Anti-Federalists accepted representa-tion reluctantly, as a necessary device in a community where the people cannot assem-ble to do their common business." My assessment of the Antifederalists has led me to make this a "seeming reluctance."

Most Americans at the founding, Federalists and Antifederalists alike, considered representative government superior in principle to direct rule by the people. To be sure, the Federalists more strongly praised the one and more severely rebuked the other. When still a Federalist, Madison said the function of representation was to "refine and enlarge" the public views. And Hamilton said that the ancient democracies, the archtype of direct popular rule, "never possessed one feature of good government. Their very character was tyranny; their figure deformity." Jefferson, who from his post in France was close to, if not at one with, the Antifederalists at the time of ratification, had mixed feelings. He both praised representation for elevating the "natural *aristoi*" to office and depreciated it as "unequal and vicious"; and he referred to the "inconvenience" of direct democracy and to the "inaptitude" of the people to conduct their own affairs. When the Antifederalist essayist Brutus said that a popular assembly could not "deliberate with wisdom or decide with despatch," he expressed more distinctly what Jefferson probably thought about the defects of direct democracy.[18]

For the Federalists, representation alone was not enough to transform republican government into good government. Tom Paine might have thought that representation would have helped Athens itself, but the prevailing opinion among the framers was, not greatly. On this point, too, Jefferson agreed. "It seems," he said, "that the smaller the society the bitterer the dissensions into which it breaks." The framers believed that even the largest American states were too small to control dissension. Indeed, the most important reason for a new Constitution, according to Madison, was to prevent the oppressive laws that majority factions in the states were enacting against the owners of property.[19]

As Publius-Madison explained in Federalist 10, the "remedy" for

18. *Federalist* No. 10, p. 62. Hamilton, "New York Ratifying Convention," June 21, 1788 (Child's version), in Hamilton, *Papers* (1962), vol. V, p. 39. Jefferson, "To John Adams," Oct. 28, 1813, in Jefferson, *Writings*, vol. XIII, p. 396; Jefferson, "To Madison," Sept. 6, 1799, vol. VII, p. 459-60; Jefferson, "To Edmund Randolph," Aug. 18, 1799, vol. X, p. 126. "Essays of Brutus," No. III, in *Complete Anti-Federalist*, vol. II, p. 279. See also Fisher Ames, "Speech in the Massachusetts Ratifying Convention," Jan., 1788, in *Works of Fisher Ames*, ed. Seth Ames (New York: Burt Franklin, 1971), vol. II, pp. 4-5.

19. Thomas Paine, *The Rights of Man* (New York: E. P. Dutton, 1944), part II, p. 177. Jefferson, "To Robert Williams," Nov. 1, 1807, in Jefferson, *Writings*, vol. XI, p. 39. Madison, "To Jefferson, Oct. 24, 1787, in Madison, *The Papers of James Madison*, ed. Robert A. Rutland et al. (Charlottesville: University Press of Virginia, 1977), vol. X, p. 212.

oppressive legislation lay in an extensive republic, more precisely, in the effects of such a republic especially on the House of Representatives. Its larger electoral districts were likely to elect more able and virtuous representatives, and its numerous and distributed factions would have greater difficulty uniting for action. At the Constitutional Convention Madison spoke as though the extended republic were sufficient, calling it "the only defense against [factions] compatible with democratic government."[20]

Hamilton was not so sure. When Madison presented his theory of the extended republic to the Convention on June 6, 1787, Hamilton noted that demagogues would be elected from large districts "more often" than Madison thought, and representatives would feel "all the passions of popular assemblies." Some days later, in presenting his own plan of government, Hamilton told the Convention: "Representation alone will not do." In *Federalist* 63, Publius-Hamilton (whom I believe its author to be) acknowledged that an extensive republic would avoid "*some* of the dangers" that beset smaller ones, and then turned to argue for a senate as a defense against the "temporary errors and delusions" of the people acting through the House of Representatives. He repeated this argument in his essays dealing with the President and judiciary. It should be noted that Madison seemed to assign a similar purpose to the Senate: as he stated in the Convention, it was to act "with more coolness, with more system, & with more wisdom than the popular branch."[21]

The framers expected the House of Representatives to be a "fluctuating" and "multitudinous" body. It might be superior to the people at large, but still its members would be only "somewhat" wise and virtuous —"in general," *The Federalist* suggests—and the ratio of the ignorant and weak in character among them would grow as it grew. Not only would the House start with a membership two-and-a-half times as large as the Senate's, but Publius predicted that it would reach 400 in 50 years and that half would be new every term. Size and turnover together would produce an unstable House, disposed to act under "sudden and violent passions," dominated by "factious leaders," unfamiliar in large part with legislative business, and lacking steadiness and restraint in its conduct.[22]

---

20. *Federalist* No. 10, pp. 62-65. Madison, "Constitutional Convention," June 6, 1787, in *Records of Federal Convention*, vol. I, pp. 134-35.

21. Hamilton, "Constitutional Convention," June 6[?], 1787 (Hamilton's notes), vol. I, pp. 146-47. Hamilton, "Constitutional Convention," June 18, 1787 (Notes for Speech), p. 309. *Federalist* No. 63, pp. 425-26. See *Federalist* Nos. 71 and 78, pp. 482-83, 528-29. Madison, "Constitutional Convention," June 7, 1787, vol. I, p. 151.

22. *Federalist* No. 47, compare pp. 384 and 385; *Federalist* No. 58, p. 396. *Federalist* No. 55, p. 375. *Federalist* No. 62, pp. 418, 419, 420-21.

The House of Representatives is the American version of the Athenian assembly. It was, in fact, often referred to as "an assembly," as were the lower houses of most colonial and state legislatures. The framers considered the House "the democratic" or "the popular" branch of American government, which would share, to a lesser degree, the defects of the original.[23]

The Senate, President, and judiciary were to be informally allied in checking the *oppressions* of the House of Representatives as well as its *encroachments*: they were to check the tyranny of popular majorities acting through the House, as well as the tyranny of the House acting for itself. The Senate would oppose unjust acts of the House; the President would oppose those of Congress when the Senate joined in them or gave way to them, and he would also resist Congressional opposition to his exercise of powers; and the courts would be a final defense. Although the framers did not see the executive and judiciary as major sources of danger to the rights of minorities and individuals, they provided checks on those branches as well.

The framers invested the other branches with the stability and energy that the House of Representatives lacked. Stability attaches itself to government in the measure that government detaches itself from the people. It adheres where officers are few, where their terms are extended, and where they are elected indirectly. The framers worked to make "the more permanent branches" less like American society in their composition than was the House. Senators would be generally "most distinguished" for their wisdom and virtue; the Presidency would "in constant probability" attract "the preeminent" and sometimes even "the noblest minds"; and judges would be selected from those very few lawyers who have integrity as well as knowledge of the laws. A stable Senate can be what the House of Representatives cannot: calm and knowing in its deliberations and steady in pursuing its policies; respected by foreign nations and the American people, and yet firm against the people's imprudence. Stability enhances the Presidency also, but it is energy, which attaches to a single person, that enables him to be prompt in executing the laws and forceful in protecting

---

23. For use of the word "assembly" to describe the House of Representatives, see, e.g., Hamilton, "Constitutional Convention," June 18, 1787 (Yate's notes), in *Records of Federal Convention*, vol. I, p. 299; *Federalist* No. 48, p. 334; *Federalist* No. 64, p. 433; *Federalist* No. 71, p. 483; Luce, *Legislative Principles*, p. 97. For use of the words "democratic" or "popular" branch to describe the House, see, e.g., Madison, "Constitutional Convention," June 12, 1787, in *Records of Federal Convention*, vol. I, p. 218; *Federalist* No. 52, p. 359; *Federalist* No. 66, p. 448.

the country. And stability makes resolute judges who would otherwise be timid in dealing with the other branches.[24]

Stability and energy are nonpartisan terms. They take no sides in the quarrels over political forms and, in fact, have no specific application to politics. Yet they embody the substance of political principles, for stability bears the features of aristocracy, and energy conjures up the figure of the monarch. It is not surprising that the Constitutional Convention experienced a "very important" difficulty in combining stability (mainly in the Senate and Supreme Court) and energy (in the executive) with republican liberty (found mainly in the House of Representatives) in arranging their government. The American Constitution contains not only the American version of the ancient assembly but the American version of the traditional mixed regime.[25]

The framers would surely say that their Constitution creates a regime that differs from mixed regimes of the past in significant ways. Indeed, they would probably insist that it is not a regime at all, but a government. It does not rule, but governs them; nor does it embody certain classes within it, but is, or strives to be, "sufficiently neutral" of society's contending forces. Its assembly, somewhat removed from the people, was intended to give them "their proper degree of influence" on its conduct, and the rest of government, somewhat further away, was intended to restrain the people when the House of Representatives could not. The Senate, President, and Supreme Court, the framers would emphasize, were invested with the *attributes* of aristocracy and monarchy, not with the real things. They would point out that all parts of their government derived their authority "from the great body of society, and not from an inconsiderable proportion or a favored class of it," and that all political offices were open without regard to wealth or other class distinctions. The underlying principle of such a government was democracy. Its model was, in a special way, Athens. The framers departed from principle and model, as we have seen, for they believed that "theoretic reasoning ... must be qualified by the lessons of practice," and they were alarmed by the practice of earlier republics. But they justified their restraints on the people in the name of the people: such restraints were necessary for securing the equal rights of all.[26]

---

24. *Federalist* No. 37, pp. 233. *Federalist* No. 52, p. 359. *Federalist* No. 64, p. 433; *Federalist* No. 68, p. 461; *Federalist* No. 72, p. 488; *Federalist* No. 78, pp. 529-30. See *Federalist* Nos. 62 and 63; 70, 71, and 72; and 78, et passim.

25. *Federalist* No. 37, p. 233.

26. Madison, "To Jefferson," Oct. 24, 1787, in Madison, *Papers* (1977), vol. X, p. 214. *Federalist* No. 35, p. 221. *Federalist* No. 39, p. 251. *Federalist* No. 43, p. 293.

The Antifederalists, generally speaking, had less faith in an extensive republic—a "consolidated government," as they called it—and more faith in democracy than the Federalists. We might say that they were unwilling to depart so much from the model of Athens. Some of them opposed the Constitution outright; more wished to limit the powers it granted the federal government and to strengthen that government's popular parts. They disapproved of connecting the Senate and the President, of the length of their terms (especially the Senate's), and of their unlimited eligibility. They criticized the proposed House of Representatives as too small to contain representatives from all classes or to know the people's wants. Some thought a term of two years was too long. Some called the proposed Senate an "aristocratic" body, the House "an assistant aristocratic branch." The President differed from a monarch "scarcely but in name." Perhaps George Mason best summarized the Antifederalist view: the new government would "commence in a moderate aristocracy" and "most probably vibrate for some years between [a monarchy and a corrupt, oppressive aristocracy] and then terminate in the one or the other.[27]

Federalists and Republicans continued to quarrel over the political character of the Constitution after the document was set in motion. Hamilton was impressed by its democratic features. He had described it as a "representative democracy" at the New York ratifying convention; and he and his party fought afterward to contain its "diseases." Jefferson described it in 1797 as wearing "a mixed aspect of monarchy and republicanism"; and he and his party would reform its "heresies."[28]

Disputes between Federalists and Republicans during the 1790s over separation of powers—some of which we have recounted—were also, inevitably, disputes over the authority of institutions closer to or more removed from the people. Indeed, one wonders if the contestants were not at times more concerned with the degree of popular influence in government than they were with preventing one branch of government

---

27. "Letters of Centinel," No. I, Oct., 1787, in *Complete Anti-Federalist*, vol. II, p. 142; "Essays of John DeWitt," No. III, [Oct.-Dec., 1787], vol. IV, p. 27; Luther Martin, "The Genuine Information Delivered to the Legislature of Maryland" (1788), vol. II, p. 34. George Mason, "Objections to the Constitution of Government Formed by the Convention" (1787), vol. II, p. 13.

28. Hamilton, "New York Ratifying Convention, Notes for Speech," July 12, 1788, in Hamilton, *Papers* (1962), vol. V, p. 150; Hamilton, "To Theodore Sedgwick," July 10, 1804, (1979), vol. XXVI, p. 309. Jefferson, "To James Sullivan," Feb. 9, 1797, in Jefferson, *Writings*, vol. IX, p. 377; Jefferson, "To John Taylor," May 28, 1816, vol. XV, p. 22.

from encroaching on another. It was typical of Republicans to discern monarchic or aristocratic designs in their adversaries' positions. To allow the President to remove executive officials would enable him to establish his "throne"; to argue that the powers of making treaties and declaring war were executive powers was to borrow from "royal prerogatives"; to allow the Secretary of the Treasury to "report" plans to the House (in contrast to merely "preparing" plans) was to clear a path for "aristocracy or monarchy."[29] Jefferson saw his party's victory in 1800 as an opportunity to put the Constitution on its "republican tack." As I have pointed out, he, in fact, sometimes followed a Federalist course during his Presidency. Indeed, he left in place such landmarks of his predecessors as the bank and the funding system, without a public word of criticism, and erected new landmarks on their constitutional design. The Republican view of the scope of national authority could not justify his purchase of Louisiana in 1803, and his embargo of 1807-1809 seemed to go further than what Hamilton (now dead) believed Congress could go under the commerce clause. Moreover, the relations that he and his agents established with Congress, by developing standing committees and substituting them for the committee of the whole in the House of Representatives, gave the legislature itself an oligarchic cast.[30]

In his own defense, Jefferson might say that he had to give way at times in steering the "constitutional Argosy" into a safe haven. Shortly after taking office, he wrote: "I am sensible how far I should fall short of effecting all the reformation which reason would suggest, and reason approve, were I free to do whatever I thought best." He covered his falling off from republican theory as best he could, for example, by disguising his Mediterranean action and not attempting a constitutional justification of the Louisiana purchase or the embargo. He paid deference to Congress even as he and his cabinet secretaries were guiding its deliberations, and Republicans in the legislature joined in the deception. They pretended they were receiving "information," not "advice," from the executive, and paid lip-service to the committee of the whole—the body that truly evinced the "sense of the majority"—as they increasingly referred legislative bills to standing committees for first discussion of their merits.[31]

29. James Jackson, *History of Congress*, 1st Cong., 1st Sess., 1789, House of Representatives, June 17, 1789, col. 507; see also Theodoric Bland, May 19, 1789, col. 381. Madison, Helvidius No. I, in *Letters of Pacificus and Helvidius*, p. 62. John Page, cited in White, *Federalists*, p. 67.
30. Jefferson, "To John Dickinson," March 6, 1801, in Jefferson, *Writings*, vol. X, p. 217. See, e.g., Jefferson, "First Inaugural Address," Mar. 4, 1801, vol. III, pp. 317-23.
31. Jefferson, "To Walter Jones," Mar. 31, 1801, vol. X, pp. 255-56. Cooper, *Origins of Standing Committees*, pp. 14, 43-44, 53.

The Congress of the future, Jefferson might explain, would be more republican in form and more restrained in activity than that of the framers. The people would elect not only Representatives but also Senators, who would serve shorter terms and whose link to the Presidency would be weakened by the near-"annihilation" of the treaty-power. Congressional authority would be confined to expressly delegated powers and to those means—implied powers—"absolutely necessary" for implementing them. The Presidency and judiciary would fall even further in stature. The President would lose his ceremonial majesty and, holding office for no more than two terms, would defer to his legislative partner to the point of exercising his veto against its enactments only in very unusual circumstances. The judges, too, serving limited terms, would be subdued in their pretensions, even to having the last word on the constitutionality of laws and executive actions. Below the national government would be the vibrant state legislatures, representatives close to the people and, below them, popular assemblies, moving in the enlarged sphere created by the diminution of national power.[32]

Conclusion

The framers' Congress has changed in significant ways over the years. The most obvious ones are signaled by amendments to the Constitution: the Senate is elected by the people, as Jefferson desired, and all elected officials are chosen by a mass electorate broader than what even Jefferson would have wished. The document has only partially noticed the great extension of national authority, of the President and courts, as well as Congress, into what was once the constitutional reserve of the states and the people—contrary to Jefferson's wishes and possibly Hamilton's, too. (I will not comment on the ways that authority has been used.)[33]

The "multitudinous" and "fluctuating" House of Representatives has become a more stable body than Hamilton thought it would. This trend began early as the House organized itself into standing committees and submitted to its Speaker for leadership, and has intensified in this century

---

32. Jefferson, "To John Taylor," May 28, 1816, in *Writings*, vol. XV, p. 21. Jefferson, "To James Monroe," Mar. 21, 1796, vol. IX, p. 329.
33. For Hamilton's view of the states, compare Hamilton, "Constitutional Convention," June 21, 1787, in *Records of Federal Convention*, vol. I, p. 359, with Hamilton, "To Edward Carrington," May 26, 1792, in *Papers*, vol. XI, p. 443.

as representatives increasingly have made careers of Congressional service and as committee chairmen, buttressed by seniority, became ever more powerful. Hamilton had not foreseen these specific changes, although he—Publius, anyway—had predicted that the "soul" that "animated" a large representative body would become "more oligarchic."[34]

Striking changes, in the name of democracy, have taken place in Congress since the early 1970s, especially in the House of Representatives. There, the power of committee chairmen has weakened, some of it falling to the numerous subcommittees and their chairpersons, some of it rising to the Speaker, and much of it subjected to the consent of the rank and file of the majority party. Deliberation and voting both in committees and on the floor have been opened in new ways to public scrutiny.

Perhaps the most vivid change affecting Congress is in its relationship to the American people. No longer does one hear about the House of Representatives giving the people "their proper sphere of influence" on its deliberations, or the Senate as a "defense" against their "temporary errors and delusions." Nor does one hear popular majorities referred to as "factions." Congress now prides itself on its continuous accountability to the people—as do the other parts of government. And the people, aided by modern communications, tend to regard all public officials as their agents—magistrates is the term used in the ancient democracies—and themselves as constituting what may be called an Athenian assembly on a grand scale. The framers generally—Hamilton specifically—would have viewed this trend with grave misgivings. What Jefferson would think, I do not presume to say.

---

34. *Federalist* No. 75, p. 507. *Federalist* No. 58, p. 396.

Motivating Deliberation in Congress

Jane Mansbridge

"The greatest deliberative body in the world," as the U.S. Senators used fondly to dub the Senate, no longer deliberates as it should. So say many of its members. The same is true for the U.S. House of Representatives. While an increased workload is the primary culprit in gradually reducing the time available for deliberation over the last forty years, a secondary cause lies in the low priority given to facilitating deliberation among political reformers and political scientists. But the situation is not immutable. We can design institutions to offer incentives for behavior we want to encourage and mild sanctions for the opposite. The key preliminary step is will—agreeing that encouraging deliberation is worth bearing some costs.

Adversary Democracy

The generation of American political scientists that emerged after World War II articulated, often unconsciously, an orthodoxy that excluded or diminished the role of deliberation. This orthodoxy brought to final fruition a revolution in political thought begun in the seventeenth century. In that century, the experience of the religious wars and the growing dominance of market economics, among other causes, helped produce not only Hobbes's vision of humans as atoms in space, hurtling on collision course one with another, but also a set of institutions based on the assumption that human interests conflict. In the theory of "adversary" democracy that has evolved from these beginnings, all is conflict. With no agreed-on standards, no individual's preferences are worth more than another's. Legitimate decisions derive from weighing each individual's preferences equally, because no fully persuasive reasons can be given for doing otherwise. While earlier assumptions of common interest could legitimate unequal power on the grounds that the more powerful would act in the interest of the less powerful, the assumption of conflict requires instead equal power for everyone's interests to be protected equally.[1]

---

1. For a fuller exposition of both the history and logic of adversary democracy, see Jane J. Mansbridge, *Beyond Adversary Democracy* (1980; rpt. Chicago: University of Chicago Press, 1983).

Until the mid twentieth century, all liberal democratic theory reflected, in lessening degrees over time, pre-adversary elements. John Locke, James Madison, and J.S. Mill, for example, all (though each less than the last) believed both that a single national interest was possible and that advancing it required representatives relatively unfettered by constituent preference. Pre-adversary theories of representation postulated much genuine common interest between leaders and led—a postulate that legitimated the representative's greater independent power.

By the second half of the twentieth century, central figures in the American profession of political science would deny the possibility of a national common interest. In 1908, Arthur Bentley declared: "We shall never find a group interest of the society as a whole."[2] By the 1950's, this denial had become an orthodoxy.[3] For this now fully developed theory of adversary democracy, Joseph Schumpeter provided a model of electoral representation borrowed from the invisible hand of the marketplace, through which the fundamentally conflicting interests of representative and constituent could achieve artificial congruence.[4]

The reigning understanding of representation in American political science today derives from Schumpeter and follows the adversary formulation. The old, crude dichotomy between the "free" trustee and the "bound" delegate has been left behind, along with the obsolete tradition of instruction. Instead we picture voters giving their representative a relatively free hand to represent their preferences in a world of complex and changing circumstances, but binding the representative to their preferences through retrospective voting. Just as the pressures of the market force the most loving capitalist to cut wages, so the pressures of reelection force the most thoughtful representative to attend to constituents' thoughtless preferences. Like the market, the system does not require voters as a collectivity to discuss, formulate and demand what they want. Politicians act like entrepreneurs, scanning the potential market, trying to

---

2. *The Process of Government* (Evanston, IL: Principia Press, 1949), p.222.

3. See Robert MacIver: "We should never imply that the people are a unity on any matter of policy. The people are always divided," *The Web of Government* (New York: Macmillan, 1947), p. 416; David Truman: "We do not have to account for a totally inclusive interest, because one does not exist," *The Governmental Process* (New York: Knopf, 1956), p. 51; or Frank H. Sorauf: "It seems clear that no interest motivates all citizens," "The Public Interest Reconsidered," *Journal of Politics* 29 (1957) p. 625.

4. Joseph A. Schumpeter, *Capitalism, Socialism and Democracy* (1942; rpt. New York: Harper and Row, 1962), chapters 21-23. For a note on Schumpeter's own concern with the common interest, see Mansbridge p. 340, n. 32.

attract the marginal vote by using the best cues they can find—including detailed opinion polls—to discover the voters' preferences. Like entrepreneurs, they also create preferences, good and bad, that they then can satisfy.

Just as the adversary assumption that citizens' interests conflict describes much of political reality, particularly in today's large nation-state, so the adversary assumption that politicians are primarily concerned with reelection—and that if they are not, the system will select them out—describes much of the reality of representation, at least in today's United States. But describing much of a phenomenon does not mean describing it all. Nor are these balances historically fixed. The adversary revolution may have run its course, both in the practice of representation and in academic description. If so, the time has come again for investigating, with a view toward encouraging, a politics of the common good, in which deliberation must have a central role. In the last five years, several political scientists have embraced the possibility that even on the scale of the nation or our largest states it makes both normative and descriptive sense to conceive of legislators as pursuing, in part, the common good.[5] The stage is now set for revising incrementally the institutions and thought processes to which we are accustomed, to promote greater attention to good public policy, and greater concern with thorough deliberation.

Conceptually, we can discard, within the old "trustee-delegate" dichotomy, the distinction between the "free" and the "bound" representative, while retaining the distinction between constituents' preferences (or "immediate preferences") and their interests (or "enlightened preferences"), and the distinction between individual and common good, or between the part and the whole. While moving from preferences to enlightened interests involves the dangers of paternalism, and while trying to discover or create a common good involves the dangers of pseudo-consensus, American political institutions and the reigning interpretations of those institutions have so emphasized these dangers that the virtues of uncovering or creating enlightened common interests have long been ignored.

5. E.g. William K. Muir, Jr., *Legislature: California's School for Politics* (Chicago: University of Chicago Press, 1982); Arthur Mass, *Congress and the Common Good* (New York: Basic Books, 1983); David J. Vogler and Sidney R. Waldman, *Congress and Democracy* (Washington, D.C.: Congressional Quarterly Press, 1985); Martha Derthick and Paul J. Quirk, *The Politics of Deregulation* (Washington, D.C.: Brookings, 1985).

The problem, both conceptually and practically, is much like the problem of group altruism in sociobiology. Sociobiologists have no trouble explaining the persistence of altruistic behaviors that result in perpetuating one's own genes. But they have not easily been able to explain how groups can persuade or socialize their members to make the group's interest their own even when this will reduce the chance that such a member's own genes will be passed on. Extending the analogy to the electoral arena, if a representative pays too much attention either to constituents' underlying interests as opposed to their preferences or to the good of the nation as opposed to the district, that representative will not survive to continue to do good, either directly or by example. Within these constraints, however, all representatives have some latitude. One important task for political science and political reform is, consequently, to discover the places in which representatives actually have the room to move toward enlightenment and the common good, make those places more accessible and more common, and reduce the penalties paid for frequenting them. I will try to take a step in this direction through a brief analysis of Congressional deliberation.

Facets of Deliberation

The word "deliberation" invokes a cluster of concepts, of which I will use, unfortunately for analytical clarity, more than one. I will not assume that deliberation involves, or should involve, only real interests, but I will assume that one goal of deliberation is to reveal real interests rather than present preferences. I will not assume that deliberation involves, or should involve, only common interests, but I will assume that one goal of deliberation is to search out or even create a common interest, which may not be visible at the first stages of a decision. While deliberation will also often reveal fundamental and irreconcilable conflict that must be dealt with through the formulae of adversary democracy, I will stress in this discussion the search for the common good in deliberation, on the grounds that this element has until recently been neglected by political scientists trained in the adversary tradition. I will also adopt here Joseph Bessette's useful distinction between bargaining, negotiation, and deliberation.[6] In this discussion deliberation will mean contemplating and dis-

---

6. Joseph M. Bessette, "Deliberation in Congress," paper delivered at the annual meeting of the American Political Science Association, Washington, D.C., 1979, pp. 10-12. This is, at the moment, the definitive treatment of the subject.

cussing the substantive merits of a proposal.[7] Bargaining will mean the discussion of strategy. Negotiation will mean a mixture of deliberation and bargaining in which agreement involves not only an accomodation to the respective power of the participants but consideration of substantive issues as well.[8]

When members of Congress have changed their minds, taken positions for the first time, or strengthened previous positions as the result of discussion on the merits of legislation, we may fairly say that deliberation has taken place. We can, further, tell good deliberation from bad by looking at the outcome in those cases in which we have reliable criteria for distinguishing good outcomes from bad. When we do not have such criteria, we can look at the process for new information, careful reasoning, accuracy, and the generation of a full range of options. The characteristics of careful weighing and lack of haste, implicit in the ordinary meanings of the English and French word "deliberation," often contribute as much as new information or reasoning to a good final decision. So too face-to-face interaction, in the right circumstances, enhances communication and mutual empathy. Yet because the very circumstances that generate better information and reasoning also at times generate greater haste, prevent face-to-face interaction, or build in professional or expert bias, the processual criteria of new information and reasoning alone cannot guarantee good deliberation.

Down and Out in the Corridors of Power

The growth of the nation's population and of the duties legitimately performed by government has, over time, caused the locus of deliberation in the Congress to move down from the assembly floor to the committees, from the committees to the subcommittees, from the subcommittees to the staffs, and out the door to the executive branch, party policy groups, and, most recently, to ad hoc meetings of interest groups, foundations, academic subspecialties, and the press. This movement does not necessar-

---

7. A full treatment of deliberation would spend more time on individual contemplation than does this paper, which focusses on two-way communication, particularly in discussion.

8. In a negotiation, for example, one might bring out long-term implications of a policy that one believed the other parties would not want, or suggest in trade not what the others asked for but a substitute that one believed they might actually want as much or more.

ily mean that the quality of deliberation has deteriorated. It may even have improved. But it does not seem to occur in the same places or to involve the same people. We do not yet know how these changes affect either the character of the deliberation itself and its outcomes, or how to influence the groups now emerging in the deliberative process to move the outcomes closer to the public interest.

We have known for a long time that little genuine deliberation now transpires on the floor of the House or Senate. Much of what is said on the floor is designed primarily for the record or for home consumption.[9] Yet read or heard, speeches in these bodies still play some educational role, disseminating new information and reasoning to supporters, opponents and the uncommitted. On the basis of interviews with Senators in 1956, Donald Matthews concluded that "despite much folklore to the contrary, Senate speeches *do* influence votes."[10]

---

9. Donald R. Matthews, *U.S. Senators and Their World* (Chapel Hill, N.C.: University of North Carolina Press, 1960), "The Nature of 'Debate'" pp. 243-49 et passim.

10. Matthews, p. 249. Speeches introducing a bill are particularly likely to have this function (p. 244). Matthews' observations come from the Senate. As for the House, John Kingdon reported, from interviews in 1969, that "in [the unspecified number of] cases in which the congressmen did report some uncertainty about how to cast a vote, they decided how to vote during the debate 23 percent of the time . . . ." John W. Kingdon, *Congressmen's Voting Decisions*, 2nd ed. (New York: Harper and Row, 1981), p. 229. Regarding the debate's information function, he concluded (p. 102), ". . . it is still a regular occurance that a quarter or so of the House membership will spend hours in the chamber listening to the debate; if not to change their minds, then at least to gain more information, to listen to new arguments, or perchance to formulate an opinion when they do not hold a strong view." In the early 1950's Bertram Gross concluded that "Floor statements are often the quickest and most effective method of passing the word around." Bertram M. Gross, *The Legislative Struggle: A Study in Social Combat* (New York: McGraw Hill, 1953), p. 366, cited in Matthews, p. 247. Finally, Bessette (pp. 26-27) gives vivid examples from 1946 and 1959 of debate in the Senate changing members' minds. He points out as well that "making up minds" is as important as changing them, and that debate often has this function.

The direct transmittal of information from debate to individual members through the *Congressional Record* may have declined over time. In 1956, Senator Richard Neuberger described his typical day as beginning, "6:45 - 7:45 A.M. rise, read *Congressional Record* of the previous day which was left on doorstep during night, also two daily newspapers" (cited Matthews, p. 80). Similarly, for the House in 1969 John Kingdon concluded that "Members often at least scan the *Record* to find out what transpired the previous day" (p.102). On the other hand, in 1985 David Vogler and Sidney Waldman concluded that "staff members often look through the transcripts of debate available in the *Congressional Record* the next day, but it is doubtful much of the content of the debate gets to senators that way" (p. 88).

Not attending debate may enhance the larger deliberative process. Skimming through the speeches the day after, or having a staff member pick out and highlight the important ideas, is undoubtedly a more efficient way to pick up new information and reasoning than attending the debate. Reading or being briefed, does not, of course, allow the two-way communication on which much effective deliberation depends, nor the nuances of facial tone, posture and voice that communicate more than formal logic and dry fact. Conciousness of this loss may explain why members of Congress often act as if attendance at the formal floor debate were an important obligation.[11] Some argue for televising floor debates, for example, on the grounds that it would shame members into attending,[12] while others recall with nostalgia the era of "real debates" on the floor.[13] Yet while citizens might be interested in and informed through debate on the floor, particularly if televised, it is not clear that the quality of deliberation in the Senate itself is improved by members using their time this way. Productive deliberation often requires privacy, relative

---

11. E.g.: Senator Howard Baker: "... increasingly the important work of this branch of the Congress, it seems to me, has been done, is being done in committees rather than on the floor of the Senate. I think it is a matter of national loss that the Senate as a body has forfeited a great amount of its status as the Nation's prime forum for the debate of public issues. To elaborate that only briefly, I would like once more to see the Senate well attended, the participation of all Members in meaningful and significant debate on a range of issues." *Hearing of the Temporary Select Committee to Study the Senate Committee System* on S.R. 127, 98th Cong., 2d sess.(hereafter called *Hearing*, Part 1, July 31, 1984, p. 2. Senator Daniel Evans: "On the first time I had a chance to sit in the Senate I listened to some rather splendid statements from my colleagues but I was one of the only ones to listen, other than those who heard the hollow voices through the squawk box, and that's a thin substitute for traditional live debate the Senate was once noted for. [I propose that] we recreate traditional, meaningful and probing debate . . . ," p. 42. Senator Ted Stevens: "It seems to me that we ought to find a way to get back to the floor, and have major debates on major issues that affect our Nation . . . ." *Hearing*, Part 2, August 2, 1984, p. 5. See also Senators Dixon and Stennis, pp. 16,59, 61, and in *Report together with Proposed Resolutions*, Temporary Select Committee to Study the Senate Committee System, U.S. Senate, 98th Cong., 2d sess., December 14, 1984, Senator John Stennis: "The Senate has lost much in the way of ability to debate and be heard, transmit ideas to other leaders and thereby produce conclusions," and Senator Howard Baker on concern for "the loss of the status of a public forum in the Senate" (p. 3).

12. *Hearing*, Part 2, August 2, 1984, p. 17.

13. ". . . in 1948, the first calendar year that I was here—the war had ended in 1945, as you remember—there were still a lot of big problems pending. . . . [Yet] there was very complete consideration and debate, at times enlightening debate on the floor by competent members. . . . we had real debates . . . ." Senator John Stennis, in *Hearing*, Part 2, August 2, 1984, pp. 59-60.

informality, and a forum that facilitates back and forth interchange in which each person desiring to speak has no difficulty getting the floor. This unrestrained interchange emerges most easily in small groups in which each member has a chance to speak spontaneously.

Committees facilitate this kind of genuine deliberation. Even in the First Congress (1789-91), although Madison argued that "it was much better to determine the outlines of all business in a Committee of the Whole,"[14] other members urged establishing committees and subcommittees to think matters through before they reached the floor.[15] As both the nation and demands for collective action through government grew, the number of committees and subcommittees grew apace.[16] Not only for specialization, but also because the committees provided a place for the relatively private discussion of delicate issues that needed negotiation, over time more and more effective deliberation shifted to the committee room.[17] Yet as the work load increased further, and as the committees themselves were opened to public scrutiny,[18] much of that deliberation shifted to the subcommittees.

Most recently, the subcommittees themselves have suffered some of the fate of the committees. Members of Congress, with from seven to seventeen assignments to committees or subcommittees as well as their other duties,[19] often cannot attend many of the meetings. They are briefed by

---

14. *Annals* 1 Cong. 1 (May 19, 1789), p. 370, cited in Joe Cooper, *The Origins of the Standing Committees and the Development of the Modern House* (vol. 56, Rice University Studies), p. 9.

15. "Mr. Jackson wished the motion had been referred to a subcommittee to digest: it seemed to him that they [The Committee of the Whole] were building the house before the plan was drawn. He wished to see the system reduced to writing, that he might leisurely judge of the necessity and propriety of each office and its particular duties." *Annals* 1 Cong. 1 [May 19, 1789], p. 374, (cited in Cooper, p. 10).

16. The development was not linear. See Figures 1-1 and 1-2 in Steven S. Smith and Christopher J. Deering, *Committees in Congress* (Washington, D.C.: Congressional Quarterly Press, 1984), pp. 9, 29.

17. For examples of deliberation in committees, see Smith and Deering, pp. 98-103: "Policy Committees" (e.g. Education and Labor, and Judiciary).

18. The number of closed committee hearings dropped from 35 percent of all hearings in 1960 to seven percent in 1975. Gregg Easterbrook, "What's Wrong with Congress?" *The Atlantic Monthly* 254 (December 1984): 59. In 1982 Senators singled out "most often" as a reason for the decline in negotiation and political self-sacrifice the rule opening committee meetings to the public. "Special Report: The Individualist Senate," *Congressional Quarterly Weekly* 40 (1982): 2177.

19. *Report of the Study Group on Senate Practices and Procedures to the Committee on Rules and Administration, United States Senate* (Washington, D.C., U.S. G.P.O., 1984) (hereafter *Report of the Study Group*), pp. 19-21.

their staffs on what to say, rush in and say it, and are briefed by their staffs later on what happened after they left. While this process allows new information and new forms of reasoning to emerge, it does not allow in the subcommittee itself the careful weighing of the reasons for and against a measure that the word "deliberation" connotes. The proliferation of subcommittees also means that key decisions are sometimes left, through self-selection, to a narrower range of members, and, through the pressure on the members' time, to fewer and fewer members. As a result, such deliberation as may occur takes place not among, say, the twelve members of a committee, but between the subcommittee chair and ranking minority member in one of their offices.[20] As John Stennis fondly recalled the 1940's in Congress:

> [In committee] the consideration was thorough and complete and disposed of on merits. You could not go back to that because the volume is too much. . . . I do not know where we are on these committees [today]. In the old days I knew. We talked to each other freely. We are not enemies now, understand, but there was a freedom, an exchange of opinion and facts and everything in between the membership. . . . The volume has just outrun us. But we did have that freedom of thought and talk and exchange of views, and it helped.[21]

Where, then, if anywhere, does this unhasty weighing take place? Some deliberation still takes place on the floor, in the committees, and in the subcommittees.[22] Some takes place when the member of Congress reads, or is briefed, on others' ideas.[23] Some takes place in the offices of the

---

20. For these reasons former Senators James B. Pearson and Abraham A. Ribicoff recommended abolishing all standing subcommittees. *Report of the Study Group*, p. 4. The later Quayle Committee, following the same logic, suggested at least a limitation. "Summary of Proposals" adopted unanimously by the Temporary Select Committee to Study the Senate Committee System, November 29, 1984. I would like to thank Senator Dan Quayle's staff for making this report available.

21. *Hearing.* Temporary Select Committtee to Study the Senate Committee System, U.S. Senate, 98th Cong., 2d sess., August 2, 1984, pp. 59-60.

22. Kingdon, while not asking what proportion of the members' talk is devoted to the merits of legislation, quotes several members as follows: "There's always a lot of talking among members. 'What are you going to do on this? Why is that?' Just checking around, getting ideas, making sure you're not missing something important that you haven't thought of. You do a lot of talking on the floor. This is mostly to confirm that you have your facts straight" (pp.77-78); "As the debate goes on, a lot of talk among the members takes place. This discussion in the chamber is extremely important" (pp. 103-4); "You get more information in the cloakroom than you do out on the floor" (p. 104).

23. E.g. Kingdon p. 79: "I read the minority views and felt they made some good points." Kingdon (p.102) reports members' reading "Dear Colleague" letters from other members, as well as printed committee reports and minority views. He adds (p. 215) that in the members' self-report, their reading affected the way they thought about an issue 49 percent of the time.

members of Congress, in the lunchroom, or on the golf course. Much information relevant to deliberation is conveyed by cue-giving, simply taking the vote of another member or group of members as a short-hand summary of the merits of a bill.[24]

Deliberation by and among members of Congress has not, then, vanished. But by both subjective and quantitative measures it has declined dramatically. Qualitative reports suggest an increasing substitution of reading or briefing for actual participation in debate; quantitative reports show a decline in reading itself. According to one report, representatives in 1965 spent almost one full day every week on "legislative research and reading"; by 1977 that time was down to an average of eleven minutes a day.[25]

By the accounts of the members of Congress themselves, their increased policy workload is the prime reason for their curtailed opportunities for deliberation. That workload has increased in part because of the expanding demands of a growing polity,[26] in part because more staff make it possible for the Congress to process more information and accordingly take on more work, and in part because the new "individualism" in both Senate and House has allowed more members to become policy entrepreneurs.[27]

At the same time that the policy workload has been increasing, so has the representatives' load of constituency service. Partly because increased travel budgets and increased staffs have made it possible, partly because the increased role of the federal government has made it necessary, and

---

24. See Kingdon, pp. 98-99, and 196, 228 and 231 on satisficing behavior, and Matthews pp. 252-53.

25. Micheal J. Malbin, *Unelected Representatives: Congressional Staff and the Future of Representative Government* (New York: Basic Books, 1980), p. 243, citing U.S. Congress, n.d., pp. 17-20.

26. Most of this demand lies in the expansion of the politiy itself, not in the demands made on it, if the federal budget is an indicator. The federal budget has not grown much as a share of GNP since the mid 1950's. *Economic Report of the President* (Washington, D.C.: U.S.G.P.O., 1986), Tables B-1, B-73, comparing 1955 and 1985. See especially on-budget outlays.

27. Barbara Sinclair, "Senate Styles and Senate Decision-making, 1955-1980," paper delivered at the annual meeting of the American Political Science Association, New Orleans, 1985, pp. 2, 4, 6, reports increases in roll call votes, in contested bills as a proportion of all bills passed, and in filibusters. See also Michael Foley, *The New Senate: Liberal Influence on a Conservative Institution* (New Haven: Yale University Press, 1980). Neither of these discussions presents clear evidence that the new "individualism" in the Senate has hurt the quality of deliberation, except by increasing the workload.

partly, perhaps, because of increased fears regarding reelection, members of Congress have come to spend more and more of their time on constituency service. Senator Gaylord Nelson, a Wisconsin Democrat who lost his bid for a fourth term in 1980, complained: "Seventy-five percent of my time, or maybe 80 percent, was spent on non-legislative matters. . . . Constituents seem to judge their senators on how much crap the senator is sending them. . . . There isn't much thinking in the Senate any more."[28] The trend to constituency service has a mixed effect on deliberation. On the one hand, by insulating the members from constituency policy pressure, it can allow them to consider more policies from a national perspective. On the other hand, the advantage it gives to incumbents keeps out new ideas, and the time it takes distracts members from their lawmaking activities.[29]

The at-home workload has not only reduced the time available for deliberation, it has also eaten dramatically into the informal, face-to-face socializing that provides both a backdrop and a forum for traditional deliberation. "Most of the senators of the 1950's," the *Congressional Quarterly* reminisces, "arrived in Washington each January on the train. Nine months later they left on the train. During the months in between, they stayed in Washington, making no weekend trips home because there were no jet planes to get them there and back that fast."[30] But with jets and increased travel allowances, most Senators have now joined the Easterners' "Tuesday-Thursday Club," and no longer have the time for breakfasts, dinners, and drinks at 4:30 with fellow members. Moreover, as more members bring their families to Washington, they tend to take their breakfasts and dinners at home. "I used to sit on the floor of the House and talk to people about their districts and where they come from. I developed close friendships," Senator Thad Cochran told *Congressional*

---

28. "Special Report: The Individualist Senate," *Congressional Quarterly Weekly* 40 (1982) 2175-82, pp. 2176-77. John Saloma's data suggest that in 1965 members spent at least 28 percent of their Washington work week on constituency service, and the percentage has probably increased since then. John Saloma, *Congress and the New Politics* (Boston: Little, Brown, 1969), cited in Morris P. Fiorina, *Congress: Keystone of the Washington Establishment* (New Haven: Yale University Press, 1977). See also Richard E. Fenno, *Home Style: House Members in Their Districts* (Boston: Little, Brown, 1978), pp. 192-203.

29. Fiorina (1977) concentrates on the negative effects of incumbency for the goals of adversary democracy (see especially pp. 13 and 14, italicized sections). But see later below (pp. 37-38), for other ways of promoting adversary goals. Fiorina touches on but does not stress (pp. 60, 61, 82) the non-adversary or deliberative effects of increased constituency service.

30. "Special Report," p. 2176.

Quarterly in 1982. "There is very little socializing here [in the Senate]. If I have any free time I spend it with my staff."[31] "I meet senators now and mention a colleague," remarked former Senator James B. Pearson, "and they say they hardly know him. Most of my career, I individually knew every guy on the floor."[32] The recently installed electronic voting boards also eliminate the many times during roll calls when members conferred together on the floor and in the cloakroom.[33] As the time spent with one another decreases, so does the emotional margin the members can allow one another. "There's much less civility than when I got here ten years ago," Senator Joseph R. Biden Jr. told the *Congressional Quarterly.* "There aren't as many nice people as there were before. It makes working in the Senate difficult."[34] Indeed, as the traditions of seniority and deference have weakened, so too has the explicit tradition of civility that, formal as it often was, provided a language with which members could surmount their antagonisms. Finally, the new professional spirit—along with the diminished influence of Southern culture in Washington and the lower consumption of alcohol—has had mixed effects on deliberation. While encouraging the accumulation of facts and figures, it has discouraged informal interchange.

With the time and energy of the members consumed by a greater workload, much deliberation these days takes place among the members of Congressional staffs, discussing the issues within the office, between offices, with committee staffs, and with interested outsiders. Indeed, some observers believe that staff deliberation has almost driven out deliberation by the members themselves, for the staff's ubiquitous presence discourages informal, private, one-to-one, face-to-face meetings of member with member, and makes members more circumspect, preferring not to comment on issues without consulting their staff. Michael Malbin reports that the number of committee staff in the House has increased from 62 in 1891 to 167 in 1947 and 2,073 in 1979.[35] He also argues that the large and "new-style" staffs have "impeded the deliberative process" in the Congress.[36] "Debate and discussion," He concludes, "have lost their central place in the legislative process."[37]

---

31. "Special Report," p. 2175.
32. "Special Report," p. 2176.
33. Easterbrook, pp. 69-70.
34. Idem.
35. Malbin, pp. 11, 13. See also Smith and Deering, Figure 7-1, p. 205.
36. Malbin, p. vii.
37. Malbin, p. 242.

The question is whether substituting staff for Congressional deliberation changes the quality of that deliberation. Malbin provides evidence that staff have different policy preferences from the members, promote more work for the Congress, aim at the short rather than the long run, emphasize policies that will look good to the press, hold information back from the Congress, approach issues in an adversary manner as if they were writing a legal brief for one side, promote their own reputations, do not make explicit the underlying normative assumptions of their research, and indulge in unnecessary quantification that promotes false certainty.[38] He does not answer the question of how, if at all, the deliberation that ensues differs from that which would ensue if the members of Congress did their own work. His most telling points are those regarding overload and quantification. It is not clear from his account that the preferences of staff differ from those of members in any particular direction (e.g. more or less liberal or conservative), that they have a shorter time perspective than the members, that they are more concerned with the press, more likely to hold information back, more adversary in their orientation, or less able to clarify their underlying assumptions than are the members of Congress they work for.[39] While they are undoubtly interested in their reputations, it is not clear in what direction this influences deliberation. One could at least conceive of a situation in which staff members' wanting to develop a reputation for expertise, say, could improve the overall quality of deliberation. Their role as policy entrepreneurs, avoiding controversial legislation, gives them an incentive to search out projects in the public interest. Malbin's own in-depth account of staff work on an actual piece of legislation ("Shepherding a Bill Through the Senate: The Sunset Bill") paints a picture of staff members who "did a great deal of reading and thinking and research," resolved difficult issues in ways that were apt to command consensus, discussed issues with the relevant interest groups without being dominated by them, met with staff from the other Senate committees in a forum that promoted collaborative interchange, and joined to "deliberate as a group" in a setting in which all or most of the

---

38. Malbin, pp. 30, 31, 44, 151, 130, 163, 150, 205, 164, 200, 229, 232-34.
39. As Kingdon points out (pp. 207-8), "It might be more fruitful to conceive of staff not as an influence *on* a member, but rather as an extension *of* a member. Because of the highly personalized hiring and firing practices, the strong tendency of staff and member to hold similar orientations and ideologies and even to have been closely associated prior to the aide's employment, and the close working relationship between staffer and boss, it may be more appropriate to think of staff and member as parts of a single decision-making unit than as separate entities."

committee's different interests were present.[40] Malbin also indicates that the most effective arguments against Sunset on the merits came in a staff working paper from the Rules Committee.[41] He does not indicate what kinds of incentives Congressional norms and institutions can offer staff to make them more likely to deliberate in the public interest.

Sporadically, deliberation goes half-way out the door to policy councils within the Republican and Democratic parties. When the Democrats are out of office they are particularly likely to set up policy councils, like the Democratic Policy Advisory Council of the 1950's (which President John Kennedy disbanded upon coming to office), the present Democratic Policy Commission, the committee on New Directions for the Democratic Party, or the reactivated Congressional Democratic caucus. Members of the Democratic caucus's Committee on Party Effectiveness, created in 1981, commented in 1984 that "it's one of the few places where a broad cross section of Democrats can sit down and get to know each other," and "the truth is scattered and the caucus committee is a place for an exchange of disparate views."[42] The Republicans have not been as self-conscious about deliberating on policy in their national organizations, although their better funding does allow them to field a journal designed to provoke policy debate among party members. In general, in spite of the increasing length of party platforms over the years, the parties do not seem to have become fundamentally more deliberative. They may move in that direction when they need to get publicity or satisfy the needs of their members for substantial intellectual interchange, but these demands tend to become eclipsed on a regular basis by the imperatives of organizing materially and strategically to win elections. Thus, although the parties are now deliberative centers by default, they have expanded only a little to accomodate that function, and it is unclear what incentives might make them do so.

Out the door, however, lies another potential arena for deliberation—that of the interest groups themselves. The relation of individual member of Congress with individual lobbyist has for a while provided one form of deliberation. Elizabeth Drew, for example, recounts an interview with Charles E. Walker, consumate lobbyist for "corporate clients on the

---

40. Malbin, pp. 51, 54, 57, 58 and 61.
41. Malbin, p. 63.
42. Quoted in Steven S. Smith, "New Patterns of Decision making in Congress," in John E. Chubb and Paul E. Peterson, *The New Direction in American Politics* (Washington, D.C.: The Brookings Institution, 1985), p. 226.

energy bill" circa 1978:

> I ask Walker if he talked to [the Chair of the House of Representatives' Ad Hoc Committee on Energy] during the golf game.

> "I didn't talk about energy on the golf course. I don't lobby on the golf course—maybe a word here or there, like 'Hey Joe, you're not going to vote for that dumb bill, are you?' We got to the [Secretary of Energy's house] about six-thirty, and we talked energy before and after dinner, and it was a great debate."

> I ask Walker what kinds of points he tries to make in such a situation.

> "First of all, you're in a person's home, and you don't press the issue," he replies. "Or you might say, 'I can't understand why two bright people like you would be for a dumb-ass proposal like that.' We start talking about the broad aspects of it—natural-gas pricing, the crude-oil equalization tax, the conversion to coal. Not the nitty-gritty but the philosophy of whether to go for those things or let the market raise the price and increase production and produce conservation."[43]

By most standards, the talks Walker describes were discussions on the merits. Walker worked by letting his information and point of view integrate itself slowly into the consciousness of the members of Congress he was cultivating. Obstacles the members faced in absorbing his way of thinking and the information he was presenting might emerge in the course of a quick chat outside a committee room, or in discussions with staff. Sometimes Walker could provide a way of thinking or more information that overcame those obstacles; sometimes he could not. As a Ph.D. in economics and a former deputy secretary of the Treasury, he took pride in his expertise, believing that in his firm's lobbying "we were protecting our clients' interests, but we were also serving the public interest."[44] The deliberation that his lobbying provoked meets the procedural criteria of eliciting and conveying new information and modes of reasoning; it also meets the criteria of lack of haste and face-to-face interaction. Whether it meets the ultimate criterion of helping uncover one's own, one's constituents' or the nation's real interests depends in part on the degree to which points of view other than Walker's made their way

---

43. Elizabeth Drew, "Charlie: A Portrait of a Lobbyist," in *Interest Group Politics* ed. Allan J. Cigler and Burdett A. Loomis (Washington, D.C.: Congressional Quarterly Press, 1983), p.225.
44. Drew, p. 227.

to the member's synapses and received an equally favorable reception there.[45]

Another process, with some potential for creating and discovering a common good, goes on within and between interest groups. Within interest groups, diversity of membership has always required not only negotiation between components of the group as to what the group position would be, but also discussion of potential points of common interest, in which reasoning and new information play important roles. Between interest groups, in areas characterized by shifting coalitions,[46] negotiation and bargaining also include some deliberation on the merits. Most importantly, in both cases, these strategic calculations usually have to incorporate, if only in response to anticipated public reactions, arguments addressed to the public interest.[47]

To these more common cases of deliberation within and among interest groups, we can add a relatively recent development. In several recent instances, members of Congress (or their staffs), who are interested not in making enemies through legislation, but in claiming credit for solving a public problem, have in essence delegated the task of hammering out legislation in the public interest to an ad hoc committee of opposing interest groups. Take the copyright law of 1978, in which Congressional committees spent more than two decades working out most of the important provisions of the act. Three or four major stumbling blocks remained, including the provision on photocopying. The Association of American Publishers and the Authors League of America had been lobbying Congress for five years to institute strict prohibitions against photocopying, while the Ad Hoc Committee of Educational Institutions and Organizations on Copyright Law Revision had been lobbying equally vehemently on the other side. Acting independently, the major opposing interest groups, with their lawyers, finally worked out their own compro-

---

45. Such equal access is, of course, an ideal that we can hope only to approximate, not to achieve; nor is it an absolute requirement for good public policy.

46. Theodore J. Lowi, in "American Business, Public Policy, Case-Studies, and Political Theory," *World Politics* 16 (1964): 677-715, argues that unstable, shifting coalitions are typical of the regulatory arena.

47. These conclusions are based on conversations with two analysts of interest groups, Kay Schlozman and John Tierney, and several practitioners. As far as I know, little detailed academic work has been done on the processes by which organized interests arrive at the policies they will support as a group. See Douglas W. Costain and Anne N. Costain, "Interest Groups as Policy Aggregators in the Legislative Process," *Polity* 14 (1981): 249-272, for the way interest groups "predigest" policies for members of Congress.

mise, embodied in a formal "Agreement on Guidelines," signed by representatives of the three groups. When Congress passed the copyright law, it took no official position on what would constitute "fair use" in photocopying, but commented, "This committee believes the Guidelines are a reasonable interpretation of the minimum standards for fair use.[48]

Such instances of delegating deliberation to interest groups, though infrequent, have inspired contemporary reformers. A former assistant secretary of the army, for instance, proposes for issues like energy regulation, consumer product safety, occupational health and safety, and environmental pollution, a regulatory "partnership" in which "business and government, representatives of labor and special interest groups . . . work to resolve problems and to build a consensus on industry rules and standards."[49] This kind of quasi-corporatist process, relatively alien to the Anglo-American tradition of adversary democracy, has democratic potential when genuinely common interests can be discovered or created.[50] In other instances, it risks reflecting in the solutions it generates no more than a compromise based on the relative raw power of the groups involved, unmediated by the tempering adversary ideal of one citizen/one vote. Evidence from some of the European corporatist experiments may indicate how to stucture such partnerships to increase the chances of their deliberations generating public policy in the common interest rather than simply ratifying the exercise of unequal power.

Finally, out the door, but with an occasional foot in it, lie the foundations and the universities. Foundations, with their conferences and sponsored projects, and academics, with their books and studies, have come to play, over time, a larger role in the Congressional deliberative process. These groups have the advantage of a relatively long time horizon. In 1986, for example, when Congress had its agenda devoured by the budget and when neither house had much important legislation affecting the welfare system in the offing, scores of academic conferences, and conferences that brought together scholars and policy makers, were held on the problems

48. House Committee on the Judiciary, "Copyright Law Revision," Report No. 94-176, 94th Cong., 2d sess., Sept. 3, 1976, p. 72, referring to the "Agreement on Guidelines for Classroom Copying in Not-for-Profit Educational Institutions."

49. J. Ronald Fox, "Breaking the Regulatory Deadlock," *Harvard Business Review* 59 (1981): 99.

50. For an attempt to use this technique in Pennsylvania, which seemingly foundered on the persistence of real and irreconcilable interests, see Charles L. Kennedy, "A Laboratory of Democracy," *News for Teachers of Political Science*, 1986, p. 7.

of welfare reform.[51] In many of these conferences, participants exchanged new information, absorbed new ways of looking at the issues, and in some cases even changed their minds—becoming, for example, more concerned with the potential dependency-prolonging effects of the welfare system. When the time comes, some of the facts, figures and ideas from these conferences, projects, books and studies will have their effect on the direction and content of Congressional deliberation. Staffs will get ideas from all these sources, will schedule hearings with the authors and participants, and will quote material from their works.

In some cases the role of academics can be immense. Martha Derthick and Paul Quirk, asking how it came to be—against all political science wisdom—that in the deregulation of the airline, trucking, and telephone industries the powerful and organized interests lost while the diffuse consumer interest won, give as their first answer the extraordinary influence of academic economists. In the case of deregulation, the commitment to a competitive microeconomic model that underlies the discipline of economics itself almost guaranteed that there would be a "virtually unanimous professional conclusion" in favor of deregulation.[52] Moreover, many economists were, in the late 1960's and early 1970's, in powerful positions in the executive branch.[53] In the Congress, one academic, a professor of law at Harvard, had a crucial influence as special council to one of the Senate's subcommittees.[54] Members of Congress, Derthick and Quirk point out, "are perpetually in search of program material—posi-

---

51. For example, in the Spring of 1986 in Washington conferences were sponsored by, among other groups, 1) Americans for Intergenerational Equity, 2) the National Academy of Science, 3) the Public Agenda Forum, and 4) the Yale Institute on Policy Studies (with two other groups). In the same year, the Ford Foundation initiated a multi-million dollar program for studies of the welfare system, and the Project on the Federal Social Role sponsored seminars on the welfare system in various universities.

52. Paul L Joskow and Roger G. Noll, "Regulation in Theory and Practice: An Overview," in *Studies in Public Regulation*, ed. Gary Fromm (Cambridge: MIT Press, 1981), p. 8, cited in Derthick and Quirk, p. 36. This review, Derthick and Quirk point out, included a bibliography of 150 items.

53. They were "members of the Council of Economic Advisers or its staff, in the Office of Management and Budget, the Justice Department, or the Department of Transportation, or with presidential task forces and study groups." Derthick and Quirk, p. 37.

54. Senator Edward Kennedy became attracted to deregulation when Stephen G. Breyer, professor of administrative and antitrust law at Harvard, became special council to Kennedy's Subcommittee on Administrative Practice and Procedure of the Judiciary Committee. Breyer suggested that Kennedy hold hearings on airline deregulation, expecting that these hearings would set up a theme of competition versus regulation for a series of investigations into other industries. Derthick and Quirk, pp. 41-44.

tions to advocate on the problems of the day—with the result that advocates, as the offerers of positions, have a fair chance of making matches with politicians who will become advocates in turn."[55] When the advocates are academics, their positions have been tempered in a fire in which factual accuracy, logical rigor and at least a surface concern with the public interest are usually required.

The entry of academics into the deliberative process can, of course, produce the unconsciously obscurantist citing of facts and figures that rightly bothers Malbin. It can easily promote the professional bias of the academic discipline, as in the example of deregulation. And the kinds of academics most likely to be heard in Washington will not usually be those with radical ideas. Yet the academic enterprise can also produce information that ought to enter the deliberative process. To take a small example, in the 1970's the conventional wisdom was that the elderly were more likely to be victims of crime than younger adults. Concern over this problem had generated a set of prospective policies and programs designed to protect the elderly from crime. However, when the House and Senate committees on aging encountered in their hearings academic analyses of national crime surveys demonstrating that the elderly were much less likely to be victimized and were no more likely to suffer physical and economic consequences than younger adults, those committees redesigned the legislation to be neutral on the question of age.[56]

This brief summary cannot look in detail at how staffs, political parties, interest groups and academics have come to play an important role in Congressional deliberation. It has particularly neglected the way key moments of deliberation come at the agenda-setting stage, where staffs and interest groups are particularly important, and how extensive deliberation in the executive branch and to a lesser degree in the press heavily influences the Congress. But the summary may at least set an agenda for future research. Deliberation in Congress has, for the most part, gone down and out. While members of Congress continue to deliberate incrementally over the course of several years on different pieces of related

---

55. Derthick and Quirk, p. 39.
56. Indeed, in the Senate John Hines, chair of the Special Committee on Aging in the Senate, strongly advocated the resulting legislation. This may have been the only time in their respective histories that this committee and the House Select Committee on Aging sponsored a piece of age-neutral legislation. See Fay Lomax Cook, "Toward a Theory of Issue Decline on Policy Agendas," paper delivered at the Northwestern University Symposium on New Directions in the Empirical and Normative Study of Public Policy, September, 1982.

legislation that require their votes, their central deliberative role today seems to be to aggregate and operationalize the deliberation of others. Only when we come to understand the strengths and weaknesses inherent in staff, party, interest group and academic deliberation, as well as the processes of deliberation in the executive branch and in the press, will we be able to begin to judge whether this evolution has affected the quality and content of Congressional deliberation as a whole for better or worse, or devise incentives to change the situation.

Mattering, Respect, and Learning:
The Representative's Incentive Structure

What, then, of the members of Congress themselves? Are we to write them off as merely useful aggregators of preferences, busily running their own small businesses from their offices, generating supply, satisfying demand, meeting their payrolls? Should we concentrate our conceptual and entrepreneurial energies on devising ways in which staffs, parties, interest groups and academics can be induced to deliberate more upon the common good? Presuming that the members of Congress still have some desire and time for deliberation, it is also worth asking what innovations could increase both their desire and their time.

I will assume that most members of Congress want, at least in some small recess of their motivational structures, to make good public policy. We need not rehearse here the tired debate over whether or not representatives care only about reelection. Neither David Mayhew nor Morris Fiorina, the two most cited exponents of the reelection thesis, actually makes this claim. Although Mayhew strives mightily to divest members' credit-claiming and position-taking of any substantive content,[57] and to portray altruistic legislation as designed to produce feelings of gratification among the givers,[58] even he finds at the end of his book that in fact, "if all members did nothing but pursue their electoral goals, Congress would decay or collapse."[59] In keeping with his relentless focus on staying in office, Mayhew reinterprets the members' goals of achieving influence within Congress and making "good public policy" so that these goals serve

---

57. David R. Mayhew, *Congress: The Electoral Connection* (New Haven: Yale University Press, 1974); pp. 52, 61.
58. Mayhew, pp. 132-33.
59. Mayhew, p. 141.

only the larger end of institutional maintenance. In this rather strained interpretation, members make good public policy only to prevent public indignation at Congress, because such indignation would undermine the institution to which they hope to be reelected.[60] Yet Mayhew's own analysis suggests that if one could find in a representative's motivational structure any desire to make good public policy, it would not be impossible to set up selective incentives within Congress to reward such behavior.

Morris Fiorina, not feeling Mayhew's need for redefinition and transubstantiation, allows the goals of "policy" and "public service" to "play their part" in a representative's motivation.[61] Policy goals, among other things, "are quite important to many legislators," and "the assumption of maximizing probability of reelection may be unacceptably inaccurate" for representatives like Frank Smith, who found his electoral goals not always consistent with the political stands he thought were right, and took those stands knowing they would hurt him at the polls.[62] Nor is such an assumption accurate for "saints," like the few Kennedy describes in *Profiles in Courage*.[63] However, because of the great uncertainty surrounding the circumstances of reelection,[64] including the possibility that a challenger might raise even the most obscure vote into an issue,[65] enough representatives act enough of the time as if they were primarily concerned with reelection to give Fiorina's calculations interest.

Nothing in Mayhew's or Fiorina's analysis requires that the present mix of incentives for representatives stay the way it is. The *sine qua non* of representation, as Fiorina points out, is that the member be reelected. But reelection can be accomplished, as we have discovered in the course of United States history, in a good many ways. The first steps toward con-

---

60. Although early in his book (p. 16) Mayhew promises to give attention to "making 'good public policy'. . . further on in this discussion," there are few specific references to this goal further on. Mayhew's larger point is that the selective incentives to induce members "to do grueling and unrewarding legislative work" (p. 141), to spend money at optimal and fair levels (p. 142), and to avoid contradictory policies (pp. 143-44), which he admits weigh against the incentives to pursue reelection, "work quite clearly in the interest of institutional maintenance and *not* in the interest of general programmatic performance" (n. 133, pp. 146-7, emphasis mine).

61. Morris P. Fiorina, *Representatives, Roll Calls, and Constituencies* (Lexington, MA: D.C. Heath, 1974), p. 31.

62. Frank Smith, *Congressman from Mississippi* (New York: Pantheon, 1964), cited in Fiorina, p. 35.

63. Fiorina, *Keystone*, p. 41.

64. Fiorina, *Keystone*, p. 29.

65. Fiorina, *Keystone*, p. 33.

ceiving of a different mix of incentives are to establish that many representatives have at least some desire to make good public policy, and then attempt to discover the institutional incentives that presently reward and foster that desire.

It is not particularly difficult to establish that at least a noticable minority of representatives have a desire to make good public policy. Richard Fenno, a reasonably shrewd observer, pointed out in 1973 that the members of the Education and Labor and the Foreign Affairs committees wanted to get on those committees because they wanted to help make good public policy.[66] Subsequent researchers have confirmed the existence of a policy orientation, although they might have made their academic reputations by showing it had declined.[67] As Charlie Walker, the lobbyist, put it:

> You got to understand what motivates the politician. Dummies, even in this town, think that politicians just want to be reelected. Well, first of all, the day of the sinecure in Congress is past. More and more of the members get bumped off by some young tiger. But what is the purpose of getting reelected? A handful will use it to try to become President of the United States. But what motivates a Lud Ashley? He doesn't want to run for President of the United States, or for senator or governor. He's a House man. He takes extreme pride in doing a good legislative job. So if I'm talking to Lud I'm taking merits—of course, there may be a hooker in there, like about storm windows. In fact, I'm talking merits with most of them.[68]

What motives can make members of Congress spend their time on good public policy when that activity can demonstrably detract from their chances of reelection? The desire to make good policy for its own sake is reinforced by at least three other motives that I believe most members experience: the motives to matter, to earn the respect of one's peers, and to learn and then act on what one has learned.

Wanting to matter or make a difference is a frequently overlooked motive for all kinds of political participation, not just on the legislative

---

66. Richard F. Fenno, Jr., *Congressmen in Committees* (Boston, Little, Brown, 1973).
67. Kingdon, 1981; Sinclair, 1983; Smith and Deering, 1984.
68. Drew, p. 249. See also Fenno (1978), pp. 215-16, and one of Kingdon's legislators (p. 46): "You'll find congressmen most of the time will want to vote according to their obligations and principles as they see them. The political considerations are less important." (p. 46). [The meaning of "principles" in this sentence is evident; the meaning of "obligations" is less clear.]

level.[69] Logically, one could want to make a difference for the worse, but in practice most people want to make a difference for the better. Logically one could want to make a difference in a particularistic way (to get more for Massachusetts), but the internal dynamic of a concern for mattering makes the bigger stage more attractive. Logically, one could want to make a difference by reflecting constituent preference, but in the role of mere conduit the representative as an individual does not matter much. Wanting to matter thus seduces a representative beyond the local to the common, beyond preference to interest.[70]

Many institutions and rituals in the House and Senate reinforce the desire to matter. They make it clear that here one can matter more than ever before. Historical references to the great achievements of earler representatives or earlier Congresses strengthen the temptation to shape history. Even the blandishments of lobbyists inflate the member's sense of capacity to matter. But often constituents and political analysts see the motive to matter as sinful. If we see in Potomac fever the potential for inducing members of Congress to deliberate, we may want to shift our distribution of praise and blame, fear power less, and begin to reward the desire to matter.

Wanting the respect of one's peers also plays a role in the motivational structure of almost every representative. One wins respect in part, it is true, by playing political hardball, by savvy parliamentary maneuvering, and by winning election after election. But one also earns respect by doing one's "homework," and by developing in a few areas an expertise that others can trust. Nor does the importance of solid work seem to have diminished recently, even though many of the folkways once associated with it—like silent freshmen and long apprenticeships—are quickly fading.

Respect for technical expertise and for sound judgment encourage, in their turn, the idea that facts matter, and therefore that problems have

---

69. See Russell Hardin, *Collective Action* (Baltimore: Johns Hopkins, 1982), pp. 108-112, on the citizen motivation to be a part of history.
70. In explaining why many members voted for deregulation even when they thought it might hurt them in their districts, Derthick and Quirk comment (p. 143) that:
    at least for many, clearly, much of the attraction of serving in Congress is the opportunity to debate issues, form opinions, and make efficacious judgments on matters of public concern. Such activities hold interest and satisfaction for many persons ... and not the least for politicians. Exercising a certain amount of political independence and voting on the merits of issues is for such members part of the point of having the job.

solutions that are more or less feasible, more or less good or bad for the nation as a whole. Doing one's homework and developing areas of expertise also draw one away from the constituent's often superficial view of a problem. Colleagues' praise and blame, and even the staff's scorn or admiration, reinforce the desire to be at least competent in one's specialty. So does the experience of relying, oneself, so frequently on substanceless cues guaranteed only by one's trust in the expertise and judgment of the cuegiver. Precisely to the degree that particularistic, face-to-face communication diminishes in the Congress, each member must rely even more on the universalistic expertise of the others. Any increase in the formal education of the members or in the professionalism of the staff will reinforce this trend. Again, rather than deploring these trends, we can recognize in them some unexpected benefits for deliberation. That recognition itself helps shift the balance of incentives.

Finally, there is the motive to learn, and having learned, to act upon that learning. Some of the most enthusiastic reactions of new Senators or members of the House center on how much they feel they learn in their first years in Washington. Yet learning often brings with it the desire to act upon what one has learned, or in any case not to act against it. Having ingested evidence that airline deregulation will not drastically reduce flights to small towns but will lower prices, a representative will have greater difficulty voting against a deregulation bill. The California legislature seems to demonstrate that selected legislative institutions can greatly reinforce the motive to learn, and can, in so doing, increase the threat to cognitive consistency that comes from voting against a measure one believes to be, on balance, for the good of the whole.

Other conditions will undoubtedly affect the degree to which members of Congress feel compelled not only to vote for what they believe is the public interest, but to spend their time trying to figure out what that is. Derthick and Quirk's three cases of deregulation in which members of Congress came to vote against the reelection interests and for good public policy point to the mixed, though in this case somewhat benign, effects of executive pressure, Congressional positions of leadership, and the academic infiltration of government.[71] John Kingdon points out that self-selection often insures that the representative rarely has to choose on policy matters between constituent preference and the representative's understanding of good public policy.[72] When this is true, a representative

---

71. Derthick and Quirk, pp. 36, 55, 103-104, 111-114, 145-146.
72. Kingdon, p. 45.

becomes used to voting on the basis of good policy, and both habit and self-image provide a disincentive for changing. The public demand for an explanation of one's vote also tends to encourage some time and thought on the subject.[73] So will a member's own demands for cognitive consistency,[74] and the expectations of the members' colleagues that he or she will act according to certain principles.

Issues that are primarily technical, rather than matters of principle, will lend themselves to an approach of trying to find the best solution. Issues like the ERA or abortion, on the other hand, often appear on the agenda as matters not only of principle, but of the kind of immutable principle that bears no discussing. On these matters, deliberation seems useless, and proponents turn to the tactics and formulae of adversary democracy to resolve an issue that they, more than anyone else, actually formulate as a question of the common interest.[75] However, when public deliberation has proceeded to a point in which principles are not opposed so starkly—as is the case now regarding "workfare," for example—then legislators, their staffs, and even the representatives of interest groups have a chance to devise and hammer out ways of approaching the problem that come closer to the public interest.

In influencing all these motives, and affecting the way that representatives approach even matters of seemingly immutable principle, what William Muir calls "the legislative culture" can have a major impact.[76] While reelection is necessary, the members of the legislature are the people one sees every day, and whom, moreover, one's own efforts have defined as winners. Social psychologists have demonstrated how a severe initiation increases one's liking for a group, and how liking a group discourages potential deviance.[77] Electoral campaigns act as a powerful

---

73. Matthews, p. 191; Fenno 1978, p. 78; Kingdon, p. 266; Derthick and Quirk, p. 145.

74. Kingdon p. 277.

75. The dynamics of failed deliberation on such an issue form the theme of my *Why We Lost the ERA* (Chicago: University of Chicago Press, 1986).

76. William K. Muir, Jr., *Legislature: California's School for Politics* (Chicago: University of Chicago Press, 1982).

77. E.g., Elliot Aronson and Judson Mills, "The Effect of Severity of Initiation on Liking for a Group," 59 *Journal of Abnormal and Social Psychology* (1959) 177-81, reprinted in *Interpersonal Behavior in Small Groups*, ed. Richard J. Ofshe (Englewood Cliffs, N.J.: Prentice-Hall, 1973), pp. 4 - 10. The more severe their initiation into a group, the less boring subjects judged a taped discussion of that group. The larger phenomenon is that of cognitive dissonance. See Leon Festinger, *A Theory of Cognitive Dissonance* (Evanston, IL: Row, Peterson, 1957). For many studies of how members who are highly attracted to a group conform more to its norms, see A. Paul Hare, *Handbook of Small Group Research*, 2nd. ed. (New York: The Free Press, 1976), p. 30.

initiation; they are likely to make legislators attend to the norms of the group they have paid so dearly to join

William Muir's study of the educative norms of the California legislature suggests that several institutions in the California legislature socialize legislators into the norm of promoting the public good.[78] Among other institutions, he lists the Buddy System Rule (having to state your objections on the merits in certain circumstances), the Third Reading Analysis (a nonpartisan analysis prepared by a special research office), and the office of the Legislative Analyst.[79] Muir, unfortunately, has no measure of outcomes. He presumes, in a way that is distinctly open to challenge, that the processes of which he approves will lead to outcomes in the public interest. Yet the legislative socialization he describes may, like some Progressive reforms of an earlier era, mask strong biases. This possibility, inherent in all claims to represent the common good, makes it important at least to try to look at outcomes. If the California legislature passes this test, we may then address ourselves to understanding which features of the California incentive system might be transferable to the national level, and how.

The Role of Philosophical Analysis

The language with which we think about representation today is misleading. The words "trustee" and "delegate" focus attention on forms of being free and bound that fit uneasily into our present understanding of retrospective voting. Yet the conceptual distinctions that can be drawn from Edmund Burke's thoughts on representation in 1774 remain important.[80] In the context of common interests, which Burke assumed, the job of the representative must be to deliberate on the sustantive merits of a proposal, trying to judge its worth from the perspective of the polity as a whole. In the context of conflicting interests, I would now add, the representative's job must be to puzzle out the real locus and meaning of that conflict, and in its democratic resolution represent his or her constituents at least in proportion to their numbers. These two tasks are compatible,

---

78. Muir's own formulation is using "the public trust justly and efficiently to help the less fortunate in a free country" (p. 156).

79. Muir, pp. 43, 130, 112-116.

80. Edmund Burke, "To the Electors of Bristol," from Edmund Burke, *Selections*, ed. L. N. Broughton (New York: Scribner's, 1925), pp. 118-126.

although not easy to manage at one time. Their compatibility becomes evident if one's theory of representation specifically prescribes deliberation in the service of good public policy in moments of common interest, and a combination of deliberation and parliamentary combat in moments of conflict. Such a formulation allows any one representative to shift modes as the situation demands. The words "trustee" and "delegate," on the other hand, tend to describe individuals rather than situations. They imply, accordingly, a "zero-sum" spectrum on which a representative must become less of a delegate the more he or she becomes a trustee, and vice versa. No individual can, on this analysis, become more of both.

Moving from the "zero-sum" trustee-delegate model to an understanding of representation that prescribes different behavior in different contexts makes it conceivable through institutional reform to increase the quality of deliberation on good public policy without decreasing the quality of the gladiatorial pursuit of local or individual interest. Let us imagine, for instance, a pie-in-the-sky package of reforms that would at the same time 1) give the incumbents an even greater advantage than at present (through increased at-home staff for constituency service, let us say), thereby alleviating constituency policy pressure and allowing greater attention to national affairs; 2) limit tenure to two (or three) terms in the Senate and four in the House in order to bring in new ideas and curb some negative effects of both incumbency and wanting to matter (e.g. excessive commitment to legislation that bears one's own mark); and 3) drastically limit or abolish the funding that interest groups can give campaigns or use to pay lobbyists in order to increase the degree to which constituents' preferences will be represented in proportion to their numbers. A package like this, while politically impossible in today's context, makes the philosophical point that it is possible to improve at the same time both the facets of a representative's job that involve good overall public policy and those that involve insuring proportional benefits to one's constituents.

As we move from a zero-sum focus, we see also that legislative deliberation need not always be bought at the price of citizen deliberation. Just as greater incumbency need not mean the diminished representation of conflicting interests as long as changes are made elsewhere in the system, so the lessened responsiveness to immediate citizen policy demand that greater incumbency allows can be balanced with other measures to increase citizen activity in politics. Benjamin Barber recently concluded *Strong Democracy* with a set of far-reaching suggestions for envigorating citizen deliberation through neighborhood assemblies, television town meetings, postal subsidies for civic information, office-holding by lot, lay juries for dispute arbitration, universal citizen service, and a multi-choice, two-stage legislative initiative and referendum process on selected issues, with a mandatory tie-in to neighborhood assemblies.[81] Particularly if implemented all at once, as Barber suggests, these innovations would have a massive effect on the quantity and quality of citizen deliberation in this country. Yet, with the exception of the referendum scheme, none would greatly affect the Congressional legislative process. Even the referenda, limited to one or two issues a year, would not affect most of the work of Congress. Citizens politicized this way would undoubtedly be more likely to vote in Congressional elections and put greater policy pressure on their members of Congress, thus restricting their freedom in deliberation. But such citizens, through their own experience in office, might also become more sympathetic to the legislator's deliberative job. In principle, there-fore, more direct citizen participation could increase both the ability of legislators to represent their constituents in proportion to their numbers and their ability to deliberate on and promote the common good.

Life is not neat, and few if any issues involve only the common good or only conflicting interests. But at least in the legislative arena, our repre-sentatives are already adroit at unconsciously shifting and mixing—as their estimation of the underlying reality requires—the different modes of representation appropriate for conflict and for common interests. A philosophical analysis that recognized the dual job they are aleady doing would allow us to ask where both processes of representation are now most distorted, which institutional innovations would help the represen-tatives do both jobs better, at what points in the system costs could most easily be born or substitutions provided for either set of functions, and where, no viable substitutions being possible, change would cost too much.

---

81. Benjamin Barber, *Strong Democracy* (Berkeley: University of California Press, 1984), chapter ten.

Concluding Essay

John Marini

The legislative body has always proved troublesome for democratic or republican government.[1] Indeed, the historic problem of all republics may be summed up in Madison's own words: "in republican government, the legislative authority necessarily predominates." Yet, according to *The Federalist*, previous republics failed precisely because of the usurpation and abuse of power by the legislature. Consequently, in terms of good government, Madison insisted that legislative predominance is an "inconveniency" which must be remedied in order to ensure reasonable or moderate government. The American Constitution, therefore, as Harvey Mansfield has noted, "introduced a strong, single executive who was taken not from a monarchical tradition, but from a constitutional tradition which would teach republics (of) their necessary dependence on the virtue and decisiveness of a single leader . . . ."[2]

Perhaps the great practical problem of the Constitutional separation of powers is to find the means of ensuring the predominance of the legislative authority, while at the same time preventing the domination of the government—or administration—itself, by the legislative body. In other words, the constitutional order is a means of institutionalizing the rule of law, and not legislative will, as fundamental to good government. This can be accomplished by devising a framework in which the legislature is essentially a deliberative body in which reason, not will, is its primary virtue. An energetic executive ought to have the capacity to exercise will, but, in normal circumstances, only in the service of reason, or reasonable laws.

At the conference the panel on "Congress: Representation and Deliberation," was to address several general questions: "In any regime the character of the laws is of primary importance," it was noted, "but, in liberal democracy, the laws must reflect the popular will, and must seek prudently to secure the common good." This crucial issue was posed in deceptively simple terms. "How is Congress as an institution designed to

---

1. The views expressed here are those solely of the author, and do not reflect the official position of the Equal Employment Opportunity Commission.
2. Harvey C. Mansfield, "Dialogue," *The Center Magazine*, vol. 19, September/October, 1986, p. 56.

reconcile these two potentially antagonistic goals: the capacity to make laws which reflect the popular will, and at the same time, prudently seek to secure the common good?" These two essays show clearly the great difference in the manner in which the framers, as opposed to our contemporaries, have sought to reconcile the tension that exists between the popular will and the common good.

In addition, these essays pose a number of more practical and specific questions concerning the problems of the contemporary Congress. Have changes in Congress, such as the transformation of its staff into a major bureaucracy, worked to decrease its capacity for deliberation and representation of local interests? Is Congress still a deliberative body whose primary function is lawmaking, which entails a reasonable attempt to reconcile public and private interests with a view to the common good? Or is Congress now organized in such a way as to allow individual members the ability to enhance personal power by indirect control or oversight of the federal bureaucracy? In this case, the specific needs of interested constituencies, decided at the center, become its main concern. If so, the characteristic product of government is no longer general laws made by the representative of the people, but administrative rules formulated by technical experts for the regulation of the minute details of life in society.

The normal activity of the legislative body appears to have been transformed by the growth of the administrative state. As a result, the primary function of the legislator is no longer deliberation, or even representation of local constituencies. Rather, the administrative state presupposes the centralized control of the political, economic, and social details of life in a complex society. It requires a vast executive bureaucracy. Consequently, selective intervention and control of the various functions of the executive branch becomes the legislator's most characteristic and important activity. Ironically, centralized administration requires a decentralized legislative body, and a feeble executive.

In the absence of lawmaking in the public interest, the Presidency is increasingly identified with a general interest, and Congress with the particular interests of organized constituencies. Hence disputes between the branches appear to be but reflections of the tension between the particular, often private, interests of organized groups and the general interest embodied in the notion of a common good. In the absence of the possibility of discovery of a common good, only the will of the most powerful branch can prevail. In disputes between the branches, it is assumed, contrary to the intention of the founders, that the *will* of Congress, and not the *reason* of the constitutional order, ought to prevail.

Indeed, in our time, it can be said that the distinction between politics and administration has replaced the political distinction between the executive and the legislative branches. Politics is perceived as the arena in which the will of the people—embodied in the positive theory of the state—is contrasted with administration, the non-partisan means by which the will of the state is transformed into action by a rational bureaucracy. Whereas the founders expected the legislators to act reasonably, at least some of the time, only the administrators are now considered capable of rationality—in the sense of utilizing the technical or rational methodology of modern science. Yet in an ironic reversal of the constitutional order, passion or will dominates in the political process, for a rational bureaucracy becomes the instrument of fulfilling the willful passions of the people. Consequently, since the progressive era, the will of the majority party in the legislature, when faithfully executed by the executive branch bureaucracy, has come to be seen as the only source of legitimacy in democratic politics.

Professor Scigilano, in his essay, insists that the framers sought to temper the popular will by creating powerful institutions such as the Senate, the Presidency, and the independent judiciary not directly subservient to the popular will. In this view, reason, which is embodied in the constitutional order, would tend to check any popular passion that threatens to become a will independent of the constitutional order itself. Characteristically, a constitutional majority will likely be a reasonable majority. If so, the popular will is unlikely to become destructive of the common good because destructive measures could rarely pass the test of rationality, let alone constitutionality. Hence the framers opted for a reasonable constitutional order, characterized by a dependence on the separation of powers.

Professor Scigliano makes it clear that "the framers accorded Congress precedence over the other branches of government in arranging the Constitution's articles." Yet, he cautioned against drawing the conclusion that they "made Congress the dominant *branch* of American government." If they had intended to do so, he suggests, "they would not have placed the powers of those (other) branches in the Constitution itself nor have protected the salaries of their officers from Congressional interference, nor have provided as they did for the election of the President and the tenure of judges." The history of ancient democracies taught that a part of the people—even a majority—could act oppressively when in control of the government, and the separation of the powers of government was intended to increase the safety of the people from the oppression of government. The most likely vehicle of a majority tyranny in a representative government is the unchecked power of the legislature, or the people's representatives.

Scigliano's thesis may be summarized as follows: "In a republic such as that created by the Constitution," the *Federalist* informs us, "the legislative power is [mainly?] exercised by an assembly which is inspired by a supposed influence over the people, with an intrepid confidence in its own strength; that assembly is sufficiently numerous to feel all the passions which actuate a multitude, yet not so numerous as to be incapable of pursuing the objects of its passions by means which reason prescribes; and thus it is against the enterprising ambition of this department that the people ought to indulge all their jealousy and exhaust all their precautions." To check the popular body, mainly the House of Representatives, whose passions can be masked by a kind of instrumental reason adverse to the common good, is the task of the Constitutional separation of powers. As Scigilano indicates, "to help check the House of Representatives, the Senate was drawn towards the President by being given a share in his appointment and treaties. Publius depends on the Senate to use its legislative veto to help prevent 'schemes of usurpation or perfidy' by the House, just as he depends on the President to use his veto to help prevent it—'the representatives of the people in a popular assembly'—from seeking 'to exert an imperious control over the other departments.' " He notes the "judges, too, were brought into the arrangement."

The separation of powers, in the *Federalist's* view, was the Constitutional means of institutionalizing reason in the political order as a whole by utilizing passions conformable to reason and negating unreasonable passions. The executive and legislative branches are pitted against each other in such a way that the legislature performs best by being able to reason or deliberate, without the capacity to act. The President can, ordinarily, only exercise his will in support of the reasonable legislation of the Congress. In the simplest terms, the legislative body reasons best when it cannot will, because the passions which most frequently animate a small body of men are likely to be dangerous. And as Madison insisted, because of its small size, such a body can use reason to mask its real intention, it can use reason in the service of passions adverse to justice or the common good— which is hardly possible in a large diverse multitude which constitutes the political society of an extended republic.

The opposite is likely to be true of a single executive. Because he cannot exert his own will exclusive of the body of men who compose the legislature, he is likely to resist those dangerous passions common to such a body when they are adverse to reason. Rather, the passions of ambition, love of honor, and love of fame—which are qualities found only in superior individuals—may in effect be virtues that can be utilized in the defense of a reasonable constitution. Hence, prudence in a democratic statesman would seem to require the exercise of will in the service of reason, rational will as opposed to arbitrary will.

This kind of juxtaposition of passion and reason within the practical operations of the separation of powers presupposed the superiority of reason to passion within the constitutional order as a whole. Consequently, Madison argued against Jefferson's method of solving disputes among the political branches of government by holding a constitutional convention and thereby recurring to the people themselves as the "only legitimate fountain of power." He objected because the public passions likely to be engendered in the future would be less amenable to reasonable resolution of the issues than was the case just after the revolution. "Notwithstanding the success which has attended the revisions of our established forms of government, and which does so much honor to the virtue and intelligence of the people of America, it must be confessed that the experiments are of too ticklish a nature to be unnecessarily multiplied," Madison observed in *Federalist* 49. He reminds Jefferson that "all the existing constitutions were formed in the midst of a danger which repressed the passions most unfriendly to order and concord; of an enthusiastic confidence of the people in their patriotic leaders, which stifled the ordinary diversity of opinions on great national questions; of a universal ardor for new and opposite forms, produced by a universal resentment and indignation against the ancient government; and whilst no spirit of party connected with the changes to be made, abuses to be reformed, could mingle its leaven in the operation."

Indeed, it could be said that Madison believed that circumstances would never be more fortuitous than at the time of the Constitutional convention for determining the question "whether societies of men are really capable or not of establishing good government from reflection and choice." Subsequently, to recur to the people for such a great public exertion as constitution-making would be a mistake. In such circumstances, "the passions, therefore, not the reason, of the public would sit in judgment. But it is the reason, alone, of the public, that ought to control and regulate the government. The passions ought to be controlled and regulated by the government." The Constitution uniquely embodied the "reason of the public," in one of the very few moments in which reason and not passion predominated in the affairs of those men involved in the fundamental act of creating a framework of government. The Constitution is the law of laws, the supreme law that enshrines the principle of reason—or rule of law—as fundamental to the political system.

The first partisan disputes, Scigliano notes, between the Federalists and Antifederalists, concerned the wisdom of a constitutional republic itself. Subsequently, the debate revolved around the meaning of the separation of powers. As Scigliano observes, the Federalists continued "to support the executive power against the encroachments, the ambition, and the superior strength of the popular branch . . . and their opponents continued to take the side of legislative power. Only now the dispute concerned the document's meaning, and the Antifederalists were replaced by the Republicans." Disputes over separation of powers, "were also, inevitably, disputes over the authority of institutions closer to or more removed from the people." As a rule, Scigliano contends, "the two parties fought over the boundaries of power between Congress and the executive branch and the propriety of contacts across those boundaries." Much of the subsequent history of American government tended to confirm the wisdom of the framers' constitutional separation of powers. Indeed, it may not be too much of an overstatement to suggest that the substance of American politics has revolved around the tension between these two political branches and the two majorities which form their respective constituencies, i.e. the Presidential national majority, and the Congressional locally-derived national majority.

The growth of Congressional power would appear to have strengthened the local and popular elements in the regime. However, it is a mistake common to our time to forget the framers' reasons for the limitation on the power of the people. The institution of Congress, itself, prefigures the answer. As Scigiliano has written, "Congress re-presents the people in government as a substitute for their presenting themselves in an assembly." Nearly all the founders "considered representative government to be superior in principle to direct rule by the people." Hamilton was not atypical when he said of the ancient democracies, the archetype of direct popular rule, that they "never possessed one feature of good government. Their very character was tyranny; their figure deformity."

However, for the Federalists, "representation alone was not enough to transform republican government into good government." Although a large, diverse society might mitigate the effects of a majority faction, "Hamilton was not convinced that Madison's remedy for the problem of faction was enough," says Scigliano. He believed "demagogues would be elected from large districts 'more often' than Madison thought, and representatives would feel 'all the passions of popular assemblies.' " Hamilton believed only "that an extensive republic would be exempted from *some* of the dangers' that beset smaller ones." Hamilton thus argued "the need for a Senate as a defense against the 'temporary errors and delusion' of the people acting through the House of Representatives. He repeated this argument in his essays dealing with the President and judiciary." Nonetheless, nearly all the framers would have "justified their restraints on the people in the name of the people: such restraints were necessary for securing the equal rights of all." The common good could not be achieved if the passions, of even a majority, could become the unfettered, perhaps unreasonable, will of the people.

A measure of the distance we have traveled since the framers' day is made apparent in Professor Jane Mansbridge's essay. Mansbridge suggests that the contemporary Congress solved the problem of reconciling the popular will with the common good in a wholly novel way. Congressmen, as well as those who study politics in a scientific way, "the American profession of political science, [denied] the possibility of a national common interest." Consequently, deliberation, or public reasoning concerning the public interest, ceased to be a primary function of the legislative body. "The greatest deliberative body in the world ... no longer deliberates as it should." Indeed, lawmaking itself is no longer the principle task of the legislature. Increasingly, Congress has delegated that authority to specialized bureaucracies supposedly better equipped to administer the complex tasks of solving the problems of industrial or post-industrial society.

Professor Mansbridge laments Congressional inability to deliberate with a view to the national interest. Professor Fiorina, too, noted at the conference that the contemporary Congress was very well organized to represent various interests, but ill-equipped to deliberate concerning a common good. However, neither Professor Mansbridge nor Professor Fiorina, both political scientists, could find anything within their discipline which enabled them to discern or even define a common interest. The capacity to deliberate presupposes the capacity to reason, which is essential in the determination of a common good. In abandoning the notion of the common good, the public interest, too, has disintegrated into the view that satisfaction of the private interests of interested publics is the best that can be achieved in the political arena. Moreover, the discipline of political science, from its inception, has denied the possibility of objective knowledge concerning a common good.

The faculty of reason, which is a presupposition of the capacity to deliberate, was undermined by the development of modern social science methodology, as well as the development of the positive theory of the state. This view of the state, which developed out of Hegel's thought, became the cornerstone of progressive thought in America in the 1880's and after. The modern state was considered the rational embodiment of the will of the people. The state was thought to be a living and evolving organism. Moreover, the power of government, once thought to be a danger to the liberties of the people, could be used for positive purposes in the interest of the nation and hence the people themselves. Consequently, the power of government need not be limited, as it could not be a danger to the people, because the rights of individuals are no longer in conflict with those of community, or the people themselves. The tension between the demands of the individual and the community, between the private and public, or government and society, which formed the basis of modern liberal constitutionalism, was said to be resolved in the Hegelian idea of the state. In the view of Hegel and the historicists who followed his view, reason and will are no longer in conflict. Reason becomes the means of carrying out the will of the people. Paradoxically, this was to be done by utilizing those persons who are devoid of a personal passion for power. Their very disinterestedness would ensure the kind of rationality necessary to carry out the will of the state. This universal class, the bureaucrats, "is at the apex of the social pyramid," Sholomo Avineri has observed, because "it is the only class of society whose objective is knowledge itself, not nature, artefact or abstraction, as is the case with all other classes."[3] Lorenz Stein, an early German theorist of public administration who greatly influenced Woodrow Wilson, pointed to the character of this class of bureaucrats immune from human passion. The bureaucratic class has "the capacity to care deeply for the welfare of the whole and to subordinate to it any special interest. These men are therefore predestined to state service, to service on behalf of the idea of the state." The American founders had no such view of the state. The notion that the disjunction between state and society, individual and community, and reason and will could be resolved—as Hegel and others held—is mere "utopian speculation" in the view of Federalists and Anti-federalists alike. The state cannot be rational, will cannot replace reason, nor can history replace nature. For the founders, reason was the means by which the "self-evident truths" are made intelligible. Nature gives men, as individuals, the capacity to reason

---

3. Shlomo Avineri, *Hegel's Theory of the Modern State*, (London: Cambridge University Press, 1972), p. 108.

which in turn informs them of their natural rights as human beings. The role of government is the protection of those natural rights of individual moral beings. Consequently, a common good is ascertainable because of a common denominator, which is, or has always been, reason. Indeed, Edward S. Corwin could still say in 1929 that liberalism's "most fundamental assumption" is the notion "that man is primarily a rational creature, and that his acts are governed by rational considerations." It is this assumption upon which "the doctrine that the people should rule rests."

However, the growth of the influence of the scientific study of politics itself did much to undermine not only the belief in reason, but those "self-evident truths" which are the product of that reason. The discipline of political science was born at the end of a century in which history had replaced nature in political philosophy, and will had replaced reason, all in the service of progress. As Corwin has written:

> the extension of certain implications of evolutionary thought challenges some of the more fundamental elements of classical American political thought. The cornerstone of the latter at its inception was the notion of a natural law of final moral and political values which were the discovery of reason. The natural law of experimentalism, on the other hand, is the natural law of the sciences, which exists independent of and indifferent to moral values. So there are no final truths, and reason as such is left without any reason for being. In its place is that continuous mental activity which we term planning, man's capacity for which is the explanation of his survival in the struggle for existence, and his only ground for hope for the future. Truth, in short, is a plan of action which is operationally successful. It is therefore relative and variable, the pliable instrument of an ever shifting problem of adjustment to "specific situations."[4]

The growing influence of the new discipline of political science was instrumental in popularizing—and subsequently undermining—the notion of rational politics and with it the possibility of discerning a common good. A. Lawrence Lowell noted: "the elder breed of political and economic philosophers erred in regarding man as a purely rational being." On the contrary, as Graham Wallas suggested, "the empirical art of politics consists largely in the creation of opinion by the deliberate exploitation of subconscious non-rational inference." The young Walter Lippman expressed the new realism implicit in the new politics. "No

---

4. Edward S. Corwin, "The Impact of the Idea of Evolution on the American Political and Constitutional Tradition," in *Corwin on the Constitution*, vol. I, ed. Richard Loss, (Ithaca: Cornell University Press, 1981), pp. 192-193.

genuine politician treats his constituents as reasoning animals," he writes, "the successful politician—good or bad—deals with the dynamics—with the will, the hopes, the needs and the visions of men." If the actions of the people are not governed by rational considerations, their leaders, too, could hardly be considered rational men. Rather it is the passions in the service of will that become decisive. As Lippman noted, "we find reasons for what we want to do." Consequently, he insists that "man when he is most creative is not a rational, but a willful animal."[5]

Although will embodied in the idea of the state replaces reason, on the assumption that passion or will can be rational, it is hardly an unmediated popular will. On the contrary, the various disciplines in the social sciences must provide the method and the expertise to solve the problems of modern society. Harvey Mansfield has pointed to this subtle sleight of hand:

> Social science, with its expertise in modeling, can guarantee choice—that is, get the people what they want—only if the people do not exercise their choice of getting what they want in their own way. From this result we see that the initial aloof objectivity of social science—in seeming not to care what the people's wants were and whether they were good—was actually the only way of getting them what they want, which is also the most effectual way of caring for them. To have offered a frown at the meaner and more bizarre wants of the people would have been attempting to set their reason against their will with no sure prospect of victory for either and the likelihood of a tense debate. The trick, then, is to leave the people their will and take away their reason; then social science can bring *its* reason to serve *their* will, showing them how to get more of what they want. The value neutrality of social science is the best or only means by which government can bring value to the people.[6]

But in the end no one is fooled and everyone is unhappy. Those public bureaucracies designed to serve the will of the people are the source of the greatest public skepticism toward—if not outright hatred of—government. Indeed, in every Presidential election since 1968—the first election after the American government began widescale bureaucratization—when the people have had reason to think in terms of the national interest, they have opposed the extension of the bureaucratic state. As for

---

5. All quotations in this paragraph are found in David M. Ricci, *The Tragedy of Political Science: Politics Scholarship and Democracy*, (New Haven: Yale University Press, 1984), pp. 78-79.

6. Harvey C. Mansfield, "The Constitution and Modern Social Science," *The Center Magazine*, pp. 51-52.

the so-called superior rationality of bureaucracy, no one is persuaded that a popular will, executed in matters of the smallest detail, can substitute for the freedom of the individual will. So when American citizens are faced with the worst of all worlds, deprived of reason in general affairs and of will in particular affairs, it is not accidental that many have become preoccupied with the most private and subjective needs and passions of the private individual. It is not suprising, as Walter Dean Burnham has noted, that the greatest mass movement in recent times is the movement away from the polls. Administrative centralization, and all that it entails, has succeeded in turning citizens into bourgeoisie, preparing the way for the enticement, among the most thoughtful and aware of the elites, of a new kind of community—that animated by Marxist ideology.

Professor Mansbridge rightly notes that Congress no longer functions primarily as a deliberative body. Moreover, as a representative body, it is less effective in reconciling particular interests in light of the general interest. But her solution only shows the difficulty of confronting this issue with an approach based on the authority of the social sciences. Deprived of reason, she is left with the value-free tools of the social scientist: psychological or behavioral motivation, technical expertise, and more nearly equal numerical representation of interests.

In terms of motivation, she suggests that individual Congressmen can look to the common by looking beyond the local, which entails an appeal to the personal motives of politicians. "Wanting to matter thus seduces a representative beyond the common, beyond preference to interest." Similarly, she insists that "respect for technical expertise and for sound judgment encourage, in their turn, the idea that facts matter, and [therefore] that problems have solutions that are more or less feasible, more or less good or bad for the nation as a whole." Ultimately, Mansbridge identifies the common interest as nothing but the opposite of local interests. In utilizing simple and neutral geographical terms, she determines that the local interest cannot provide a standard because it is not all-inclusive. The nation, or the state, must be the standard because it allows for the equal representation of all interests. She suggests, "in the context of common interests . . . the job of the representative must be to deliberate . . . from the perspective of the polity as a whole. In the context of conflicting interests . . . the representative's job must be to puzzle out the real locus and meaning of that conflict, and in its democratic resolution represent his or her constituents [at least] in proportion to their numbers."

Mansbridge differs from Madison, who believed that a public interest could be achieved by reasonable representatives precisely because the multiplicity of interests would negate each other in such a way as to allow representatives the freedom to ignore the most harmful interests and thereby give them the opportunity to transcend private interests with a view to the common good. Without the ability to reason concerning the common good, representation can be nothing more than the all-inclusive, and faithful *re-presentation* at the center of the passions and interests of all the diverse groups which constitute the society, good as well as bad.

Professor Mansbridge makes a notable attempt to "entice Congress toward deliberation." But the discipline of political science itself contributed to its demise, and social science methodology cannot bring about its resurrection. Professors Mansbridge and Fiorina provide empirical evidence of the great difficulty confronting those whose presuppositions are derived from modern political science methodology or political theory when trying to come to grips with such value terms as the common good or the public interest. The deliberative function of Congress was eroded by the attack on reason itself, which was a product, in philosophical thought, of the triumph of historicism. Public reason was no more defensible than the faculty of reason itself against the corroding influence of Hegel, Darwin, and Marx, and the success of the experimental method in science, which dominated nineteenth-century thought. Edward S. Corwin long ago pointed to the effectiveness of that attack. He observed:

> when we turn to the philosophy of instrumentalism or experimentalism and its conception of thought as planning ... [such] a conception simply passes by as obsolete the idea of thought as the fine fruit of a cognitive, reasoning faculty which, just because of its detachment from the daily concerns of men, is able to arrive at abstract and permanent truths. ... The autonomous reason of the eighteenth-century Enlightenment, the power to see things *sub specie aeternitatis*, is demoted by instrumentalism to a planning device for meeting the shifting demands of an ever changing environment, and is then further reduced to the ignoble role of a tool of propagandists. The eternal verities become, first relative truths, then half-truths, or less than half-truths, even deliberate falsehoods.[7]

The attack on reason could not but succeed in undermining the idea of a common good which is discerned by rational deliberation. The "Framers' Congress" was deliberative because the framers assumed that the distinctive characteristic of man was his capacity to reason. The institutions of government were constructed in such a way as to augment those passions hospitable to reason and diminish support for unreasonable

---

7. Corwin, pp. 191-192.

passions, even those which purport to be in the service of a majority will. The current Congress and Professor Mansbridge, not to mention Fiorina, both have difficulty deliberating concerning a common good because both doubt what the framers took for granted, the possibility that "societies of men" really are capable of "establishing good government" and perpetuating it "from reflection and choice." Deprived of any authoritative support for reason—either in science, social science, or modern philosophy—there is no common denominator from which to deliberate in order to discern a common good. In the contemporary view, reason itself is nothing more than the rationalization of a passion or interest, whether of class, race, sex, or whatever. Consequently, there can be no reasonable or principled defense of limited or constitutional government. In the absence of reason, only will, whether of the majority or minorities, remains.

Chapter Three

The President: Executive Energy and Republican Safety

In claiming the right even to violate a law in order to carry out his duties, Lincoln asked, "are all the laws, but one, to go unexecuted, and the government itself to go to pieces, lest that one be violated?" Now that the President is the head of government for a superpower in a nuclear age, how far should his authority extend beyond the mere execution of the laws?

Executive and Prerogative: A Problem for Adherents of Constitutional Government

Richard H. Cox

I

Are all the laws, *but one*, to go unexecuted, and the government itself to go to pieces, lest that one be violated?

Abraham Lincoln[1]

It is the nature of war to increase the executive at the expense of the legislative authority.

Alexander Hamilton[2]

Adherents of constitutional government are troubled by these statements. The first implies that the necessities of civil war entitle the President to ignore his duty "faithfully" to execute the laws, the second that those of foreign war entitle him to arrogate the legislative powers. Both, in appealing to "necessities," make an implied claim on behalf of the doctrine of "executive prerogative."[3] That doctrine at very least is problematically constitutional, and at worst may be simply a euphemism for tyrannical rule carried out under the guise of zeal for the public good.

My purpose is to consider the question of "executive and prerogative"

---

1. See Lincoln's "Message to Congress in Special Session," July 4, 1861, in *The Collected Works of Abraham Lincoln*, ed. Roy P. Basier (New Brunswick, N.J.: Rutgers University Press, 1953), vol. IV, p. 430.

2. *The Federalist*, ed. J. E. Cooke (Middletown, Conn.: Wesleyan University Press, 1980), No. 8, para. 5. In order to facilitate use of other texts of *The Federalist*, I refer to papers by Number and paragraph, thus: (8:5).

3. See, for example: Larry Arnhart, "'The God-Like Prince': John Locke, Executive Prerogative, and the American Presidency," *Presidential Studies Quarterly*, vol. 9 (Spring, 1979): 121-30; and Richard Pious, *The American Presidency* (New York: Basic Books, 1979), Ch. 2, "Prerogative Powers."

from the perspective of The Founders. My plan is to present three short essays: on Hamilton, on Locke, and on Aristotle.[4] And my rationale is as follows: The Constitution is the authoritative statement of the nature of executive power but it requires interpretation. Who, then, among The Founders shall interpret it? My choice of Hamilton, in his portion of *The Federalist*, rests on these considerations. First, *The Federalist* is the most systematic, theoretical interpretation of any of The Founders. Second, because that interpretation precedes the actual implementation of The Constitution it is of exceptional importance in throwing light on what its authors anticipated would be the mode of governance under the new Constitution. Third, although both Hamilton and Madison render elements of an interpretation of the executive power, Hamilton writes the majority of the papers in the whole work—fifty-one of eighty-five—and he also writes the thematic interpretation of the executive power, in Nos. 67-77.[5] Fourth, Hamilton generally is perceived as that founder who is most favorable to extensive executive powers.

The subsequent turning to Locke and Aristotle rests on this further premise: The precise character of Hamilton's interpretation of executive power comes most fully to light by seeing it within the wider horizon of political philosophy, modern and ancient. For the moderns, I turn to Locke, because, first, he is rightly known as "America's philosopher"; second, he originates the explicit modern notion of "the executive power"; and third, his treatment of "pre-rogative" is the most explicit and systematic by any modern political philosopher. For the ancients, I turn to Aristotle, because, first, Locke obliquely draws upon Aristotle's treatment of *pambasileia*, or "kingly rule over all matters," in his treatment of "prerogative"; and second, Aristotle's ambivalent treatment of such rule reveals a perhaps insoluble problem concerning governance.

---

4. To facilitate following the argument in the text, without burdening the text with excessive detail, I have placed, in the Appendix, analytical outlines of the materials being treated.

5. The question, Who wrote which Numbers of *The Federalist?*, is not capable of absolutely definitive resolution given the absence of key documents—most notably, the manuscripts of Hamilton's and Madison's contributions. However, I think that Douglass Adair's very detailed arguments persuasively allocate the papers this way: Hamilton (Nos. 1, 6-9, 11-13, 15-17, 21-36, 59-61, 65-85); Madison (Nos. 10, 14, 18-20, 37-58, 62-63); and Jay (Nos. 2-5, 64. See Douglass Adair, *Fame and the Founding Fathers: Essays by Douglass Adair*, ed. Trevor Colbourn (New York: W. W. Norton, 1974), pp. 27-74, 257-58.

II

Our first task is to situate Hamilton's interpretation within the horizon of thought and within the general structure of the argument of *The Federalist*.

The horizon of thought of *The Federalist* is that of public deliberation on whether to adopt a new "constitution" for the American states. Its arguments are thus constrained by the necessity to act, which is in tension with the freedom simply to reflect concerning government. This constraint operates with peculiarly great force in Publius' treatment of the executive power. For the opposed positions of the time are rooted in the question, "What is the nature of the best regime?"; but the answers they give are skewed in the direction of what, from a completely impartial perspective, must appear to be a partisan preference for republican over monarchical —or, more generically, royal, or princely—government. But because the executive power most clearly squints in the direction of princely government it also is the most alarming of the three powers to republicans, hence most in need of rhetorical as well as reasoned defense. Hamilton, in his capacity as Publius, understands this difficulty very well, as we shall see.

As for the general argument of *The Federalist*, Hamilton, in his guise as Publius, opens by posing this question: Can men institute "good government" by "reflection and choice" rather than submit to one that "accident and force" chance to institute (1:1)? Nos. 2-36 articulate the general principles of good government: "safety" is the first if not the loftiest object; "energy" is the necessary means. Nos. 37-84 relate these principles to those of republican government. Hamilton does so particularly with respect to "the executive power" in Nos. 67-77. At the end, he urges adoption of The Constitution for the "prosperity" as well as "safety" of "the people" (85:5).

The meaning of "safety" and of "energy" in *The Federalist* needs clarification. "Safety" means, first, security of men's bodies and properties against the dangers emanating necessarily from external or internal war and is rooted in what Madison once calls "the great principle of self-preservation" (43:29). It is an emphatically modern principle, emanating from the doctrines of Hobbes and Locke. "Safety" means, secondly, safety of the "liberty" of "the people," and is rooted in "dependence on the people" and "due responsibility," to use Hamilton's formulation (70:5).

"Energy" means the ability to do work. In the context of *The Federalist*, it means the ability of the government to do the work that is essential to securing the objects of government, the first object being the "safety" of men, insofar as practicable, against the dangers inherent in war. It is much worth noting, here, two general points concerning Hamilton's treatment of "energy." First, in No. 23, which introduces the explication and defense of "energetic government," Hamilton asserts that the powers requisite to such "safety"—those concerned with military force—must "exist without limitation, *because it is impossible to foresee or define the extent and variety of national exigencies, or the correspondent extent and variety of the means which may be necessary to satisfy them*" (23:4, emphasis by Hamilton). Second, although the government as a whole is often referred to as being "energetic," only the executive power, as such, is ever explicitly said to be necessarily "energetic," and that is said by Hamilton (70:3).

It is then a good question whether the executive power is, for Hamilton, the very core of governance as such—the original, most necessary and yet also potentially the most dangerous power, hence the power least capable of final constitutional delimitation and yet, simultaneously and even paradoxically, the one most in need of such delimitation.

The problem may be restated as follows. The thrust of Hamilton's general argument concerning government is that in conditions of exigency the power of the government to act is necessarily unlimited. But the great difficulty is how to determine whether exigency truly exists, and then what actions are to be taken to meet it. The strict principle of republican government suggests that "the people," who are posited as the ultimate source of all government powers, should make these two determinations. Yet in the conditions posited, it is utterly problematic, at very least, whether "the people" can so act. The alternative, then, is to entrust these momentous determinations to "the government," which is comprised of "representatives" of "the people." But the problem only then takes on a new form: Are all three powers equally "representative" with respect to such determinations? Are they all equally capable? Or is one preeminent, and if so which, on what grounds, and to what extent?

Not surprisingly, given both the delicacy of these questions and the fact that Publius writes in full recognition that the adoption of The Constitution is still very much in doubt, one searches in vain for a direct, clear answer in *The Federalist*. It is therefore necessary to infer one from a close study of the actual arguments, and to recognize that Hamilton, like Madison, was schooled and artful in the use of ancient principles of rhetoric.

Madison introduces the crucial theme of "the conformity of the Constitution to the true principles of republican government" in No. 37. Hamilton applies it to "the executive power" in Nos. 67-77. I will begin with the relationship of Hamilton's argument to that of Madison in No. 37. I will then turn to selective comments on Hamilton's argument as such.

The President: Executive Energy and Republican Safety

Hamilton's argument, as the analytical outline shows, falls into two parts. He says at the beginning that the "arrangement" of the executive power was attended with very great "difficulty" but does not say precisely what that difficulty was. However, the immediate sequel suggests that it consisted simply in differentiating the power of the Presidency from that of English monarchy, for the first three papers treat that theme. They do so at first with hyperbole that seems to exceed that of the anti-Federalist critics; then with sober, even pedantic textual analysis; and finally with two sets of comparisons, the last of which takes the form of a kind of primer. By the end of No. 69 it seems that the fears of those who oppose The Constitution because they fear the Presidency squints at monarchy should be fully allayed.

All the more striking, then, is the opening into what proves to be a new treatment; for Hamilton, at the beginning of No. 70, now tersely formulates a deeper difficulty: some men believed that a "vigorous executive is inconsistent with the genius of republican government" (70:1). Whether he is as successful in meeting this difficulty as he was in meeting the first is the crux, as I shall now argue.

The sense of "difficulty" that opens each of the two parts is intended, I believe, eventually to remind the reader of Madison's argument in No. 37. That argument is rhetorically very subtle and substantively very troubling. It deserves, if there were but space enough and time, a very careful investigation. It must suffice, here, to make these observations: First, Madison discriminates among readers/critics, and appeals, ultimately, to a kind of "middle" sort, who will discern, on reflection, that "a faultless plan was not to be expected." Whether that shortcoming is accidental or inevitable is a large question. Second, Madison sketches five "difficulties": (1) the "novelty" of the undertaking; (2) combining "stability and energy" with "republican form"; (3) delineating the powers of the central and state governments; (4) mediating conflicts of large and small states; (5) mediating conflicts of regional and other interests. All five entail theoretical and practical considerations. But the theoretical is dominant in the first three, and thus the central theoretical difficulty is, perhaps not surprisingly, how to combine the requisites of energetic government with those of republican government. The three elements of the latter are: (1) derivation of all powers from "the people," (2) shortness of term of office, and (3) plurality of offices. Hamilton will have his work cut out for him in reconciling each of these with his fundamental principle that "Energy in the executive is a leading character in the definition of good government" (70:1). Third, within the treatment of the third difficulty, Madison engages in a digression that David Epstein shrewdly characterizes as "the most astonishing passage in *The Federalist*."[6] The digression is a compressed, highly skeptical reflection on human understanding that reminds one of Locke's *Essay Concerning Human Understanding*, and that includes the sobering contention that not even the "greatest adepts in political science" have been able "to discriminate and define, with sufficient certainty" the exact bounds among the three powers of government.

As we return now to Hamilton it is necessary to keep most particularly in mind the two salient difficulties that have emerged: First, "how far" is it possible to combine energetic with republican government? As for Madison, he is chary, in No. 37, about responding directly and unequivocally to his own question. And one has to wonder whether "how far" logically entails the possibility of the unpleasant conclusion "not altogether." Second, how to construe the lack of "certainty" as to the limits of "the executive power" in relation to the other two? Does this perhaps ominous deficiency pertain most particularly to the three powers at rest, so to speak, in the definition that can be given to them in any written constitution? Or to the three powers in motion, so speak, in the dynamics of government at work? Or to both? Here is a problem of the first magnitude concerning political mechanics for the founders of the new "science of politics" (9:3).

Hamilton orders his treatment of the reformulated difficulty in three parts: (1) a short defense of "energy" in the executive; (2) a terse statement of three questions: (a) what are the "ingredients" of "energy"?; (b) "how far" do these consist with those of "the genius of republican government"? (c) does The Constitution embody such consistency? (3) a lengthy answer to the questions: (a) a terse statement of the "ingredients" of "energy" [unity, duration, adequate compensation, competent powers] and of "safety in the republican sense" [dependence on the people, responsibility]; (b) a lengthy answer to questions (a) and (b); and (c) a summary reply to question (c).

I shall now comment on three aspects of Hamilton's treatment, each of which indicates the ultimately problematic consistency of an energetic executive with republican orthodoxy. That orthodoxy consists, to repeat, in (1) derivation of all powers from the people, (2) short terms of office, and (3) plurality of holders of office, all of which, in principle, combine to produce dependence and responsibility.

---

6. David F. Epstein, *The Political Theory of* The Federalist (Chicago: The University of Chicago Press, 1984), p. 114.

A first difficulty is that the two primary ingredients of Hamilton's energetic executive, "unity" and "duration," are manifestly in tension with the third and second of the republican principles. Hamilton's response to this difficulty consists, upon rigorous comparison of his arguments with the strict sense of the principles, of palliations rather than resolutions. One example, but a telling one, must suffice: At the center of his treatment of "unity," which is manifestly in tension with the principle of plural offices, Hamilton adverts to the notion of "responsibility" (70:15). He distinguishes two senses thereof, "censure" and "punishment," and seeks to show that each is more readily fulfilled when there is a single "executive" who may be blamed. But both senses necessarily operate *ex post facto*, hence necessarily permit great latitude of executive action for which no prior grant of power may be proved.

A second difficulty is that the first part of Hamilton's response to the "idea" that an energetic executive is "inconsistent with the genius of republican government" is, given the weightiness of the difficulty, an astonishingly brief, elliptical and curiously phrased three-part defense of the "necessity" for such an executive, prior even to the statement of the "ingredients" thereof. The defense consists of two dense, abstract arguments that surround a single historical example, the whole occupying some twenty-four lines. On so slight a base a very considerable structure is erected, hence it seems highly desirable to look closely at that base.

Hamilton begins the first argument from a curious perspective: At the outset, he posits "enlightened well wishers" to "republican government" who "must at least hope" that the contention that there is an inconsistency between a vigorous executive and republican government is not true. But by the end of the sentence those well-wishers seem to have become simple adherents of such government who must either deny the truth of the contention or give up their adherence. What seems to be excluded is an admission of the contention and at least a well-wishing to republican government that falls short of simple adherence. In any case, what may not be given up is the premise that an energetic executive is "essential" to protect men against foreign attack and against three species of domestic ills: bad administration of the laws, assaults on property, and assaults on "liberty" from "ambition, faction," and, most terrifying one must suppose, "anarchy."

Hamilton now turns abruptly from "argument" to a single "example." And what an example it is!—the office of Dictator in the Roman Republic, which Hamilton styles "the absolute power of a single man." The example seems simply, at first, to reinforce the conclusion reached at the end of the first argument: it suggests that not even the greatest republic of antiquity could dispense with such an executive in conditions of exigency, even if it meant a *de facto* suspension of the most essentially republican features of the Roman constitutional order. But what is curious is that Hamilton now restates the need for an energetic executive—which is, to repeat, an important (and shall we dare to say, perhaps, the most important?) element in the definition of "good government." The restatement consists, first, in a reversal of the order of considerations so that domestic ones now precede foreign; and second, in a new formulation of domestic ones, which now falls into but two divisions: the Dictator is said to have afforded protection against the ambitions of those who aspired to "the tyranny," and against seditions of "whole classes" that threatened the "existence of all government." Thus there is a reduction of the internal threats to those of tyranny and anarchy, the latter becoming the central element in a triad which culminates in the threat of destruction by foreign arms. The premise of Hobbes and of Locke, that man's greatest danger is to be without a supreme power to protect him, thus comes into its proper light as the true foundation of the whole argument.

But how are we to construe Hamilton's use of this particular example that forms the center-piece, as it were, of his amazingly brief defense of the "necessity" of an "energetic executive"? Though he readily notices that the Dictator's power is "absolute," he does not say it is "arbitrary." Though he contrasts the absolute power of the Dictator to that of the aspirant tyrant, he does not vouchsafe to the reader a set of criteria by which to tell one from the other. And though he recognizes that there is a departure from strict republicanism, he does not make clear whether that departure is itself authorized by republican action, but says only that the "republic was obliged to take refuge" in the office of Dictator. In short, he leaves the reader, it appears, to ponder these troubling difficulties on his own.

We turn, finally, to the second argument. This compresses the problem posed to its bare outline: (1) feeble executive = feeble execution of government; (2) feeble execution = bad execution; (3) bad execution = bad government. This series of equations seems intended to dramatize the consequences of rejecting an energetic executive by its concluding with the phrase "bad government"—which, presumably, not even the most ardent republican will desire. But the troubling points raised by the nuances of the adversion to the Roman Dictator remain.

The third difficulty concerns an essential ambiguity in Hamilton's treatment of the first and most fundamental republican principle—that all power derives from the people. In order to see just how ambiguous that treatment is we have, first, to recognize a great difficulty in the principle itself; and second, to consider, albeit elliptically, Hamilton's treatment of the qualities most desirable in the executive.

The principle that all powers ultimately derive from the people posits power essentially in the sense of three powers of governance. But the activity of governance is, by its nature, a compound of such power and the power consisting of the possession and exercise of the natural faculties of the individual human soul—the passions, spiritedness, and reason, to use an ancient formulation. How these two senses of power may be conjoined in such a way as to meet the test of republican orthodoxy is a conundrum. The qualities that inhere in the exercise of the second kind of power are essentially insusceptible to consitutional formulation, yet most critical in giving real substance to the dynamics of actual governance, a difficulty that is most acute in the exercise of "the executive power."

Hamilton begins the defense of "unity" by ascribing to the executive the qualities of "decision, activity, secrecy and dispatch," and to the legislature those of "deliberation and wisdom." The former seem intended to stress the ministerial nature of the executive, the latter the determinative nature of the legislature. But as he proceeds, Hamilton slowly changes the relationship of the two by re-modelling the qualities of the executive, particularly in relation to the conditions of exigency. In the treatment of "unity"—the property that most is akin to princely govern-ment as such—Hamilton is content to stress "vigor and independence" of the executive as requisite. But along the way, in a series of three references to the use of plural magistracies in Rome—Consuls, Tribunes, and Decemvirs—he warns of the dangers from dissensions that afflicted all three institutions, but does so most emphatically with respect to the first and last. His near-silence about dissensions among the Tribunes—that plural magistracy most dependent on "the people"—is broken, later, when he tersely speaks of the "importance, perplexity, and disorder" characteristic of that popular institution (75:6).

In the treatment of "duration," Hamilton progressively remodels the desirable qualities of the executive. To the first four posited he gradually adds "courage," "magnanimity," "fortitude," "daring to act on his own opinion," "firmness," "wisdom," "integrity," and "experience," which is "the parent of wisdom." But the most notable, problematic and troubling remodelling of all occurs at the middle of this treatment, where the theme of the "love of fame" comes very briefly to the surface of the argument. Hamilton asserts that that love is "the ruling passion of the noblest minds," and seeks to show that it can be safely directed to pursuit of "the public benefit" on the basis of these premises: first, all men ardently seek rewards; second, the "best security" for fidelity to the public good is to make a man's interest coincide with his duty; third, men of the noblest minds will be willing to assume the executive power only if they can expect to exercise their great personal powers in the planning and under-taking of "extensive and arduous enterprises for the public benefit" that require long periods for maturation and perfection (72:4).

It hardly needs to be said, I suppose, that the second of these premises is both the most problematic and dangerous. For as Lincoln will later warn, in his 1838 speech on "The Perpetuation of Our Political Institutions," there is among men a tiny tribe of the eagle—and Caesar seems to be the most notable historical example—that will have fame at any cost, even that of destroying a free political order. Hamilton's seeming confidence in joining interest to duty in the soul of those thirsting for fame, and coming, at last, to the exercise of "the executive power," particularly in conditions of alleged or real exigency, should give adherents of constitutional govern-ments pause.

III

Locke, "America's philosopher," is, in the language of antiquity, a "philosophic lawgiver." Our inquiry is: What is his teaching, or "law," on "executive and prerogative"?

We must begin from his placement of that theme within the structure of his *Second Treatise*, and from certain subtle features of his arrangement of the sub-parts. On these related points, John Collins has made the following astute and persuasive argument: First, Locke orders the whole of the *Second Treatise* into two main sub-parts: (I) Chs. I-VI treat pre- and non- governmental topics; (II) Chs. VII-XIX treat governmental topics. Second, Locke further divides the 13 chapters on governmental topics symmetrically into sub-parts: [1] Chs. VII-XI (five); [2] Chs. XII-XIV (three); [3] Chs. XV-XIX (five). Third, within Chs. XII-XIV, which treat "executive and prerogative," and which contain 26 sections, he divides the argument into two sub-parts of 13 sections each: (1) 143-155 treat the "executive" prior to the introduction of "prerogative"; and (2) 156-168, treat it in relation to "prerogative." In the latter, he speaks of "prerogative" 26 times.[7]

---

7. John Collins is, at the time of this writing, a Ph.D. candidate at Harvard University. He made his observations and arguments in the course of work on a dissertation on Locke's understanding of natural law, and very kindly conveyed them to me in correspondence, in September, 1984.

It is problematic whether these structural aspects and these details of Locke's ordering are intended to convey anything substantive about executive and prerogative. But it is suggestive that he places that theme at the center of his treatment of governmental topics: that he orders and divides it with what appears to be mathematical exactness; and that that exactness involves "3," "26," and "13." But to what purpose? Observing and reflecting on these and related features, Collins argues that they are rhetorical devices intended to remind the thoughtful reader of Machiavelli's infamous treatment of "princely government" in the 26 Chapters of *The Prince*. I believe Collins is correct. And reflecting upon his and my own observations, I have reached the conclusion that Locke's teaching on executive and prerogative is intended to be a deliberate albeit oblique correction of Machiavelli's teaching on "princely government," and that that correction is deliberately rooted in a return—albeit an oblique, ambiguous and problematic one—to Aristotle's teaching on *pambasileia*, or "kingly rule over all matters."

My argument in support of this conclusion is necessarily truncated. It rests on the general premise that the philosophers' teachings on political rule are rooted in an understanding not just of "human nature" but of man's place in and relation to "nature" as a whole. It focusses primarily on three of Locke's thematic treatments, "state of nature," "prerogative," and "tyranny." It rests on the specific premise that Locke intends these themes to be seen as closely linked parts of his treatment of executive and prerogative. And it relates aspects of these, first, to Machiavelli's "princely government," and, second, to Aristotle's *pambasileia*.

Locke originates the explicit form of the modern notion of "the executive power" of government. It is tacitly articulated, first, in the treatment of the "state of nature" in Ch. II, and is rooted in every man's possession of "the executive power of the law of nature" (II.13). That power gives every man the right to punish breakers of "the law of nature," which wills the preservation of all men, and to exact reparations from those who do. Locke's awareness of the originality of this teaching—and, by implication, the correlative teaching on "the executive power of government"—is indicated by his twice pointing out that some may call it a "strange doctrine" (II.9,13). Just how "strange" remains to be seen.

Locke's treatment is a complex fusion of argument and appeal, real or problematic, to the authority of Hookers' *Laws of Ecclesiastical Polity* and of *Genesis*. He orders it in 12 sections. All the sections are either simply Lockean argument, or a blend of such argument and appeal to authority, except for the second, sect. 5, which is simply an appeal to the authority of

Hooker. The consequence is that Locke orders his own argument in 11 sections. But to what purpose? To anticipate, we shall see that Locke also orders the treatments of "prerogative" and "tyranny" in 11 sections. Again we may ask, To what purpose?

I suggest that it is an exact, though most unobtrusive, rhetorical device to indicate that Locke's teaching on executive and prerogative is, in part, a turning to Machiavelli's teaching on "princely government," within which Machiavelli himself uses the "11" in two very different senses: First, he assigns the number "11" to the chapter that treats of "ecclesiastical principates," even though, according to Augustine, "11" is the number signifying "transgression of the law"—or Decalogue—for 11 goes beyond 10.[8] Second, in Ch. XV, which boldly announces that he brings "new modes and orders," he gives a list of what traditionally are known as virtues and vices. In this case, he orders the list in 11 pairs, to signify he is taking issue with Aristotle's 11 sets of moral virtues and vices in the *Ethics*. A crucial sign that Machiavelli does take such issue is his conversion of Aristotle's triadic sense of virtue (vice of excess—virtue as mean—vice of deficiency) into sets of merely virtue and vice with no "mean."

But to return to Locke. The critical point is that he seeks to discover a standard by which to judge the exercise of power by individual men and by rulers. More precisely, he seeks a standard that is simple, easily comprehended, rooted in "nature," universally and certainly applicable, and reflective of the utterly passionate side of human nature—above all, of the first and most powerful passion, which is to be safe. He does so in order to resolve the ages-old difficulty that men disagree about the standard by which to judge political rule, hence tend to fall into civil broils and even anarchy, which may then give way to tyranny. In seeking such a standard, Locke cautiously follows the way taken by Machiavelli, and then Montaigne, Bacon, Hobbes, and Descartes. Each, in his way, takes issue with the classical understanding of "nature," for it yields a standard that is utterly problematic, according to the modern view, not least because it posits "natural right" in the form of *teloi*, or "ends." Locke, like the other moderns, will find the standard of "nature" in the beginning, or in that which men flee because of an impulse of nature itself.

Locke's origination of "the executive power" takes place, second, in his treatment of the ambiguous relationship of "the legislative" and "the executive," which culminates in the thematic treatment of "prerogative."

---

8. Sarah Thurow called my attention, many years ago, to the fact that St. Augustine, in the *City of God* XV.21, so characterizes "11."

We must sketch how this takes place and how it is intended as a deliberate correction of Machiavelli by means of a partial return to Aristotle. We must begin, here, from the fact that Chs. XII-XIV of Locke's argument are intended, at one level, to be understood as parallel to Chs. XII-XIV of Machiavelli's argument. But to see something of the subtlety and tendency of each argument, we have to turn back for a moment to Ch. XI of each book.

Machiavelli's XI, is, on the surface, a pious treatment of "ecclesiastical principates." But its underlying argument reinforces the sense that its placement and numbering suggest, and that is a sense of "transgression of the law." Locke's XI, "Of the Legislative Power," treats primarily of human law, but twice traces its ultimate basis to "the law of nature," which, in turn, is equated with "the will of God" (II.135). Locke repeatedly insists in XI that "the legislative" is the "supreme power; that it must never act "arbitrarily" with respect to the "end of government, which is dictated by the "law of nature"; and that it must always, as to means, act not in "arbitrary" ways but only through "promulgated and established laws." In short, Locke, through his rooting of positive law in the "law of God and Nature," and through his repeated inveighing against "arbitrary" rule, whether as to the end or to the means, appears fundamentally to oppose Machiavelli's bold association of "11" with "transgression of the law"—so much so that Locke associates it rather with rule by and through law alone, a rule mindful, it seems, of the ultimate basis of "the law" in "the Will of God."

But at the end of XI, a difficulty very unobtrusively emerges: In the thematic treatment in the main part of the chapter, Locke places the primary emphasis on "ends" and the secondary emphasis on "means." But at the end of the chapter, in what at first appears merely to be a summary of the main points, Locke reverses the order. That reversal opens the way into *the* problem of XII-XIV: Is rule exclusively by and through the law politically possible? In this literal and thematic center of his treatment of governmental topics, Locke argues with amazing care and subtlety, and constantly has in mind Machiavelli's Chs. XII-XIV, on the one hand, and Aristotle's treatment of *pambasileia*, on the other hand. Only a sketch of my reasons for so thinking can be given here.

First, on Machiavelli: Machiavelli's Chs. XII-XIV treat the problem of "arms," Locke's that of "executive" and "prerogative." Machiavelli, operating from the premise that "nature" is essentially hostile to man, who is driven by a "natural necessity to acquire," begins Ch. XII with the flat assertion that since all states rest on "good arms" and "good laws," but the former beget the latter, he will speak only of "arms." Locke begins his XII with a reiteration of the supremacy of the law, and thus seems to negate Machiavelli's startling depreciation of the law. But then, mindful of Machiavelli's argument, Locke tersely first distinguishes the "executive" from the "legislative," and then the "federative" from the "executive"; calls the "federative" "natural," the only one of the three powers ever to be so called; entrusts to it the great, dangerous powers of "war and peace"; concedes that the "federative" cannot be much guided by "laws"; and concludes that it must be guided, instead, by "prudence," "wisdom," and again "prudence" (II.145-147). The necessity of "wisdom" for the conduct of the "federative" thus precedes, and necessarily precedes, the necessity of "prerogative" for the conduct of the "executive," given the necessitousness of the condition of a state of nature among polities. In that state, the "law of nature" is the only law. And just as it gives an indefeasible right to individuals arbitrarily to save themselves in the extreme condition, so does it give an ultimately arbitrary right to "public persons," or "states," to save themselves in the extreme condition.

As for "the executive power" strictly understood, it is characterized, as to its relation to "positive law," by an increasingly explicit emphasis on the necessity of "prerogative." Locke treats that notion, as already noted, in 11 of the 13 sections in the second half of XII-XIV, thus linking it backwards to the "state of nature" and forward to "tyranny." When he begins to speak explicitly of "prerogative," in sect. 156, he simultaneously begins to speak of "the prince," thus joining the two themes. He progressively modifies the definition of "prerogative" culminating with the assertion that it is simply the "power of doing public good without a rule" (II.156). And as for examples of so doing, Locke gives only two that pertain to individual subjects: destruction of an "innocent" man's house to stop a fire that threatens others' houses; and pardon of a "guilty" man if that does not "prejudice" the "innocent" (II.159). In both cases, the root of the executive power's discretion is "the law of nature," that wills "the preservation of all" as much as possible. It is adherence to that one, simple standard, legislated by "nature," that is intended to hedge "the executive power" in from engaging in "arbitrary" rule in the realm of "means."

As for the turning to Aristotle: That takes place entirely in the treatment of "prerogative" within Chs. XII-XIV. To see what Locke intends, we have to digress to take an overview of Aristotle's treatment of *pambasileia*.[9]

---

9. Aristotle, *The Politics*, Translated and with an Introduction, Notes, and Glossary, by Carnes Lord (Chicago: University of Chicago Press, 1984), 1286 a7—1288 a32.

Aristotle departs from the fundamental question whether it is "more advantageous" to be ruled by the best man or the best laws: *pambasileia* is the former, for it is rule over all matters by a man of superior "virtue," wholly according to his own deliberation and will. Aristotle orders the treatment in three phases. In the first two, he presents a dialectic in which the arguments for *pambasileia* and for a certain rule of law join, with the latter having the edge. In the first, he sketches a kind of "history" of regimes, beginning in ancient times with "kingship," moving through "polity," "oligarchy," and "tyranny," then ending in modern times with "democracy." In the second, he posits law, in its essence, as "god and intellect" alone ruling, with no admixture of "the human," which necessarily includes aspects of "the beast"—i.e., "desire" and "spirit" (*thumos*). In the third, he presents a terse, highly ambiguous case for *pambasileia*. It is ambiguous, to say the least, because it depends on men's being willing to be ruled by one of such "virtue" as to stand to them as gods do to men, analogous to the way the law, essentially, is "intellect without appetite."

Within the 11 sections on "prerogative," Locke sketches two "histories" of the use of "prerogative." The first history is a general one: it indicates that, originally, rule everywhere was princely and almost entirely "prerogative," then was modified as "the people" sought to prevent abuses of such rule. In principle, Locke completes the constraint on possible abuse of "prerogative" by his discovery and promulgation of "the law of nature" as the standard. This is Locke's adaptation and correction of Aristotle's "history" of regimes. Locke's second "history" is a particular one: it is a sketch of d the "History of England" which indicates that "our wisest and best princes" possessed "prerogative" in greatest degree, for they were, according to a certain "argument," "God-like princes" who ruled the way God rules the universe, through "wisdom and goodness." This is Locke's adaptation and correction of Aristotle's positing of "law" as essentially a rule of "god and intellect" without any mixture of "desire" or "spirit." Locke transmutes the argument on behalf of law as "godlike" into an argument for a "prince" who is "godlike."

Both adaptations and corrections rest on the necessity of the exercise of "prerogative" by a single man, who conducts what we may for the moment call "executive government," but which is, in essence, a modified form of "princely government" disguised, in part, as a government in which "the legislative" is "the supreme power." The necessitous aspect of such government reflects the Lockean view that "nature" gives men nothing but "almost worthless" materials, from which they must wrest their welfare by "industry" and "rationality," and that government, as such, both by

116

"established laws of liberty" and by a prudent "executive" use of "prerogative," must protect them in such conduct. The limit on such government,
in turn, is prescribed by that single, simple rule or standard we previously
have noticed, "the law of nature."

Locke's third and final origination of "the executive power" is in the
treatment of "tyranny" in Ch. XVIII. Both the surface of this treatment
and one most unobtrusive example indicate Locke's correction of
Machiavelli by a partial return to Aristotle: Locke, like Aristotle, explicitly
distinguishes "prince" from "tyranny," but Machiavelli never even speaks
of "tyrant"; and whereas Locke's only example of a single man who is a
"tyrant" is Hiero II, Machiavelli calls him a "prince," placing him as
second only in rank to "founders" such as Moses, Cyrus, Romulus and
Theseus in Ch. VI.

But much less manifest than Locke's surface correction is an underlying agreement which is shown in three ways. First, Locke structures XVIII
just as he does II: He orders the whole treatment of "tyranny" in 12
sections, but the second section is an appeal to the "authority" of a "king,"
James I, whose antithesis of "king" and "tyrant," which turns on ruling
under the law or not, Locke gladly adopts. But this reduces Locke's own
argument to 11 sections, exactly as had been done in the treatments of the
"state of nature" and "prerogative." What is more, by appealing to
"authority" in the second section of the first and last treatments—here, a
King of England, there a learned English Divine—Locke all the more
emphasizes the peculiar and exact mixture of argument and such appeal.
In the last of the three treatments which originate "the executive power,"
the surface appeal to a "king" is accompanied by and rooted in an
underlying appeal to a "philosopher." Second, Locke resolves, insofar as
any resolution is possible, the ambiguity of "prince" and "magistrate" that
permeates his book. For at the center of the treatment of "tyranny," he at
first uses "prince," and then "magistrate," echoing a parallel ambiguity in
his first usage of a nomenclature for the ruler, which occurs in the
treatment of the "state of nature" (II.9). But at the end of the section, for
the only time in his book, he refers to a "republic," of which either a
"prince" or "magistrate" is the head (II.205). In so concluding, Locke
tacitly follows Machiavelli's obscuring of the traditional distinction
between "princely" and "republican" forms of government, an obscuring
most evident in Machiavelli's Ch. IX. Third, returning to the theme of
"arbitrariness," so prominent in the treatment of "law" and "prerogative,"
Locke twice condemns "arbitrary" rule. Yet in between those two
extremes, in a parenthesis in his final section on "tyranny," he says that

117

"prerogative" is "an arbitrary power in some things left in the prince's hand to do good, not harm to the people" (II.201, 210).

Locke's confidence in the ability of "the people" to distinguish "the prince" from "the tyrant" rests, first, on his confidence that the standard of "the law of nature" is sufficiently clear and compelling to guide such judgment. It rests, second, on his confidence that modern "princes," guided by Locke as philosophic lawgiver, can more readily become "wise princes" than could rulers in former times precisely because they share that standard with "the people" (II.168). Locke's discovery of "the law of nature" as *the* standard is intended to ensure a high degree of probability of the convergence of prudent rule with adherence to "the law."

IV

Aristotle's treatment of *pambasileia* is a subtle, dense, highly ambiguous set of inquiries into the fundamental problem of what kind of political rule is best. It is the culmination of his extended inquiry into the nature of *politeia*, or "regime." In articulating the *arche*, or "beginning," of his treat-ment, Aristotle says that *pambasileia* is a "kind of regime" and that "it is necessary to theorize [*theoresai*]" concerning it, and to "run through" the "difficulties [*aporias*]" it brings to the surface.

The initial formulation of the greatest—or seemingly greatest—*aporia* is this: Whether it is "more advantageous" to be ruled by "the best man" or "the best laws"? But as the inquiry proceeds, what comes increasingly to the surface is this still greater *aporia*: Whether—and if so, in what sense—*phusis*, or "nature," supplies, or supports, or gives direction to the resolu-tion of the first difficulty? This second, more fundamental *aporia* is differ-entially treated within the three phases of the "theorizing" and involves a dialectic among five concepts: "advantage," "law," "virtue," "nature" and "justice." In the course of that dialectic, "justice" is the last of the five concepts to emerge, imitating the way in which "justice" emerges, in Bk. I, only when the *polis* is properly founded.

The ultimate difficulty, for our purposes, may be reduced to this form: To what extent does "nature" supply, or bring forth, or make possible, a single man *and* a multitude mutually capable of the rule of supreme human "virtue," such that what is both "advantageous" and "just" will coincide in so great a degree that "law," in the ordinary sense, is not needed—indeed, would be against what is right?

The argument suggests the immense difficulty, verging on impossibility, of the convergence required, such that the "advantageous" and the "just" will "naturally" coincide. The conclusions of the first and third parts of the *logos*, taken together, point to the fundamental problem: At the end of the latter, which coincides with the end of the whole *logos*, Aristotle says a man of truly superlative virtue should be obeyed—using a form of the verb *peitho*, which conveys the sense of "to be persuaded." But at the end of the former, Aristotle speaks of a particular *aporia*: Whether a *basileus*—even one ruling according to "law"—will need "force" (*ischun*) to "compel" those who do not "will to obey"? His conclusion that "force" will be needed stands, to say the least, in some tension with his conclusion that the man who is naturally best should be obeyed "by persuasion," as it were. That tension reflects a perhaps natural tension between what by nature persuasion may achieve and force must accomplish in rule over humans. In that tension lies the root of the problem of executive and prerogative.

V

Our brief inquiry into the views of "founders" has shown that that problem remains a great one for adherents of consitutional government. Indeed, today it may be even more of a problem than ever before in the sense that Hamilton, Locke, and Aristotle, each in his way, at least saw it as a problem rooted in the problematic sense in which "nature" may supply a standard, whereas today the very notion of turning to "natural right," whether modern or ancient, for a standard, is virtually beyond the horizon of serious discussion.

One sign of that is the assertion by Leszek Kolakowski, in the 1986 "Jefferson Lecture in the Humanities," that the appeal to the "self-evident truths" of The Declaration of Independence—truths rooted in "the Laws of Nature and of Nature's God"—are "banned beyond recall from permissible philosophical or theoretical idioms."[10] If that be granted, then the attempt to return to The Founders' standard for judging the discretionary use of "the executive power" must prove futile. Indeed, so must *any* attempt to discover such a standard in "natural right," whether modern or ancient, for that notion itself increasingly is, or seems to be, driven beyond the horizon of thought of the great majority of contemporary intellectuals and academic students of government. As that happens, the consigning to

---

10. Leszek Kolakowski, "The Idolatry of Politics," *The New Republic*, 16 June 1986, p. 29.

the ashbin of "History" of the very notion of a standard of judgment, supplied from "nature," that transcends and gives guidance to mere human will comes to be understood as Progress. To the lips of that demi-god are then imputed strange doctrines—such as that what we have been calling "constitutional government" is really a repressive regime, in spite of the fact that "the people" do not realize that they are repressed, and must, therefore, be guided to a new stage of "History" by a self-appointed elite that will exercise virtually unlimited discretion that is tyrannical in character.

But there are intrepid doubters. One of the most notable is Harvey Mansfield, Jr. His thoughtful, wide-ranging reflections on the institutional and theoretical foundations of "the executive power" proceed from a steadfast recognition that that modern notion is a special form of the problem of the nature of rule, and that that problem, in turn, is fully intelligible only within the horizon of some understanding of what is *kata phusin*, or "according to nature," including the possibility that there is "natural right."[11] It seems to me that such inquiries are peculiarly fitting during this, our prolonged period of inquiry into and celebration of the bicentennial of American "constitutionalism," for they do what the political philosophers have always sought to do, and that is to be radical in the sense of going to the root by uncovering foundations.

---

11. Harvey Mansfield, Jr., "The Ambivalence of Executive Power," in *The Presidency in the Constitutional Order*, ed. J. Bessette and J. Tulis (Baton Rouge: Louisiana State University Press, 1981), pp. 314-33; "The Absent Executive in Aristotle"s *Politics*," in *Natural Right and Political Right: Essays in Honor of Harry V. Jaffa*, ed. T. B. Silver and P. W. Schramm (Durham, N.C.: Carolina Academic Press), pp. 169-96.

Appendix

I. ANALYTICAL OUTLINE OF *THE FEDERALIST*, Nos. 67-77.

    Part I: On Presidency and Monarchy. Nos. 67-69.

        A. Polemic against critics who speciously liken the two. No. 67.

        B. Praise of mode of election. No. 68.

        C. Analysis and comparison of powers of President and English Monarch. No. 69.

    Part II: On Presidency and Republican Government, Nos. 70-77.

        A. Considered predominantly under the aspect of the principle of "energetic government." No. 70. No. 77, para. 10.

            1. Positing of the "necessity" of "an energetic executive" for "good government." No. 70, paras. 1-2.

            2. The problem: How to combine "ingredients" of "energy" with those of "safety." No. 70, paras. 3-5.

            3. Detailed analysis and justification of the "ingredients" of "energy." No. 70, para. 6 - No. 77, para. 11.

                a. Unity, No. 70, paras, 6-23.

                b. Duration. Nos. 71-72.

                c. Adequate compensation. No. 73, paras, 1-2.

                d. Competent powers. No. 73, para. 3 - No. 77, para. 10.

        B. Considered predominantly under the aspect of the principle of "republican safety" ("due dependence on the people"/"due responsibility"). No. 77, para. 11.

II. ANALYTICAL OUTLINE OF LOCKE'S "SECOND TREATISE."

        A. Part I: On Pre-and Non-governmental topics. Ch. I-Ch. VI. I. Introduction: Definition of "political power."

        II. State of Nature.

        III. State of War.

        IV. Slavery.

        V. Property.

        VI. Paternal Power.

(Strictly speaking, the first part extends into Ch. VII, where the first 10 sections treat non-political society, especially "conjugal society." Thus, a re-ordering of the book would give a Ch. VII entitled "On Non-political Societies." The whole first part would then be in 7 chapters, extending from Sect. 1-Sect. 86, and would center on "slavery" as the central pre-political problem.)

B. Part II: On Governmental Topics. Ch. VII-Ch. XIX.
(As noted above, this part, strictly speaking, begins with section 87 within Ch. VII. The whole second part is in 13 chapters, extending from Sect. 87-Sect. 243, and centers on "prerogative" as the central political problem —a problem that emerges within Ch. XIII, at Sect. 156.)

VII. Political Society.
VIII. Beginning of Political Society.
IX. Ends of Political Society.
X. Forms of Commonwealth.
XI. Extent of Legislative Power.
XII. Legislative, Executive, and Federative Powers.
XIII. Subordination of Powers.
XIV. Prerogative.
XV. Paternal, Political, Despotic Power.
XVI. Conquest.
XVII. Usurpation.
XVIII. Tyranny.
XIX. Dissolution of Government.

III. ANALYTICAL OUTLINE OF ARISTOTLE ON *PAMBASILEIA*.
A. First *logos*: 1286 a7—1286 b 40.
   1. On rule of one best man vs. best law.
   2. On "history" of regimes, with respect to "virtue."
   3. On two difficulties:
      a. On whether a king will—against "human nature"—pass over his own sons for the rule.
      b. On whether a king must use "force."
B. Second *logos*: 1287 a1—1287 b35.
   1. On *pambasileia* as one who rules in "all things."
   2. On such rule as being "against nature."
   3. On what "the law" can and cannot "decide."
C. Third *logos*: 1287 b36—1288 a32.
   1. On "nature" in relation to various "regimes."
   2. On the special "virtue" needed for *pambasileia*.
   3. On its being "against nature" for a man of preeminent "virtue" not to be "obeyed."

The President: Executive Energy and Republican Safety

Larry Berman

Among the difficulties encountered by the convention, a very important one must have lain in combining the requisite stability and energy in government with the inviolable attention due to liberty and to the republican form.

James Madison, *Federalist #37*

Energy in the Executive is a leading character in the definition of good government. It is essential to the protection of the community against foreign attacks; it is not less essential to the steady administration of the laws; to the protection of property against those irregular and high-handed combinations which sometimes interrupt the ordinary course of justice; to the security of liberty against the enterprises and assaults of ambition, of faction, and of anarchy .... A feeble executive implies a feeble execution of the government. A feeble execution is but another phrase for a bad execution; and a government ill executed, whatever it may be in theory, must be, in practice, a bad government.

Alexander Hamilton, *Federalist #70*

They [our enemies] are asking for it and they are going to get it. We have not used this power in this first four years as you know. We have never used it. We have not used the bureau and we have not used the Justice Department, but things are going to change now. And they are going to do it right or go.

Richard Nixon, White House Tapes

We cannot win the race to the future shackled to a system that can't even pass a federal budget.

Ronald Reagan, 1986 State of the Union Message

The President: Executive Energy and Republican Safety

Overview

This essay addresses the question: how much energy in the executive is necessary within a separation-of-powers system for government to function effectively? This inquiry leads inexorably to the broader question of whether America's 200 year-old constitutional blueprint can still meet policy demands and popular expectations that the constitutional framers could not possibly have envisioned. The Framers would be puzzled by the scope and complexity of problems that only the President, in his capacity as *The Government*, is expected to solve.[1]

Since 1789 no institution of American government has changed so dramatically and with such profound consequences for society as the Presidency. The Framers could not possibly have anticipated the role played by an activist, interventionist federal government in American life—with the President symbolizing the health of the nation. Throwing out the first pitch of a World Series, leading the July 4, 1986 Statue of Liberty celebration or providing Presidential urine for an anti-drug campaign, the President as spokesman for a national interest represents America. Successful (and popular) Presidents have crossed the parchment constitutional boundaries in expanding the power and reach of their office. The faces of these former Presidents are displayed on the nation's currency; schools, streets, national holidays, and athletic stadiums are identified by their names.

America's original constitutional blueprint for a government of balanced institutions competing for power has evolved into a distinctly *Presidential* government which is sustained by popular expectations that only strong Presidential leadership can solve national problems. In perhaps the greatest irony of the Framers' constitutional blueprint, separation of powers led inexorably to the "first among equals" President. As James Sundquist explained:

> the powers of the modern presidency, clearly were not wrested by self-seeking chief executives from a struggling but ultimately yielding Congress, in a series of constitutional coups-d'etat. On the contrary, every transaction embodying a shift in power and influence was one of mutual consent, for the shifts were made pursuant to law, and the Congress wrote and passed the laws. ...Indeed, one of the striking

---

1. For an extensive discussion see Larry Berman, *The New American Presidency* (Boston: Little, Brown and Co., 1987). (I want to acknowledge the assistance of my research assistant, Linda Norman.)

factors of the modern presidency is the extent to which it was built through congressional initiative.[2]

Yet, today's President operates within the framework of an 18th-century document carefully designed to prevent Presidential primacy and, by implication, legislative program success. The Framers viewed executive energy as more of a defensive rather than offensive capacity. Their generation had suffered firsthand the consequences of concentrated power used for tyrannical purposes. Individual liberty could not exist if legislative and executive powers were united in the same person or governmental body. The newly devised institutional relationships diffused tyranny in any form: legislative, judicial, or executive. Every aspect of our nation's founding reflected the suspicion of concentrated power. The Framers sought a proper balance between grants of governmental power and guarantees of individual liberty. They created a government which was strong enough to govern the new nation, but sufficiently restrained not to infringe on individual liberties or engulf the companion institutions. Madison's strictures have worked exceedingly well against aspiring King Georges, but not so well in helping Presidents as political leaders formulate majoritarian public policy from which citizens can derive a basis for political accountability.

The Framers sought and encouraged conflict between the separated branches. Yet, they could not anticipate that a divided government would be characterized by a Legislative branch controlled by one party and the Executive by another. When Congress and President fail to agree, the result denigrates the integrity of legislation—merely postponing hard political choices from one election to the next. Diffusion in policy-making responsibility under separated institutions has led to confusion in voters' minds on whom to hold accountable for governmental deadlock.[3] When Congress does not pass the *President's legislative program*, voters have difficulty fixing responsibility for failure since neither Congress nor the President constitutes *The Government*, just part of it. Divided government is the result of ticket splitting by voters who seem unconcerned with the linkage between their private voting act and the President's subsequent need to form a government over the next four years. Americans, I dare say, expect

---

2. James Sundquist, *Decline and Resurgence of Congress* (Washington, D.C.: Brookings Institution, 1981), p. 4.

3. See James Sundquist, *Constitutional Reform and Effective Government* (Washington, D.C.: Brookings Institute, 1986), and James MacGregor Burns, *The Power to Lead* (New York: Simon and Schuster, 1984), p. 193. Lloyd Cutler, "To Form a Government," *Foreign Affairs*, Fall 1980.

their President to resolve these issues and formulate public policy by leading Congress; they do not expect Congress to take the lead itself. As House Minority Whip Trent Lott (R. Miss.) observed, "It's like a 3-D movie house around here—we're good at delaying, deferring, and dallying."[4]

The 1984 Presidential election epitomized the lack of linkage between the act of voting for President and the formation of a government to carry out that President's program. President Reagan amassed 525 of the 538 electoral votes, but the House remained Democratic, 253-182. Just what type of mandate could Ronald Reagan claim from "the people"? Had "the American people" actually intended for this Democratic Congress to check the legislative programs of a personally popular President? The 1986 Congressional election left in its wake a personally popular but lame duck Republican President with a House and Senate controlled by Democrats. Moreover, the Framers expected government service to be a temporary, not a lifetime occupation. Yet members of Congress are reelected at a rate approaching 90% because their institutional resources are organized purely to achieve another term.[5]

The Framers' Philosophical Perspective

The issues addressed by this essay are timeless, not period pieces. The Framers' philosophical views about human nature, governmental power and republicanism are still valid, but their structural arrangements may no longer be suited for today's conditions. The fundamental constitutional values of the Framers incorporated the assumption that governmental authority be *accountable* to the popular will and that governmental power be *checked* and *balanced*. "The Framers were aware," wrote Robinson, "that these values were sometimes in tension, but they were convinced that they were not contradictory, and they believed that the viability of the Republic—indeed, the future of republican government —required that they both be achieved."[6]

---

4. "A Formula for Chaos," *U.S. News and World Report*, 25 Aug. 1986, p. 16. Richard Strout, "What the Founders Wrought," rev. of *The Power to Lead*, by George MacGregor Burns, *The New Republic*, 9 Apr. 1984, pp. 39-40. See also Richard Strout, *TRB: Views and Perspectives on the Presidency* (New York: Macmillan, 1979), p. 433.

5. See David Mayhew, *Congress: The Electoral Connection* (New Haven: Yale University Press, 1974).

6. Donald Robinson, "The Renewal of American Constitutionalism," in *Separation of Powers—Does it Still Work?*, ed. Robert Goldwin and Art Kaufman (American Enterprise Institute, 1986), pp. 48-9.

Separation of powers allowed the Framers to create a government which accomplished the reconciliation of republicanism and liberty. In *Federalist* #9 Hamilton referred to improvements in the science of politics which provided "powerful means by which the excellencies of republican government may be retained and its imperfections lessened or avoided." Protection of liberty could not be guaranteed by these parchment barriers. Instead, ". . . some more adequate defense is indispensably necessary for the more feeble against the more powerful members of the government. The legislative department is everywhere extending the sphere of its activity and drawing all power into its impetuous vortex." Madison's solution involved connecting and blending the branches, "as to give to each a constitutional control over the others, the degree of separation which the maxim requires, as essential to a free government, can never in practice be duly mastered."

Energy in the Executive: From Theory to Practice

There is a distinctly pejorative connotation to the question, "Now that the President is the head of government for a superpower in a nuclear age—how far should his authority extend beyond mere execution of laws?" Except for rare genetic flaws in a handful of White House occupants, the President's answer to the question "how far should my authority extend beyond the mere execution of the laws," has been answered, "as far as I claim." Therein lies the constitutional dispute involving the Reagan administration's Iran/Contra initiatives.

Nowhere have the personalities of political actors had more impact on political events than in the interpretation of executive power in Article II. The *stewardship* theory of Presidential power was defined by Theodore Roosevelt, based on his conviction that "the executive power was limited only by specific restrictions and prohibitions in the Constitution or those imposed by the Congress under its constitutional powers." Taken literally, this is a writ to do virtually anything, since the Constitution restricts the President from almost nothing. As holder of the executive power the President is obliged to do whatever is necessary to serve the interests of the people.

In his autobiography, Roosevelt analyzed the stewardship theory in detail, placing himself within the Lincoln-Jackson rather than the Buchanan-Taft school of thought:

The most important factor in getting the right spirit in my Administration, next to the insistence upon courage, honesty, and a genuine democracy of desire to serve the plain people, was my insistence upon the theory that the executive power was limited only by specific restrictions and prohibitions appearing in the Constitution or imposed by the Congress under its constitutional powers.

My view was that every executive officer, and above all every executive officer in high position, was a steward of the people bound actively and affirmatively to do all he could for the people, and not to content himself with the negative merit of keeping his talents undamaged in a napkin. I declined to adopt the view that what was imperatively necessary for the nation could not be done by the President unless he could find some specific authorization to do it. My belief was that it was not only his right but his duty to do anything that the needs of the nation demanded, unless such action was forbidden by the Constitution or by the laws. Under this interpretation of executive power I did and caused to be done many things not previously done by the President and the heads of the departments. I did not usurp power, but I did greatly broaden the use of executive power. In other words, I acted for the public welfare, I acted for the common well-being of all our people, whenever and in whatever manner was necessary, unless prevented by direct constitutional or legislative prohibition . . .

The course I followed, of regarding the Executive as subject only to the people, and under the Constitution, bound to serve the people affirmatively in cases where the Constitution does not explicitly forbid him to render the service, was substantially the course followed by both Andrew Jackson and Abraham Lincoln. Other honorable and well-meaning Presidents, such as James Buchanan, took the opposite, and as it seems to me, narrowly legalistic view that the President is the servant of Congress rather than of the people, and can do nothing, no matter how necessary it be to act, unless the Constitution explicitly commands the action.[7]

In contrast to Roosevelt's stewardship theory of executive power is William Howard Taft's *constructionist* view. Taft believed that the only true view of the executive function was that the President could exercise absolutely no power that could not be traced to a specific grant or be implied from the express grant in either the Constitution or an act of

---

7. Theodore Roosevelt, "The Stewardship Doctrine," in *Classics of the American Presidency*, ed. Harry Bailey (Oak Park, Ill.: Moore, 1980), pp. 35-36. See also *The Autobiography of Theodore Roosevelt* (New York: Scribner, 1913), pp. 197-200.

Congress. "There is no undefined residuum of power," Taft wrote, "which he can exercise because it seems to him to be in the public interest."[8]

Most students find it remarkable that Roosevelt and Taft could read the same Constitution and arrive at such disparate conclusions. Could the Framers have intended that "the President has the right, in law and conscience," as Woodrow Wilson believed, "to be as big a man as he can be"? History demonstrates that Presidents have claimed responsibility to preserve and protect the nation as well as the Constitution. This "wild card" has allowed the President to go beyond what is narrowly prescribed in the Constitution when conditions call for extraordinary action—or when the President thinks such action is necessary. As a result, members of Congress tend to tell this story about the origins of government: Once upon a time there was a powerful king who lived in a forest. But having all of this power bored him and he decided to give some to his followers, who eventually became judges and legislators. But "the indefinite residuum, called 'executive power,' " he kept to himself.[9]

The linkage of power and purpose does not yield neat and tidy constitutional solutions. Who should determine the extent of national security? How far should emergency powers extend? Virtually every justification for executive energy in national security involves one's world view and partisan policy preferences. History demonstrates that Presidents have claimed responsibility to preserve and protect the nation as well as the Constitution. This "wild card" has allowed the President to go beyond what is narrowly described in the Constitution when conditions call for extraordinary action or when in the President's judgment such action is necessary. There is no avoiding the tension between executive energy, executive paranoia and republican safety. This *doctrine of necessity* received its explicit formulation by Lincoln; but President Nixon boldly went

---

8. William Howard Taft, *Our Chief Magistrate and His Powers* (New York: Columbia University Press, 1916), pp. 138-145.

9. Edward Corwin, *The President: Office and Powers* (New York: New York University Press, 1957), p. 3. See Charles Thach, *The Creation of the Presidency 1755-1789* (Baltimore: Johns Hopkins University Press, 1923), pp. 138-139.

where no predecessor had dared in declaring, "When the President does it, that means it is not illegal."[10]

The claim to *inherent executive power* is usually based on the President's own judgment of a crisis or emergency. For paranoid Presidents who see enemies everywhere, this may cause problems in constitutional balance. Does the President possess an inherent power to break into Daniel Ellsberg's psychiatrist's office because he or his political lieutenants determine that national security is involved? Does the President have an inherent power to place phone taps on administration personnel who are suspected of leaking information to the press? Nixon admitted that even though he could see no military comparison between the Civil War and Vietnam, "this nation was torn apart in an ideological way by the war in Vietnam, as much as the Civil War tore apart the nation when Lincoln was President."[11]

Nixon reasoned that as holder of the *executive power* a President can go beyond his enumerated powers and take whatever steps are necessary to preserve the country's security, even if his actions might be unconstitutional. This reasoning worked during the Civil War but could not pass muster during Watergate. During a televised interview with David Frost,

---

10. Thomas Jefferson wrote to John Colvin in 1810 that "a strict observation of the written laws is doubtless one of the higher duties of a good officer, but it is not the highest. The law of necessity, of self-preservation, of saving our country when in danger, are of higher obligation. To lose our country by a scrupulous adherence to written law would be to lose the law itself, with life, liberty, property ... thus sacrificing the end to the means." This "doctrine of necessity" was expanded in a letter from President Lincoln to Albert Hodges:

   I did understand, however, that my oath to preserve the Constitution to the best of my ability, imposed upon me the duty of preserving, by every indispensable means, that government—that nation—of which that Constitution was the organic law. Was it possible to lose the nation, and yet preserve the Constitution? By general law life and limb must be protected; yet often a limb must be amputated to save a life; but a life is never wisely given to save a limb. I felt that measures, otherwise unconstitutional, might become lawful, by becoming indispensable to the preservation of the Constitution, through the preservation of the nation. Right or wrong, I assumed this ground, and now avow it. I could not feel that, to the best of my ability, I had even tried to preserve the Constitution, if, to save slavery, or any minor matter, I should permit the wreck of government, country, and Constitution altogether.

11. See *New York Times*, 4 June 1977, where the Nixon-Frost dialogue is transcribed. See also Richard Nixon, "Televised Interview with David Frost, May 20, 1977," in *Problems of the Presidency: A Text with Readings*, ed. Barbara Hinckley (Glenview, Ill.: Scott, Foresman, 1985), p. 256.

Nixon was asked: "Is there anything in the Constitution or the Bill of Rights that suggests the President is that far of a sovereign, that far above the law?" Nixon responded, "No, there isn't. There's nothing specific that the Constitution contemplates in that respect. . . . In war time, a President does have extraordinary powers which would make acts that would otherwise be unlawful, lawful if undertaken for the purpose of preserving the nation and the Constitution. . . ." For Nixon, however, domestic political dissent was defined as a state of war that justified illegal wiretaps, surveillance, and break-ins. The voluminous impeachment inquiry of President Nixon contains all too many examples of the abuse of power which violated civil liberties.[12]

The preceding discussion requires that I approach the subject of "more" executive power somewhat cautiously. Why, you may ask, make the Presidency any more powerful—Congress and the Supreme Court have already done that job. Moreover, following the abuses of power by Presidents Johnson and Nixon (coupled with the traumatic effect on our national psyche), a compelling argument was made for strengthening Congress, not the Presidency.[13] Indeed, witnesses who testified at the Congressional committee investigating Iran/Contra activities cited this Congressional resurgence as diluting executive responsibility in foreign affairs—thereby justifying the privatization of foreign policy.

How Much Executive Power?

Let us agree to transcend the truism that a President who breaks laws to save the nation is justified; a President who violates civil liberties on a generalized claim to national security is bereft of legitimacy. We can

---

12. For a broad discussion of these issues See Duncan Clarke and Edward Neveleff, "Secrecy, Foreign Intelligence, and Civil Liberties: Has the Pendulum Swung Too Far?" *Political Science Quarterly* 99 (Fall 1984), p. 508. See Walter Karp, "Liberty Under Siege: The Reagan Administration's Taste for Autocracy" *Harpers*, November 1985, pp. 53-67. The Reagan administration [in the name of national security] has taken several steps to extend intelligence gathering activities. These actions demonstrate the complexity of national security versus republic safety. Critics contend the expanded CIA role threatens basic tenets of liberty. The administration argues that the measures protect national security. Executive Order 12333 of 1981 allowed the CIA to engage in electronic surveillance when countering "hostile electronic surveillance."
13. See Richard Neustadt, "The Constraining of the President: The Presidency After Watergate," *British Journal of Political Science* 4 (1974), pp. 383-397.

consider an array of examples which involve executive energy and the national interest. In *Federalist #70* Alexander Hamilton identified *unity*, *duration*, *adequate salary* and *competent powers* as the components which constituted *energy* in the executive. I begin from the premise that Congressional reassertion over policy runs contrary to the popular desire for a qualitatively better and safer world. Congress responds, oversees, and checks, but Congress cannot lead nor speak for American interests. The demands upon and for Presidential government continue to grow. Only the President can supply the big picture. The potential for abuse is ever present—no legislation can prevent a President from attempting to break the law. Yet, the cry "remember Watergate" discredits the messenger. Checks and balances are not necessarily synonymous with separation of powers. Many European democracies maintain strong checks without separating institutions.

The Constitution designated the President Commander-in-Chief and assigned Congress the power to declare war, order reprisals, raise and support armies, as well as provide for the common defense. The history of war powers, however, has been one of Presidents' making war before Congress declares it. The development of nuclear weapons and the complexity of regional conflicts has dramatically altered the way in which wars are fought. The invasion of Grenada, deployment of U.S. forces in Lebanon or Bolivia, the U.S. attack on Libya in 1986, or Persian Gulf policy in 1987 reveal these complexities. American troops were initially committed to Bolivia to assist Bolivian police in raiding cocaine plants *without* Congressional consultation. What would happen if such troops were fired on? The War Powers Resolution requires the President to report to Congress within 48 hours after committing U.S. troops to hostile action (if no state of war has been declared). Unless Congress agrees otherwise, the troops must be withdrawn after 60 days; the President may request 30 additional days for ensuring their safety. Congress can stop the military commitment by concurrent resolution, which is not subject to the President's veto.[14]

The question of how much executive energy leads inexorably to other questions. Is aid to the Contras an act of collective self-defense on the part of the United States and other Central American countries against Nicar-

---

14. The constitutionality of this concurrent resolution is clouded by the decision in *I.N.S. v. Chadha*, in which the Supreme Court ruled that legislative vetoes violated structural provisions of the Constitution. See Joseph Cooper, "Congress and the Legislative Veto: Choices Since the Chadha Case," in *Making Government Work: From White House to Congress*, ed. Robert Hunter, Wayne Berman and John Kennedy (Westview Press, 1986), pp. 31-67.

aguan aggression or a violation of Nicaraguan sovereignty? Does executive energy extend to CIA training, arming, and financing of the Contras? Is selling arms to Iran and diverting the profits to the Contras in the national interest or even a legitimate executive activity? Is the President empowered to initiate unannounced Navy flight operations over the Gulf of Sidra which could draw Libyan military fire? Should the President be required to consult with Congress when authorizing "freedom of navigation" exercises in the Gulf of Sidra? The argument on means is often influenced by the outcome. Americans applauded Ronald Reagan's strike against Qaddafi, brushing aside constitutional questions on inter-branch collaboration. Selling arms to so-called Iranian "moderates" elicited a far more negative response.

In April 1986 President Reagan ordered an air raid against Libya *without* prior consultation with Congress. Legislative leaders were not briefed until warplanes had *already* left Britain headed for Libya. President Reagan's actions received widespread support from the American general public (not so in Britain) as well as from most members on Capitol Hill. Yet, given constitutional divisons and responsibilities, should the President have consulted with legislative leaders? As Representative Lee Thornton (D, Indiana) asked, "In this kind of world Lebanon is not Pearl Harbor, and when a decision calls for the best we can summon, it ought not to be made by one man or woman, even if that man or woman is the President of the United States. It ought to be a collective judgment." To which President Reagan responded, "I just don't think that a committee of 535 individuals, no matter how well intentioned, can offer what is needed in actions of this kind or where there is a necessity."

Within days of the air-raid a bill was introduced by Republicans in both houses of Congress which would have authorized the President to respond to foreign terrorism *without* prior consultation with Congress. The bill *exempted* the President from the War Powers Act when responding to terrorist attacks with deadly force. The President would be required to report to Congress within 10 days of any anti-terrorist action—including preemptive strikes or even presumably the assassination of foreign leaders. One of the bill sponsors said that if Col. Muammar el-Qaddafi "became deceased as the result of our counter-strike, that would have been within the intent of the bill."[15] Authorizing the President to use any means necessary to preempt acts of terrorism against U.S. citizens clearly goes well beyond "mere execution" of laws.

Libya provided a "best-case" test of Presidential energy. Qaddafi constituted a symbol of international terrorism to most Americans. Far more complex with respect to constitutional distinctions is President Reagan's program of intervening covertly on behalf of what he calls "freedom fighters" throughout the world, offering aid packages in the Angolan war on behalf of the South African supported rebels or to the Contras in Nicaragua in their fight against the Sandinistas. The openly debated "covert" aid program constitutes the linchpin for the Reagan doctrine of keeping Moscow on the defensive. Yet, from the perspective of our inquiry of "how much energy," the question falls squarely on one's faith in the President doing the defining of national security interests of the United States.[16]

The Item Veto

> The President shall have power to disapprove any items of a bill making appropriations of funds while approving the remainder of the bill. Any items of a bill so approved shall be law, and any items so disapproved shall not be law. If the President disapproves any items of a bill, he shall append to the bill at the time of signing it a statement of the items disapproved, together with the reasons for such disapproval. The house in which any bill containing items disapproved by the President originated shall have power to reconsider such items and if, after such reconsideration, two-thirds of the house shall agree to pass a bill containing any such items, to send this bill to the other house. If approved by two-thirds of that house after reconsideration, such bill shall become a law. But in all such cases, the votes of both houses shall be determined by yeas and nays, and the names of the persons voting for and against the bill shall be entered on the journal of each house respectively.
> *Hypothetical constitutional amendment.*[17]

---

15. See "In Wake of Libya, Skirmishing Over War Powers," *CQ Guide to Current American Government*, Fall 1986, pp. 59-62. See Steven Roberts, "Lawmakers Say U.S. Failed to Consult Them Properly," *The New York Times*, 16 Apr. 1986, p. 13. Linda Greenhouse, "Bill Would Free Reagan on Terror," *The New York Times*, 18 Apr. 1986, p. 9.

16. Leslie Gelb, "The Doctrine/Un-Doctrine of Covert/Overt Aid," *The New York Times*, 21 Feb. 1986, p. 12.

17. See *Reforming American Government*, ed. Donald Robinson (Westview Press, 1985), p. 259.

Most Framers envisioned the President's veto as a "negative" by which an executive could be defended against legislative excesses. The veto represented one of the most basic elements in how the Framers sought to separate and check power. The Framers intended the executive to use the veto against legislative encroachment as well as against bad legislation, which is why supporters of the item veto refer to reinstating the intent of the Framers. What criteria would a President employ in determining a poor law? In *Federalist #73* Hamilton argued that the veto was necessary to protect executive independence ("He might gradually be stripped of his authorities by successive resolutions or annihilated by a single veto") and that the veto:

> not only serves as a shield to the executive, but it furnishes an additional security against the enaction of improper laws. It established a salutary check upon the legislative body calculated to guard the community against the effects of faction, precipitancy, or any impulse unfriendly to the public good, which may happen to influence a majority of that body.

Today, many politicians have embraced the item veto as an imperfect mechanism for reinserting *accountability* into a system now virtually devoid of responsibility in resource allocation. If one believes that 200 billion-dollar deficits threaten our nation's security, the issue of accountability needs to be considered. Support for the item veto comes from both sides of the political aisle. Congressman Jack Kemp believes the:

> line-item veto will save a substantial amount of tax dollars by allowing the President to delete unnecessary expenditures tacked on to overall appropriations bills. . . . Given the severity of our current budget problems, I hope you share with us the belief that this amendment is both warranted and necessary to offset the inability of Congress to place meaningful controls on federal spending.

Senator Ted Kennedy argues that:

> by giving the President a stronger role the line-item veto will instill a new and needed measure of Presidential accountability in federal spending, and reduce the excesses of a Congressional budget process which too readily focuses on individual districts and special interests, not the national interest.[18]

---

18. See Arthur M. Schlesinger, Jr., "The Item Veto Is a Bad Idea," *Chicago Tribune*, 2 Apr. 1984. See three papers prepared for delivery at the Annual Meeting of the American Political Science Association, New Orleans, La., August 29-September 1, 1985: Thomas Cronin and Jeffrey Weill, "An Item Veto for the American President?"; Ronald Moe, "Prospects for the Item Veto at the Federal Level: Lessons from the States"; and Louis Fisher, "The Item Veto: The Risks of Emulating the States."

President Reagan has regularly requested that he be given an item veto authority. He maintains that the item veto would enforce the principle of checks and balances by restoring the original intent of the veto itself. In the effort to achieve fiscal responsibility over the federal budget, an item veto would enable the President to reject specific items within a piece of legislation rather than veto the bill entirely. In Reagan's view:

> the President is thus prevented from using the veto as the Framers intended, to increase the chances in favor of the community against the passing of bad laws, through haste, inadvertence, or design. *It is for this reason that we have proposed restoring the Framers' original design through constitutional amendment granting the President line-item veto authority.*[19]

The item veto would allow the President to strike out particular items in appropriations bills. (Each appropriation bill would be broken into individual controllable items for Presidential approval or veto.) One of the most forceful arguments in favor of an item veto is made by George Will:

> It would restore the fact of a *Presidential* budget. Congress today cannot write a budget and will not respect the President's budget. Thus we have a great nation with no budget process. A line-item veto would enable the President to control spending, but that's not my principal interest in this. My principal interest is that it would instill in the Presidency muscle badly needed. It would give the Presidency an instrument of reward and punishment that he badly needs.[20]

How much choice is involved in actual appropriations bills? The Congressional Budget Office estimates that approximately $154 billion (or 18%) of total outlays would be open to the President's scissors. Much of the budget would still be beyond the President's control: medicare, medicaid, social security, as well as the net interest on the cost of financing the federal debt would be exempted from the item veto. While the federal

---

19. Ronald Reagan, "The Presidency: Roles and Responsibility," *National Forum: The Phi Kappa Phi Journal*, Fall 1984, p. 25. Emphasis added.
20. See George Will, "The Presidency in the American Political System," *Presidential Studies Quarterly* 14 (1984): 324-334; George Will, "Power to the President," *Newsweek*, 12 Oct. 1981, p. 120. See U.S. Congress, Senate, Committee on the Judiciary, Subcommittee on the Constitution, *Hearings on Line-Item Veto*, 98th Cong., 2d sess., 1984, 172-173.

deficit would not be significantly reduced by the item veto, it is evident that political accountability would be enhanced.[21]

The President already has a limited line item veto. The 1974 Congressional Budget and Impoundment Control Act gave the President power to delay or cancel spending of appropriated funds. The President can defer spending unless a House or Senate resolution is passed directing the President to spend the money. In order to *rescind* the appropriation, a President must propose that both houses of Congress within 45 days *actually* rescind the appropriation which made the funds available. If the two houses refuse to comply, the President must release the funds. The advantage of a line item veto is evident since the President needs only one-third of the members in either House to agree with him. (He needs a majority in both on a rescission.)[22] My support for an item veto is premised on the perception that the current budget process is indeed beyond

---

21. See "Budget Accord: Programs Congress Saved," *The New York Times*, 28 June 1986, p. 8. We can get some idea of how President Reagan would try to utilize an item veto by studying the list of programs retained by the Congressional budget resolution which President Reagan sought to eliminate or reduce significantly: Export-Import Bank direct loans; Overseas Private Investment Corporation insurance programs; Advanced communications technology satellite; Rural Electrification Administration subsidies; Weatherization assistance programs; Environmental Protection Agency sewage treatment grants; Soil conservation programs; Landsat; Sea grant and coastal zone management; Department of Agriculture Extension Service; Trade adjustment assistance to firms; United States Travel and Tourism Administration; Postal subsidy; Rural housing loans; Small Business Administration; Section 202 housing; Amtrak; Interstate Commerce Commission; Washington Metro transit system; Maritime cargo preference expansion; Appalachian Regional Commission; Economic Development Administration; Urban Development Action Grants; Rental housing development grants; Section 312 rehabilitation loan fund; Section 108 loan guarantee programs; Rural development program; Small Business Administration disaster loans; Community service block grants; Impact aid for school districts (Part B); Library programs; Small higher education programs; State student incentive grants; College housing loans; Public Health Service health profession subsidies; Federal Emergency Management Agency supplemental food and shelter; Section 8 moderate rehabilitation; Rural housing grants; Legal Services Corporation; Grants for local juvenile delinquency programs; and Public debt reimbursement to Federal Reserve Banks.

22. Rescissions were not affected by the Supreme Court's ruling in *Chadha* because a rescission involves an affirmative action by Congress. This was not the case with deferrals. In May 1986, Senator Dodd introduced a bill [in response to Reagan administration deferrals] which would amend the Impoundment Control Act of 1974 to provide that deferrals of budget authority proposed by the president shall not take effect unless Congress approves the deferral within 45 days. According to Dodd, "Congress would not have vested the president with the power to defer spending without retaining the power to override those deferral decisions, if necessary."

redemption. I see the item veto as a mechanism for increasing *executive* accountability by allowing the President to speak of and shape his program—in fact, not theory. The item veto would increase the executive's influence in Congress by neutralizing the tendency of omnibus appropriation bills to reflect anything but national priorities.

Duration

Speaking during a 1986 campaign stop at Springfield, Missouri, President Reagan was interrupted by cheers of "four more years." The seventy-five year old President said, "I hope you mean you hope I'll have four more years. The Constitution speaks to the other." President Reagan's lame-duck status between 1986-88 weakens not only his Presidential bargaining position but also the new Presidentially oriented political system. Alexander Hamilton viewed "duration in office" as the "second requisite to the energy of the executive authority." The Framers understood the advantages of a four year renewable term and opposed the idea of "exclusion," which would restrict the President from serving more than two terms.

As Ronald Reagan operates within a political system in which virtually everyone else is facing an upcoming election, the Framers' reasoning bears reconsideration. The Framers viewed re-eligibility as a central component of executive energy. "To enable the people, when they see reason to approve of his conduct, to continue him in the station in order to prolong the utility of his talents and virtues, and to secure to the government the advantage of permanency is a wise system of administration." Yet, the two-term limit works to destroy a system of incentives for politicians with shared electoral needs.

The 22nd amendment does more than restrict Presidential tenure: it restricts executive power. President Reagan told Barbara Walters, "in thinking about it more and more, I have come to the conclusion that the 22nd Amendment was a mistake. . . . Shouldn't the people have the right to vote for someone as many times as they want to vote for him? They send senators up there for 30 or 40 years, congressmen the same."[23] Moreover, reelection infuses *accountability* within the political system. Politics and

---

23. See Lou Cannon, "Funny How a President's Views on the 2-Term Limit Can Change," *Washington Post National Weekly Edition*, 30 June 1986, p. 20; "Keep Limit on Presidential Terms?", *U.S. News and World Report*, 1 Sept. 1986, p. 70.

elections are inexorably linked with effective Presidential leadership and the popular will. The Framers recognized that not restricting duration in office was a leading requisite of executive energy. Repeal of the twenty-second amendment would also permit the retention of our best citizens. As Hamilton noted, "how unwise must be every such self-denying ordinance as serves to prohibit a nation from making use of its own citizens, in the manner best suited to its exigencies and circumstances."

Discussions

In *Federalist* #1, Alexander Hamilton observed that the time had come "to decide the important question whether societies of men are really capable or not of establishing good government from reflection and choice, or whether they are forever destined to depend for their political constitutions on accident and force." By 1816 Thomas Jefferson argued that "forty years experience in government is worth a century of book reading." The Framers had served their country well, but they lacked "the experience of the present." Today, with benefit of 200 years experience with our constitutional blueprint, the Framers would say their institutional inventions could do better. They would undoubtedly take great satisfaction from the way checks and balances had thwarted tyranny; but once they learned of contemporary demands upon government, almost certainly they would be less pleased with their legacy of divided government.

The Gramm-Rudman-Hollings balanced budget law symbolized the failure of government as conceived by the Framers: political institutions were intended to battle one another over choices in policy direction and resource allocation. Gramm-Rudman-Hollings has been likened to the "Son-of-Sam" killer in New York. "Son of Sam went out and killed a number of people," said John Rhodes, co-chairman of the Committee for a Responsible Federal Budget. "Then he called the police and said, 'Please catch me before I kill more people!' This Congress and this President have run up $1.5 trillion in new debt over the last five years. Gramm-Rudman-Hollings was the closest thing they could contrive to calling the cops and saying collectively, 'Stop us because we cannot stop ourselves.' "[24]

Even the most casual observer of American politics would be struck by the Son-of-Sam analogy. The budget balancing law was enacted in an

---

24. *Congressional Record*, February 18, 1986.

effort to create a mechanism for deficit reduction *should* Congress fail to make the necessary cuts. When the Supreme Court declared the law unconstitutional, Chief Justice Burger rejected what in essence technically constituted a Congressional veto. The position of Comptroller General, ultimately answerable to Congress, could allow Congress to invade executive branch prerogatives.[25] Each day the modern American President continues to confront the legacy of the Framers: a separated legislative branch which shares governing powers with the executive, each with an independent electoral base.

Citizens who seek to honor the founders on September 17, 1987 should use past experience to assess the adequacy of their government's blueprint. It is possible that the requirements of national public policy for the twenty-first century call for modifying the vehicle that has taken us this far. The effects of gridlock hurt the public interest and obfuscate political responsibility. Voters have difficulty fixing accountability since neither Congress nor the President constitutes *The Government*, just part of it. So long as these relationships characterize modern American government, the question of how much executive energy is necessary must be answered with a bold, "as much as the bounds of law and morality allow."

In legislating the dominant Presidency, Congress provided the means for trying to make government work *within* the context of the Framers' design. External demands required new institutional arrangements. Of the three branches, only the President was positioned to act for the government. Yet, the environment in which the President operates provides few stable relationships for achieving political success. The continuing tension between superpowers has created a permanent cold war climate, and American interests are generally viewed as best represented by the President. The gap continues to widen between the President's responsibility and the system's capability, between promise and performance. Presidents are also driven by an electoral calendar to "get their way" (or stall in the murk of separated institutions). Professor Hugh Heclo has identified this as the "illusion" of Presidential government:

> Both the executive and legislature seem to act independently of each other, and no party is in a position to control both branches jointly. And yet the puzzles of modern government will not go away. The claims of more and more groups affected and mobilized by government activity demand concerted attention; contradictions need to be reconciled; someone needs to see the "big picture" of what is happening.[26]

25. See Bowsher v. Synar No. 85-1377. (U.S. Supreme Court, 7 July 1986).
26. Hugh Heclo, "The Presidential Illusion," in *The Illusion of Presidential Government*, ed. Hugh Helco and Lester Salamon (Boulder, Colo.: Westview, 1981), p. 5.

Only the President can assume responsibility for making government work. For all his political responsibility, however, the President is still in a remarkably vulnerable constitutional position. The Framers were too cunning in their invention to allow for any regularity in Presidential leadership.

Concluding Essay

Ken Masugi

The challenge to executive authority posed by what has become known as the Iran-Contra affair makes all the more important the topic of this chapter.[1] The question of allowing the exercise of prudence—surely what fundamentally is at stake in the affair—was present throughout the conference. The enduring issue of how wisdom and consent are to be blended was especially prominent in the papers by Grant Mindle on judicial review, David Broyles on federalism, and Dennis Mahoney on separation of powers. By explicitly and implicitly reflecting on prudence and its scope, the essays by Richard Cox, "Executive and Prerogative," and Larry Berman, "The President: Executive Energy and Republican Safety," help us advance our understanding of the most significant constitutional crisis in American government since Watergate. Hence professors Cox and Berman illuminate the character of American constitutional government in this and times more or less stormy. I would like to suggest a means of synthesizing the two accounts of executive power and show how the philosophic and the practical can be studied in the Presidency of one man: George Washington.

Professor Cox's essay is an impressive retrospective on this age-old problem of republican government. In working up to the Founders' Constitution he considers the teachings of Aristotle, Locke, and Hamilton (writing as Publius). More than any other paper in the conference, Cox's essay places the Founding in the history of political philosophy. To understand our republican form of government, we need to consider different regimes such as monarchy (in particular Aristotle's *pambasileia*) and the prerogative of executive power as described in Locke's *Second Treatise*.

It is appropriate that such a retrospective take place in a chapter on the executive, for the executive more than the other branches of government permits such speculation. Indeed, as Cox shows, the turn to political philosophy is essential for understanding the Presidency.

Professor Berman, author of books on the Office of Management and

---

1. The views expressed here are those solely of the author, and do not reflect the official position of the Equal Employment Opportunity Commission.

Budget and the Presidency, presents us with a variety of conundrums of the contemporary Presidency—foreign affairs, the item veto, and the two-term limitation imposed by the twenty-second amendment—which indicate the vulnerability of Presidential power in foreign and domestic affairs. "The framers," Berman concludes, "were too cunning in their invention to allow for any regularity in Presidential leadership." His is a venerable argument: that the Constitution does not adequately protect Presidential power in either the domestic or foreign policy areas. Yet in a revealing step in his argument Berman observes:

> Nixon reasoned that as holder of the *executive power* a President can go beyond his enumerated powers and take whatever steps are necessary to preserve the country's security, even if his actions might be unconstitutional. This reasoning worked during the Civil War but could not pass muster during Watergate.

Does Nixon's failure indicate more the different nature of the crisis he faced or rather the determination or even ruthlessness of his enemies? That is, Nixon's forced resignation signals a smoldering crisis in our understanding of separation of powers and hence of democracy and self-government.

To bring this question up to date, what should we make of President Reagan's unwillingness to raise constitutional arguments in his defense in the Iran-Contra affair? The regnant political silence covers a plethora of potentially illuminating arguments drawn from the themes of western political philosophy, American political tradition in both thought and action, and above all from the text of the Constitution.

To see what has been overlooked in defending the Presidency, let us begin with the obvious, the words of Article II of the Constitution, which describes "the executive power ... vested in a President of the United States." The contrast with the opening of Article I—"All legislative Powers herein granted"—is quite deliberate, as Hamilton noted in his first *Pacificus* paper. As Hamilton explained:

> the difficulty of a complete and perfect specification of all the cases of Executive authority would naturally dictate the use of general terms .... The enumeration [in Article II] ought rather therefore to be considered as intended by way of greater caution, to specify and regulate the principal articles implied in the definition of Executive Power; leaving the rest to flow from the general grant of that power, interpreted in conformity to other parts [of] the Constitution and to the principles of free government.[2]

---

2. Alexander Hamilton, "Pacificus No. 1," in *Selected Writings and Speeches of Alexander Hamilton*, ed. Morton J. Frisch (Washington: American Enterprise Institute, 1985), p.400.

It is telling that Justice Jackson, in his concurring opinion in the steel seizure case, should have simply ridiculed and dismissed this argument. Similarly, Chief Justice Burger's Court opinion in the Nixon tapes case reflected no appreciation of Hamilton's argument. What does Hamilton mean by "The principles of free government?" Surely this must refer to extra-constitutional principles, in the same way that Madison, in *Federalist* 43, refers "to the great principle of self-preservation; to the transcendent law of nature and of nature's God, which declares that the safety and happiness of society are the objects at which all political institutions aim and to which all such institutions must be sacrificed."[3] This should provide a sober background against which to judge the past decade's 150 or so Congressionally induced constraints on Presidential power in foreign affairs—heralded by the War Powers Act.

Going beyond the law to preserve it can also be defended through reference to the oath specified in Article II, "before he enter on the Execution of his office": "I do solemnly swear (or affirm) that I will faithfully execute the Office of President of the United States, and will to the best of my Ability, preserve, protect and defend the Constitution of the United States." That the oath is required of the President (and not of Congressmen or judges) indicates his peculiar duty in this regard. Executing the office here clearly means more than simply enforcing or administering the laws. This may well entail going beyond them.

This, and the President's power as commander in chief of the armed forces, leads us to consider the notion of executive prerogative. Locke put it quite bluntly in his *Second Treatise*: "*Prerogative* can be nothing, but the Peoples permitting their Rulers, to do several things of their own free choice, where the Law was silent, and sometimes too against the direct Letter of the Law, for the publick good; and their acquiescing in it when so done" (paragraph 164). Later, Locke states even more tartly that the people could allow "God-like princes" prerogative, which "is nothing but the Power of doing publick good without a Rule" (paragraph 166). Separation of powers, we must remember, was not intended to weaken individual parts of the regime, but was rather designed to make each part stronger so the public good could be secured. As Publius argues in *Federalist* 71, "it is one thing to be subordinate to the laws, and another to be dependent on the legislative body." And of course, as Mackubin Owens pointed out in his discussion of Berman's paper at the conference, mere

---

3. See also the young Hamilton's "The Farmer Refuted" for a thoughtful summary of natural rights. *Selected Writings*, pp. 19-22.

efficiency cannot be the purpose of politics either. Ultimately regimes must be judged by the character of the citizens they produce, and here the executive can be an invaluable model for republican government.

Hence energy in the executive cannot be reduced to the possession and exercise of power. Moderation is, after all, a virtue. The example of George Washington indicates the extent to which *character* is central for judging the success or failure of particular Presidents. In the midst of America's first regime crisis, that of the 1790s, Washington's Farewell Address proposed to Americans means of achieving unity:

> Of all the dispositions and habits which lead to political prosperity, Religion and morality are indispensable supports. In vain would that man claim the tribute of Patriotism, who should labour to subvert these great Pillars of human happiness, these firmest props of the duties of Men and citizens.

One might misunderstand the argument of *The Federalist*, especially if numbers 10 and 51 are read through the eyes of modern political science to imply that America was to become nothing but a nation of factions. Liberal democracy's necessary condition of accommodating the consequences of liberty, and hence of faction, does not undermine its sufficient condition of unity based on higher law. In truth, the necessary conditions of politics focused on by the ancients have always remained possibilities for communities of human beings; America offers the opportunity of employing the means of the improved science of politics in service of the politics of the best regime. America presents both the eternal goods necessary for the practice of virtue and the various modes of virtue itself. Thus both consent and wisdom have roles to play. As Ambassador Krueger remarked at the conference, the people's representatives must always remember—not that most need reminding—whom they are speaking and acting for. Refining the best in the people is the task of all legislators and citizens in the American republic, but it is preeminently the task of the President. A few indications of how this is to be done can be found in Washington's speeches and writings.

Perhaps the finest examples of his fulfilling the office of educator came while Washington was still commander of the army, in his "Circular to the States" (June 8, 1783).

> The Foundation of our Empire was not laid in the gloomy age of Ignorance and Superstition, but at an Epocha when the rights of mankind were better understood and more clearly defined, than at any former period, the researches of the human mind, after social happiness, have been carried to a great extent, the Treasures of knowledge,

acquired by the labours of Philosophers, Sages, and Legislatures, through a long succession of years, are laid open for our use, and their collected wisdom may be happily applied in the Establishment of our forms of Government; the free cultivation of Letters, the unbounded extension of Commerce, the progressive refinement of Manners, the growing liberality of sentiment, and above all, the pure and benign light of Revelation, have had a meliorating influence on mankind and increased the blessings of Society. At this auspicious period, the United States came into existence as a Nation, and if their Citizens should not be completely free and happy, the fault will be intirely their own.

These themes persist through the First Inaugural, his Thanksgiving Proclamation (in which Washington takes on the role of a high priest), and his annual addresses to Congress (which elaborate on the necessary and sufficient conditions for republican government in the United States). Of course these themes are brought out marvelously in the Farewell Address.

Washington explicitly states that he wants the Farewell Address to be re-read over the generations. It was to provide an argument for political and moral unity not only during the 1790s and for the current generation but for generations to come. Famous for its attack on parties (in the sense of factions), the document united in its composition the hands of Hamilton, Madison, and Jay—the original Publius triumvirate. Can it still instruct us today?

There are some grounds for skepticism. Morality and religion—even the civil religion of the Declaration of Independence's "laws of nature and of nature's God"—have become further sources of division instead of unity. It would appear that, following Lincoln's appeal to "cold, calculating reason," we today need to reacquire the "knowledge [that] is in every country the surest basis of public happiness." Hence Washington proposed a national university, which today would surely add more to the problems we face than to the solutions. If the unity to be fostered by commerce in the 1790s is now not only assured but potentially stultifying, we face today ethnic and linguistic divisions with disastrous consequences for both domestic and foreign policy. We can only preserve our nation through recurrence to the principles that Washington defended and the means he proposed. A recovery of the moral basis of the regime—its ultimate source of unity—can still be achieved through a revival in appreciation for natural law. If we are daunted by the smug confidence in historicism today, we should recall that doctrines alien to natural rights were just as strong in the eighteenth century and in the nineteenth as well. Natural rights was never a doctrine taken for granted by a majority of the world.

And the advice concerning foreign policy may appear too indulgent of isolationism to aid us in a perilous world. Yet Washington looked forward to the time when America would become a "great nation" with a "magnanimous" people, in addition to being free and enlightened. It is clear that Washington's intention was to have helped found a nation whose Constitution allowed its statesmen the scope to act, both to protect its citizens from foreign powers and to foster in them a manly republicanism.

Turning to our present-day political crisis, we see that the Farewell Address needs re-reading more than ever. In defending the powers of the Presidency, the Congress and the people—not to mention the President himself—must keep in mind that they are charged with perpetuating a tradition beginning with Washington. It is not simply a mark of Reagan's luck in this crisis that when he demanded to know of audiences what they were doing on August 8, 1985 (the day he approved the arms sales to Iran) that he chose the eleventh anniversary of the very date Richard Nixon resigned. Washington did not serve as general, President, or Founder so that foreign plots could so readily shake a regime or an arrogant Congress could pose as the *vox populi* and repository of all morality and justice.

Writing in *The Claremont Review of Books* (Spring, 1987) Douglas A. Jeffrey posed the question facing President Reagan well: "Which is the nobler course for a democratic statesman: to risk defeat in the public arena, or to accept it, and the subversion of democratic forms, without a fight?" To Washington, the father of our country, this would be a mere rhetorical question. It reflects on our difficulties that the question is not rhetorical today. While presenting an effective case for moving beyond the current crisis, the President in his March 4, 1987 speech to the nation gave the game away when he told the National Security Council (revamped under Washington veteran Frank Carlucci) that he "wanted a policy that reflected the will of the Congress as well as the White House." The barbarians are now inside the gates. It is doubtful whether this White House now contains even a mere lieutenant colonel on the National Security Council staff who can give plausible constitutional arguments for executive authority.

Chapter Four

The Judiciary: Supreme Interpreter of the Constitution?

*In **Cooper v. Aaron** (1958) the Supreme Court declared that its interpretations of the Constitution are "the supreme law of the land," thus claiming for itself the same authority as the Constitution. Is this a fulfillment of the nature of constitutional government which secures the supremacy of the law and the protection of minority rights against partisanship and majority tyranny? Or does it undermine the constitutional government by placing one of its institutions above the Constitution itself?*

In order to reflect the extent of the current controversy over this issue we have included four essays in this chapter.

Congress and Judicial Review

Grant B. Mindle

The Federalist's defense of judicial review is well-known; unfortunately, the significance of the argument immediately preceding its introduction —Hamilton's affirmation of judicial weakness—is often overlooked.[1] The power "to pronounce legislative acts void, because contrary to the Constitution" has masked the vulnerability of the institution exercising it so much so that Hamilton's conclusion that the "natural feebleness" of the judiciary has placed it "in continual jeopardy of being overpowered, awed, or influenced by its co-ordinate branches" is apt to appear naive[2] To its champions as well as its critics, the modern judiciary is certainly more formidable than an initial reading of *Federalist* 78 might suggest.[3]

But before we conclude with Justice Stone that "the only check upon [the Court's] exercise of power is [its] own sense of self-restraint," a position which necessarily calls into question the democratic character of judicial review, it may be helpful to reconsider the views of the founders.[4] When we speak about the judiciary, we often do so as if there were but two alternatives, judicial supremacy and judicial subjection. The democratic alternative to judicial supremacy, however, is not judicial subjection, but the hybrid Hamilton thought the Constitutional Convention had achieved by mating the "natural feebleness" of the judiciary with the extraordinary power of judicial review. And even if Hamilton's prophecy has gone awry, as many believe it has, it is still more instructive to begin an analysis of judicial power with the views of the framers, if only because they do not presume the existence of Stone's virtually unfettered judiciary. Whatever its validity today, Stone's dictum simply cannot account for the growth of judicial power, let alone for the decision in which the most formidable of

---

1. See Walter Murphy and C. Herman Pritchett, *Courts, Judges, and Politics*, 3rd edition (New York: Random House, 1979), p. 15 where this passage from *Federalist* #78 is omitted; note also the absence of any recognition of the institutional weakness of the judiciary in the excerpt by Judge Frank Johnson, pp. 66-71.

2. Alexander Hamilton, James Madison, John Jay, *The Federalist Papers* ed. Clinton Rossiter (New York: The New American Library [Mentor], 1961), #78, p. 466.

3. Would anyone, for example, still maintain with Hamilton that the "judiciary has no influence over either the sword or the purse"? Cf. *Federalist* #78, p. 465 with Murphy and Pritchett, pp. 37-38, 47n.1.

4. J. Stone dissenting, U.S. v. Butler, 56 S. Ct. 325.

judicial powers was first established, *Marbury v. Madison*. In that case, the limitations the Court faced were principally external, arising from the weakness of the judiciary vis-a-vis the other branches.[5] Indeed, no case better exemplifies Hamilton's understanding of judicial power, for the line of argument Marshall chooses represents a subtle blending of weakness with strength. Although he recognizes that the Court is too weak to give orders to the executive branch, Marshall nevertheless reaffirms the Court's right to do so, and then cleverly escapes the consequences of his conclusion through the assertion and exercise of judicial review. Nor is Marshall's ringing invocation of the principles of the American regime— "The government of the United States has been emphatically termed a government of laws, and not of men. It will certainly cease to deserve this high appellation, if the laws furnish no remedy for the violation of a vested legal right"—sufficient to secure Marbury his commission, a sobering reminder of the pretentiousness of Marshall's conclusion that "the laws of his country afford him a remedy."[6]

Although the origins of judicial review have been studied assiduously, little attention has been paid to the Congressional debates of 1802.[7] Responding to Jefferson's oblique remark that "the judiciary system of the United States, and especially that portion of it recently erected, will of course, present itself to the contemplation of Congress," Senator Breckenridge introduced a resolution calling for the repeal of the Judiciary Act of 1801.[8] The motion was debated by Congress for nearly two months; because the measure called for the abolition of judicial offices already, albeit recently, established (a possible violation of the constitutional provision stipulating that judges shall hold their offices during good behavior), the participants in the debate were forced to discuss at length the purpose of the judiciary, its relationship to the executive and the legislature, and eventually the propriety of judicial review itself. More specific than the isolated remarks to be found in the constitutional and state ratifying conventions, unencumbered by the weight of Marshall's 1803

---

5. For an alternative analysis of *Marbury*, see Christopher Wolfe, *The Rise of the Modern Judiciary* (New York: Basic Books, 1986), pp. 84-89. I find Wolfe's analysis unpersuasive, particularly in light of Marshall's modification of *Marbury* in Cohens v. Virginia. See also Donald O. Dewey, *Marshall Versus Jefferson* (New York: Alfred Knopf, 1970), p. 152.

6. Marbury v. Madison, 1 Cranch 163, 168.

7. The caliber of the debate itself, however, has been noted by many. See, for example, Felix Frankfurter and James Landis, *The Business of the Supreme Court* (New York: MacMillan, 1927), p. 27.

8. *Annals*, 7th Cong., 1st Sess., p. 15.

opinion in *Marbury v. Madison*, the debate offers a fresh perspective on the theory and practice of American constitutionalism.

I

The Jeffersonians won the Presidency and control of Congress in the election of 1800. Fearful that that madman, that Jacobin, Thomas Jefferson might wreck the new nation they had labored to establish, the Federalists used their last months in office to transform the Judiciary into a bastion of Federalism. With six weeks to go in his term, John Adams nominated his Secretary of State, John Marshall, to be Chief Justice of the United States; with three weeks to go, Adams signed the Judiciary Act of 1801, relieving Supreme Court justices of the burden of riding circuit through the creation of 16 circuit court judgeships. Loyal and, for the most part, moderate Federalists were quickly appointed and confirmed to all 16 posts; and on his final day in office Adams signed "The Organic Act of the District of Columbia" creating positions for 42 Justices of the Peace, although several of the commissions were never delivered, among them the commission destined for one William Marbury.[9] Anticipating the handiwork of his predecessor, Jefferson angrily remarked in a letter to John Dickinson: "The remains of Federalism are to be preserved and fed from the Treasury, and from that battery all the works of Republicanism are to be beaten down and erased by a fradulent use of the Constitution which has made judges irremoveable."[10]

The Judiciary Act of 1801 is often portrayed as a purely partisan measure, an act of desperation by a party soon to be booted from office greedily exploiting its last opportunity to distribute patronage.[11] To accept this characterization, however, would be to do a grave injustice to the Federalists who supported it. The creation of a system of circuit courts had been envisioned and discussed as early as 1790 when Edmund Ran-

---

9. Cf. William S. Carpenter, *Judicial Tenure in the United States* (New Haven: Yale University Press, 1918), p. 55; for Jefferson's view of Adams' appointees, see Richard E. Ellis, *The Jeffersonian Crisis* (New York: Oxford University Press, 1971), pp. 32-33. When Jefferson assumed office, there were no Republican judges. See Charles Warren, *The Supreme Court in United States History* (Boston: Little, Brown & Co., 1926), vol. 1, p. 190.

10. Quoted in Dewey, p. 63.

11. See, for example, Andrew McLaughlin, *A Constitutional History of the United States* (New York: Appleton-Century, 1935), p. 288; Homer Carey Hockett, *The Constitutinal History of the United States* (New York: MacMillan, 1939), p. 304.

dolph, Washington's Attorney General, filed a report with Congress summarizing the arguments pro and con, and concluding with a recommendation that Supreme Court justices be relieved of the burden of riding circuit.[12] The Judiciary Act of 1793, reducing the number of Supreme Court justices needed to hear a circuit court case from two to one, while offering some relief, did little to alleviate "the basic awkwardness of the original system."[13] The distance Supreme Court justices were forced to travel, the time it required, the prospect that a circuit court consisting of only two members (a Supreme Court justice and a district judge) would be unable to agree, the delay that would ensue should one of the judges be ill or for some other reason unable to hold court, the likelihood that Supreme Court justices would be called upon to rehear cases they had already heard as circuit court judges, the delay and expense a system so administered imposed upon potential litigants—these were among its more notable defects.[14]

Court reform had been considered by the Senate in 1798, and had been recommended to the Congress by President Adams as early as December 3, 1799. And the following year, John Marshall, while a member of the House of Representatives, had served on the committee delegated to bring in a bill. Although their efforts were unsuccessful, they do attest to Federalism's deep and abiding interest in reformation of the judiciary. This is not to deny the presence of partisan motives (Adams could have left his successor free to appoint whomever he wished to the circuit court), but it does suggest that the impetus for reform cannot be attributed solely to Adams' defeat.[15]

By expanding the size of the federal judiciary and enlarging its jurisdiction, the Federalists hoped to facilitate the enforcement of federal law, civil as well as criminal, reduce the cost and enhance the accessibility of federal justice, neutralize the power of the state courts, and in time win back the affection of the people by showing them the benefits of an

---

12. See Kathryn Turner, "Federalist Policy and the Judiciary Act of 1801," *William and Mary Quarterly* vol. 22, no. 1 (1965), pp. 5-6; Frankfurter and Landis, pp. 14-15.

13. The phrase is from Jerry W. Knudson, "The Jeffersonian Assault on the Federalist Judiciary," *American Journal of Legal History* vol. 14, no. 1 (1970), p. 57.

14. A more comprehensive account of its defects can be found in Edward C. Surrency, "The Judiciary Act of 1801," *American Journal of Legal History* vol. 2, no. 1 (1958), pp. 60-61. See also *Annals*, 7th Cong., 1st Sess., pp. 37, 52-56.

15. Frankfurter and Landis, p. 26n. 73. Not all of those appointed to the circuit court accepted their appointment, leaving Jefferson with a few appointments of his own, which he did make. Surrency, p. 54.

efficient and uniform system of justice.[16] Judicial reform was thus an essential part of Federalism's war against states' rights sentiment. In a letter to Fisher Ames, Oliver Wolcott, Adams' Secretary of the Treasury and a leading proponent of judicial reform, observed: "The steady men in Congress will attempt to extend the judicial department and I hope that their measures will be very decided. It is impossible, in this country, to render an army of an engine of government, and there is no way to combat the state opposition but by an efficient and extended organization of judges, magistrates, and other civil officers."[17]

Not surprisingly, much of the support for repeal of the Judiciary Act can be traced to states' rights sentiment, and to the fear of its adherents that expansion of the size and jurisdiction of the federal judiciary would divert suits from state to federal court.[18] Kentucky (the home of Senator Breckenridge, the leading advocate of repeal) and Virginia were particularly alarmed by its potential impact upon the validity of state land titles, jurisdiction having been conferred in diversity cases irrespective of the value of the land itself.[19] Although the advocates of repeal also made much of the federal judiciary's declining docket—President Jefferson had sent the Congress a highly inaccurate account of the number of cases decided by the Court since its creation and the number pending on the day the Judiciary Act of 1801 was passed—their fear that new suitors might flock to federal court is evident throughout the debate.[20] Thus Senator Breckenridge's opening address to the Senate was somewhat misleading. Convinced that the judicial power should extend only to "great national and foreign concerns," that most judicial questions could and would be resolved by the states themselves, Senator Breckenridge had boldly predicted that "the time will never arrive when America will stand in need of 38 federal judges."[21] But others were less optimistic. As Senator Jackson of Georgia put it: "the more courts you have the greater temptation there is for litigation, and more suits, or rather evils, will flow from them."[22] For their part, the Federalists were quick to point out the inaccu-

---

16. Turner, p. 31; *Annals*, 7th Cong., 1st Sess., pp. 51, 110, 117-18, 122-23, 681.
17. Turner, p. 10.
18. Turner, pp. 16, 23-32; Warren p. 192; Carpenter, p. 58.
19. Carpenter, pp. 60-61.
20. Regarding the inaccuracy of Jefferson's data, see Ellis, p. 41; regarding the cost of the reform, see Max Farrand, "The Judiciary Act of 1801," *American Historical Review* vol. 5 (1900), p. 685.
21. *Annals*, 7th Cong., 1st Sess., p. 26.
22. *Annals*, 7th Cong., 1st Sess., pp. 50-51.

racy of Jefferson's data, and reiterate the importance of providing a system of justice readily accessible to one and all.[23]

But the principal, and for our purposes the more interesting question was the constitutional one. Could Congress abolish the office of a sitting judge? Article III, section 1 of the Constitution declares: "The judicial power of the United States shall be vested in one Supreme Court, and in such inferior courts as the Congress may, from time to time, ordain and establish. The judges, both of the Supreme and inferior courts shall hold their offices during good behavior, and shall, at stated times, receive for their services, a compensation, which shall not be diminished during their continuance in office."

Everyone agreed that Congress *must* establish a Supreme Court; the words, "the judicial power of the United States *shall* be vested in one Supreme Court" were imperative and commanding.[24] But the Jeffersonians, taking their cue from a letter John Taylor had written Senator Breckenridge in reply to his request for advice, argued that the existence of inferior courts was purely discretionary.[25] And since the power to ordain includes the power to revise or abolish—or at least so they maintained—Congress was free to revise or abolish the act establishing an inferior court whenever it found it expedient to do so. To butress their position, they also relied upon Article I, section 8 where Congress' power "To constitute tribunals inferior to the supreme Court" is placed amidst a list of powers otherwise discretionary.[26]

Once their offices had been abolished, the judges would cease to be judges, provided, of course, that a judge is defined as the Jeffersonians insisted he should be, by the services he renders, and not as the Federalists suggested, by his confirmation and acceptance of the appointment.[27] Although the Constitution appears to prohibit Congress from reducing the salary of a sitting judge, Breckenridge, again taking his cue from John Taylor, argued that no one should receive public money except for services rendered, noted the impropriety of sinecures in a democracy, and cited the provision in Article III that "The Judges ... shall ... receive for their *Services* a Compensation which shall not be diminished during their

23. *Annals*, 7th Cong., 1st Sess., pp. 36, 117-18, 135-36, 572, 623, 668-69, 798.

24. *Annals*, 7th Cong., 1st Sess., p. 48.

25. Taylor's role is explained in more detail in Carpenter, pp. 61-66. According to Ellis, p. 41, Jefferson initially considered the removal of Adams' appointees unconstitutional.

26. See, for example, *Annals*, 7th Cong., 1st Sess., p. 48.

27. See, for example, *Annals*, 7th Cong., 1st Sess., p. 29.

Continuance in Office" (emphasis added).[28] And finally, as proof of his assertion that Congress might, in the interest of expediency, abolish an existing court, he cited the Judiciary Act of 1801 itself, noting its abolition of the district courts in Kentucky and Tennessee.[29] If the Federalists were right, if the Constitution did indeed forbid the abolition of a judicial office while its occupant was still alive and willing to serve, then the Judiciary Act of 1801 was itself unconstitutional, and therefore subject to repeal.

The Federalists were quick to point out the absurdity of a Constitution which would guard the pay but not the office of a sitting judge. "[May we] destroy the office which we cannot take away?"[30] "Is murder prohibited, and may you shut a man up, and deprive him of sustenance till he dies, and this not be denominated murder?"[31] Nor were they sympathetic to the doctrine that it is the law, and not the Constituion, which secures the tenure of the judiciary. Such a doctrine, if accepted, would allow Congress to abolish the office of an unfriendly judge, thereby securing his removal without mustering the two-thirds majority impeachment requires.[32] Congress would then be free to recreate the office and fill it with someone whose politics was more in accord with its present disposition.[33] If there were too many judges, would it not be better, they asked, to leave all vacancies unfilled, or seek a Constitutional amendment to secure their reduction? Although the Federalists could hardly deny their abolition of the district courts in Kentucky and Tennessee, they duly noted the Judiciary Act's respect for the independence of those judges whose offices were abolished, drawing attention to its provision for their appointment to the circuit court. Congress, it seems, is free to abolish the office of a sitting judge, but it must do so "with an eye to the independence of the judges already in office."[34] It may expand the jurisdiction of a sitting judge, it may even revoke jurisdiction previously assigned, but it cannot deprive him of jurisdiction altogether.[35]

---

28. *Annals*, 7th Cong., 1st Sess., p. 28.
29. *Annals*, 7th Cong., 1st Sess., p. 26.
30. *Annals*, 7th Cong., 1st Sess., p. 39.
31. *Annals*, 7th Cong., 1st Sess., p. 57.
32. To guard against this, some of the Jeffersonians argued that Congress was not free to repeal the office of a single judge, but could only repeal the system in its entirety. See *Annals*, 7th Cong., 1st Sess., pp. 31, 63, 541, 562, 795.
33. *Annals*, 7th Cong., 1st Sess., pp. 166, 541.
34. *Annals*, 7th Cong., 1st Sess., p. 731.
35. *Annals*, 7th Cong., 1st Sess., p. 163.

Arguments such as these provoked John Randolph to declare in the House of Representatives that "if the intent of this bill is to get rid of the judges, it is a perversion of your power to a base purpose; it is an unconstitutional act. If, on the contrary, it aims not at displacing one set of men, from whom you differ in political opinion, with a view to introduce others, but at the general good by abolishing useless offices, it is a Constitutional act."[36] Randolph's approach rests the legitimacy of repeal upon two propositions, the absence of a political motive, and the inexpediency of the newly established system, neither of which is as easily established as he assumes.

The Federalists responded by insisting that to concede such a power to Congress would jeopardize, if not destroy, the independence of the judiciary, and reduce to a nullity the principle that each of the branches should be "distinct from and independent of each other."[37] How can the judiciary be expected to resist the abuses of the legislature if Congress has the power to abolish their offices at will? Were such a doctrine accepted, their dependence upon the legislature for their tenure in office and the salary that accompanies it would in time produce "a servile disposition, and destroy that manly independence so essential to an upright and good judge."[38]

II

Everyone acknowledged the importance of an independent judiciary, but there was little agreement concerning the scope of its independence. To the Federalists, the judiciary was the most beneficent of the branches, offering every individual protection against unwarranted deprivations of his person and his property. Were Congress, for example, to enact a Bill of Attainder, the judiciary could be relied upon to impede its enforcement. Standing between the legislature and the Constitution, the government and the people, the judiciary was designed to protect the people from both executive and legislative tyranny, and should the occasion ever arise, to protect the people from themselves, from the consequences of their own follies and injustices.[39]

---

36. *Annals*, 7th Cong., 1st Sess., p. 658.
37. *Annals*, 7th Cong., 1st Sess., p. 31.
38. *Annals*, 7th Cong., 1st Sess., p. 144.
39. *Annals*, 7th Cong., 1st Sess., p. 754.

To the Federalists, judges were "men of learning, wisdom, and moderation."[40] Congressman Hastings even speaks of them as "uninfluenced by popular or party views."[41] Possessing none of the prerogatives which are dangerous to liberty, the judiciary was especially well suited to guard against the weakness and wickedness of man.[42] But without the peace of mind its independence confers, the probability of its doing so would greatly diminish. There must be no menacing power to bias judicial decisions. "If, when in office, they are rendered completely independent of the party by which they were appointed, there can be but little cause of apprehension respecting the decisions of the judge, whatever may have been the politics of the man."[43] The independence of a judge "consists in having his mind elevated above the fear of any evil consequence resulting to him from rendering upright and impartial judgments."[44]

Nor could a dependent judiciary be counted upon to exercise its most formidable power—judicial review. An independent judiciary was imperative, the Federalists argued, if only for the sake of judicial review, just as judicial review was essential to the preservation of a federal and constitutional system. Eliminate judicial review, and the states will soon find themselves subject to Congress' own construction of its own powers, a conclusion the Federalists hoped the advocates of states' rights would be loath to accept.[45] Such a legislature would be omnipotent, and the limitations to its powers so carefully marked out by the Constitution would be in vain. "The people have retained power to themselves and have said to the legislature, thus far you shall go and no farther. There are certain cases wherein you shall not be the judges of what will or will not be to our advantage."[46] Believing that the judiciary was a more competent interpreter of the Constitution, the Federalists concluded that enforcement of those limits must rest with the judges. To repeal the Judiciary Act of 1801 would be "wounding our Constitution in a vital part," and would undoubtedly lead to its dissolution.[47]

The judiciary the Federalists celebrated, however, bore little resemblance to the one the Jeffersonians had come to know, and fear. If

---

40. *Annals*, 7th Cong., 1st Sess., p. 783.
41. *Annals*, 7th Cong., 1st Sess., p. 881.
42. *Annals*, 7th Cong., 1st Sess., p. 573.
43. *Annals*, 7th Cong., 1st Sess., p. 930.
44. *Annals*, 7th Cong., 1st Sess., p. 730.
45. *Annals*, 7th Cong., 1st Sess., pp. 56, 83, 87, 180, 784, 929-31.
46. *Annals*, 7th Cong., 1st Sess., p. 536.
47. *Annals*, 7th Cong., 1st Sess., p. 144.

anything, its vigorous enforcement of the Alien and Sedition Acts had taught them to regard the courts as an instrument of oppression, and not at all as a resolute guardian of our civil rights, determined to forestall their invasion by the legislature.[48] Nor were they overly impressed with the "impartiality" of its judges. Two judges of the newly created Circuit Court for the District of Columbia had already invoked the common law against libel to institute proceedings against the editor of a Jeffersonian newspaper, *The National Intelligencer*, for having published a letter railing against the partisanship of the judiciary.[49] No one asked, but many must have wondered why Federalists alone had been appointed to the judiciary, if indeed "there can be little cause of apprehension respecting the decisions of the judge, whatever may have been his politics." Although rarely mentioned in the debates themselves, Marbury's efforts to secure a writ of mandamus from the Supreme Court and the Court's request that the Secretary of State, James Madison, show cause why the writ should not be issued, convinced even those Jeffersonians least sympathetic to Senator Breckenridge's assault upon the judiciary that something would have to be done lest the Federalists use the courts to obstruct the legitimate exercise of executive power.[50] To Senator Morris' query, "But what danger is to be apprehended from an army of judges," Senator Jackson had quickly replied, "I am more afraid of an army of judges, under the patronage of the President, than of an army of soldiers .... [H]ereafter if [the sedition law] should exist, your judges, under the cry of sedition and political heresy, may place half your citizens in irons."[51]

The Jeffersonians readily conceded that the legislature might also exceed its authority by enacting laws in violation of the Constitution. In their eyes it had already done so when it passed the Alien and Sedition Acts. But their success at effecting reform through the ballot box convinced them that it was safer to entrust the power to interpret the Constitution to a body periodically accountable to the people, than to confer it upon a branch of the government as insulated from public opinion as the judiciary. "But while the elective principle remains free, no great danger of *lasting* oppression can be really apprehended" (emphasis added).[52] Were a court, however, to err in its interpretation of the Constitution, to effect a remedy could prove to be far more difficult:

---

48. *Annals*, 7th Cong., 1st Sess., pp. 47, 583, 873.
49. Ellis, p. 40.
50. Ellis, p. 44.
51. *Annals*, 7th Cong., 1st Sess., pp. 37, 47.
52. *Annals*, 7th Cong., 1st Sess., pp. 709-10.

> That there must be some place where the true meaning of the Constitution must be determined, all would agree. Where then is it? The people have constituted two departments of authority, the Executive and Legislature, emanating directly from the people. Are we then to be told that there is more safety in confiding this important power to the last department, so far removed from the people than in departments flowing directly from the people, responsible to and returning at short intervals into the mass of the people?[53]

The Federalists had assumed an independent judiciary would engender in the judges a manly determination to render upright and impartial judgments; but, since such independence would leave the judiciary unaccountable for its behavior, could it not as easily, if not more easily, rob the judges of any incentive to restrain their partisanship? Senator Mason, for example, argued that "all the departments of a popular Government must depend, in some degree, on popular opinion. Were a department to be "placed in such a situation as to be independent of the nation, it [would] soon lose that affection which is essential to its durable existence."[54] Too much independence could endanger the rights of the people as well as threaten the survival of the judiciary itself should the people ever become infuriated by its defiance of popular sentiment. Moreover, "this independence of the judiciary, so much desired, will ... if encouraged or tolerated, soon become something like supremacy." A judiciary, armed with the power of judicial review, would be "independent of all law."[55] To sanction such a doctrine would be to deny the capability of the people to govern themselves, and entail "the humiliation of the legislature."[56] Such a judiciary would cease to be a "coordinate" branch of government, and become their superior, transforming our democracy into a despotism.

Would the denial of judicial review render the Court a "subordinate" branch of the government as the Federalists assumed? Or would its affirmation make it their superior, by vesting in the Court an "unlimited and uncontrollable power of legislation"?[57] The Federalists dutifully repeated Hamilton's argument in *Federalist* 78, that judicial review did not "suppose the superiority of the judicial to the legislative power," but "only supposes the power of the people superior to both," and that when a conflict arises between the text of the Constitution and a statute enacted by Congress,

---

53. *Annals*, 7th Cong., 1st Sess., p. 531.
54. *Annals*, 7th Cong., 1st Sess., p. 59.
55. *Annals*, 7th Cong., 1st Sess., p. 532.
56. *Annals*, 7th Cong., 1st Sess., p. 180.
57. *Annals*, 7th Cong., 1st Sess., p. 554.

the judges are bound by their oath of office to give the former—the deliberate will of the people—priority.[58] Indeed, "the people want to be protected from themselves."[59]

Some of the Jeffersonians were prepared to concede the existence of judicial review, although many were not, offering one or another variant of the doctrine of departmental review.[60] Since every officer of the government takes an oath to support the Constitution, all have an equal right to construe it. Congressman Davis, for example, believed the judges need not execute a law they considered unconstitutional, but were powerless to declare it null and void.[61]

And even those Federalists who hoped that the judiciary would declare the repeal of the Judiciary Act unconstitutional expressed little confidence in the ability of the judiciary to withstand an assault from the legislature. Like Hamilton in *Federalist* 78, they were all too aware of the "natural feebleness" of the judiciary. Nor were the Jeffersonians, despite all of their talk about judicial supremacy, oblivious to the inherent weaknesses of the judiciary. Consider the following remarks by Senator Stone:

> But says the gentleman from New York, the judges are officers instituted by the Constitution, to save the people from their greatest enemies, themselves; and therefore they should be entirely independent of, and beyond the control of the Legislature. If such was the design of the wise men who framed and adopted the Constitution, can it be presumed they would have provided so ineffectual a barrier as these judges can readily be shown to be? It is allowed, on all hands, the Legislature may modify the courts: they may add judges, they may fix the times at which the courts shall sit. Suppose the legislature to have an interest distinct from the people, and the judges to stand in the way of executing any favorite measure—can anything be more easy than for the Legislature to declare that the courts, instead of being held semi-annually, or oftener shall be held only once in six, eight, ten, or twenty years? Or in order to free themselves from the opposition of the present Supreme Court, to declare that court shall hereafter be held by thirteen judges.[62]

By expanding the size of the Court, by postponing or cancelling its sessions, Congress would have little trouble waging war successfully against an unpopular judiciary, even one armed with the power of judicial

---

58. *Annals*, 7th Cong., 1st Sess., pp. 783, 866, 920.
59. *Annals*, 7th Cong., 1st Sess., p. 754.
60. *Annals*, 7th Cong., 1st Sess., pp. 115, 178-79, 698, 865, 973, 982.
61. *Annals*, 7th Cong., 1st Sess., p. 558.
62. *Annals*, 7th Cong., 1st Sess., p. 73.

review. Nor were these the only alternatives available. As Congressman Smith observed, Congress could also use the exceptions clause ("the supreme Court shall have appellate Jurisdiction, both as to Law and Fact, with such Exceptions, and under such Regulations, as the Congress shall make") to overturn an unpopular decision:

> Should any of your courts render themselves obnoxious to Congress by deciding their laws unconstitutional, what is to be done? Take from them all their jurisdiction, both civil and criminal, and transfer it to other courts, who will decide more in unison with your opinion. By this means, you remove every obstacle which the judges, by declaring your laws unconstitutional, might throw in your way.[63]

Surprisingly, the Federalists never denied, as some scholars are wont to do today, Congress' right to use the exceptions clause to alter the jurisdiction of the Court. Raoul Berger, for example, has argued that the exceptions clause must be read narrowly, that it makes no sense to confer judicial review, if the Court's jurisdiction can be limited so easily; others have argued that a literal reading of the exceptions clause "would destroy the essential role of the Supreme Court in the Constitutional plan."[64] But the Federalists thought otherwise. In these debates, one finds the most ardent advocates of judicial review and judicial independence, men such as Senator Morris of New York and Congressman Bayard, readily affirming Congress' right to modify, either by expanding or restricting, the jurisdiction of the federal judiciary. Senator Morris, noting that the appeal to the Supreme Court is "subject to such exceptions and regulations as Congress shall make," argues Congress could, if it chose to do so, defeat the appeal rendering "the judgment of inferior tribunals final."[65] These tribunals might be either the State Supreme Courts, a previously existing lower federal court, or even a lower federal court recently created by Congress to hear matters previously assigned to other judicial bodies.

According to the Federalists the limitations to the exercise of this power were twofold. First, although Congress had the right to withdraw specific subjects from the jurisdiction of the Supreme and/or lower federal courts, it was not permitted to leave a court without any jurisdiction whatsoever.[66] In short, the exception must be an exception, not a charade designed to abolish the business of the office altogether. Second, it was

---

63. *Annals*, 7th Cong., 1st Sess., pp. 701-02.
64. Raoul Berger, *Congress v. The Supreme Court* (Cambridge: Harvard University Press, 1969).
65. *Annals*, 7th Cong., 1st Sess., p. 181.
66. *Annals*, 7th Cong., 1st Sess., p. 910.

impermissible to alter a court's jurisdiction in such a way as to deprive the judges of their independence, that is, to place them in a position where they might have reason to fear their decision in a case would jeopardize their tenure in office.[67] And, of course, Congress was obliged to respect the independence of every judicial body it creates regardless of how unpopular its decisions may prove to be. Thus even a recently created judicial body would always be free to affirm, without fear of retaliation, a doctrine contrary to the opinion of Congress.[68]

III

The debate over the repeal of the Judiciary Act of 1801 is a rather telling reminder of the inherent weakness of the judiciary. Not only did Congress manage to abolish the offices of the newly created circuit court judges, but the Supreme Court in *Stuart v. Laird*, though privately subscribing to the opinion that the Constitution forbade the Supreme Court from exercising circuit court duty, nevertheless felt impelled to uphold the constitutionality of what Congress had done.[69] Constrained by political circumstances, it had little choice but to affirm an interpretation of the Constitution it considered unwarranted.

The Federalists and the Jeffersonians debated at length the purpose and the role of the judiciary in a constitutional system, the former holding that judicial review was essential to the preservation of a limited government, and implicit in the idea of a written Constitution; the latter suggesting such a view was tantamount to despotism and would, should it become dogma, leave the people and their representatives subject to a privileged few "who are themselves independent of all law."[70] But paradoxically, or at least so it must seem to those of us schooled in the contemporary debate, they chose sides in a context framed by a mutual awareness of the "natural feebleness" of the judiciary. They knew, what we seem to have forgotten, that "the judiciary, from its very nature, being the most feeble, if unprotected by the [legislature and the executive] cannot long endure."[71]

---

67. *Annals*, 7th Cong., 1st Sess., p. 785.
68. *Annals*, 7th Cong., 1st Sess., p. 790.
69. Warren, pp. 270-71.
70. *Annals*, 7th Cong., 1st Sess., p. 532.
71. *Annals*, 7th Cong., 1st Sess., p. 940.

The debate and its outcome suggest that Congress' power to control the courts by modifying their jurisdiction is broader than many scholars are willing to concede.[72] "In republican government, the legislative authority necessarily predominates."[73] Thus the finality of a judicial decision ultimately depends upon the acquiescence of Congress, a view of judicial authority which we believe is at odds with the one announced by the Court in *Cooper v. Aaron*. Indeed, the dependence of judicial review upon Congressional acquiescence has traditionally received less attention than is warranted. This is not to deny the limitations the imperatives of our federal and constitutional system impose upon any attempt by Congress to exercise its power to restrict the jurisdiction of the court. The necessity for uniformity, the role of the judiciary in securing the enforcement of federal law, as well as the prospect that State or lower federal courts, or even newly created courts, would continue to adhere to the Court's more controversial rulings suggest the difficulty a Congress bent upon mitigating the impact of a Supreme Court ruling might encounter.[74]

Nor is it our purpose to suggest that Congress should or is even likely to exercise the powers it possesses under the exceptions clause, although the democratic character of judicial review depends upon the acknowledgement of its right to do so. Whether we like it or not, and I am inclined to believe we should, Congress can, if it wishes, do much to influence the behavior of the judiciary. Its failure to do so, often in the face of considerable provocation cannot be explained by recourse to a view of the constitutional system in which relations between the branches are determined by self interest alone.[75]

The perpetuation of our system of government does not rely simply upon the assignment of specific powers to each of the branches of government. A self-interested or purely mechanical explanation of American politics cannot account for the development of judicial power, or for the remarkable restraint Congress has shown toward the judiciary, even when confronted by decisions with which it vehemently disagrees. It has been deterred not by the existence of judicial review, but by its commitment to the integrity of our constitutional system, and its fear that without an

---

72. For a comprehensive review of such arguments, see Ralph A. Rossum, "Congress, the Constitution, and the Appellate Jurisdiction of the Supreme Court: The Letter and the Spirit of the Exceptions Clause," *William and Mary Law Review* vol. 24 (1983), pp. 398-423.
73. *Federalist* #51, p. 322.
74. Rossum, pp. 423-26.
75. *Federalist* #51, p. 322.

independent judiciary the nation would suffer.[76] Like judicial review, the power given to Congress by the exceptions clause is liable to abuse. But there is no simple check for every abuse of authority. As Congressman Henderson observed, "The Government of our country is predicated upon a reasonable confidence in those who administer our public affairs."[77] Belief in judicial review should not be permitted to obscure the necessity of virtue and statesmanship, on the part of legislators as well as judges.

The judiciary has benefitted from the belief in law, a belief shared by the people as well as its legislators. It is that belief, and not judicial assertions to the effect that the Supreme Court's interpretation of the Constitution is definitive or that the Constitution means whatever the judges say it does, which is the basis for the strength of the modern judiciary. The perpetuation of its present authority will depend upon the willingness of Congress and the American people to continue to exhibit the self-restraint they have shown in the past. Any theory of judicial power must be supplemented by a doctrine of Congressional self-restraint

The restraint either branch exhibits will be determined by its interpretation of the Constitution. Whether or not an interpretation favorable to the exercise of judicial power prevails cannot be taken for granted. Not the formal powers of the Court, but the respect Americans still harbor for "parchment barriers," reinforced by their belief that the Court is not truly free to interpret the Constitution however it wishes, will continue to be the foundation of judicial power. The Court's present success should not blind us to the wisdom of Justice Jackson's observation that "not one of the basic power conflicts which precipitated the Roosevelt struggle against the judiciary has been eliminated or settled, and the old conflict between the branches of the government remains, ready to break out whenver the provocation becomes sufficient."[78]

---

76. Congress has rarely exercised its power to create exceptions; its principal use was after the Civil War, in order to ensure the validity of its reconstruction program.

77. *Annals*, 7th Cong., 1st Sess., p. 528.

78. Robert Jackson, *The Supreme Court in the American System of Government* (New York: Harper & Row, 1955), p. 9.

Does the Supreme Court Have the Last Word on Constitutional Law?

Louis Fisher

In such cases as *Marbury v. Madison* (1803), *Cooper v. Aaron* (1958), and *Baker v. Carr* (1962), the Supreme Court has insisted that it alone delivers the "final word" on the meaning of the Constitution.[1] Yet Congressional and executive practices over a number of years have had a major influence on constitutional questions. Many of their determinations never reach the courts or, when they do, are avoided through the use of threshold tests erected by the judiciary. Often the Court decides to ratify the customs and accommodations reached by the other two branches. Even when the Court strikes down their actions, it is often only a matter of time before a persistent Congress gets its way.

This essay examines the basis for judicial review, draws a distinction between its application against the states (as part of the Supremacy Clause) and its use against the coequal Congress and President, and reviews the dynamic process in which all three branches interact in a dialogue to shape the meaning of the Constitution. In this sense, no one branch is ever final if the Nation remains unsettled and seriously divided about a constitutional issue.

Sources of Judicial Review

When legislators or the chief executive make unpopular decisions the voters may remove them at the next election. The ballot box represents a periodic test of the legitimacy of elected officers. The federal judiciary cannot draw legitimacy from elections. When judges announce an unpopular decision, citizens want to know on what authority courts may overturn the judgments of elected officials who also take an oath to support the Constitution. Judges must be able to identify persuasive and authoritative sources: constitutional language, pre-*Marbury* precedents, principles

---

1. The views expressed here are those solely of the author, and do not reflect the official position of the Congressional Research Service.

announced by the Marshall Court, and convincing evidence that has accumulated since that time.

Constitutional Language

Article III, Section 1, of the Constitution provides that "The judicial Power of the United States, shall be vested in one Supreme Court, and in such inferior Courts as the Congress may from time to time ordain and establish . . . ." Section 2 extends the judicial power to various cases and controversies, but there is not a specific grant of power to declare an act of Congress, the President, or state government unconstitutional. The absence of an explicit grant is not conclusive. An implied power may exist. For example, although the Constitution provides no authority for the President to assert executive privilege, or remove appointees from office, or issue executive orders which have the force of law, or enter into international agreements without the advice and consent of the Senate, the Supreme Court has considered those powers implicit in Article II.[2] Similarly, the Court has found an implied power for Congress to investigate, to issue subpoenas, and to exercise the power of contempt.[3]

The power of judicial review can be implied from two sources. Under Art. III, section 2, the judicial power extends to all cases "arising under this Constitution, the Laws of the United States, and Treaties made . . . ." Moreover, the Supremacy Clause in Art. VI provides that the Constitution, federal laws "made in Pursuance thereof," and all treaties shall be the supreme law of the land, "and the Judges in every State shall be bound thereby, any Thing in the Constitution or Laws of any State to the Contrary notwithstanding." This language requires federal courts to review the actions of state governments and might invite review of Congressional statutes that are not "in pursuance" of the Constitution. However, judicial review over Presidential and Congressional acts raises a wholly different dimension: the relations between coordinate branches of the national government. Justice Holmes once remarked: "I do not think the United

---

2. United States v. Nixon, 418 U.S. 683 (1974) (executive privilege); Myers v. United States, 272 U.S. 52 (1926) (removal power); Contractors Ass'n of Eastern Pa. v. Secretary of Labor, 442 F.2d 159 (3d Cir. 1971), cert. denied, 404 U.S. 854 (1971) (executive orders); Dames & Moore v. Regan, 453 U.S. 654 (1981) (executive agreements).

3. McGrain v. Daugherty, 273 U.S. 135 (1927) (investigations); Eastland v. United States Servicemen's Fund, 421 (U.S. 491, 505 (1975) (subpoenas); Anderson v. Dunn, 19 U.S. (6 Wheat.) 204, 228 (1821) (contempt power).

States would come to an end if [the Supreme Court] lost [its] power to declare an act of Congress void. I do think the Union would be imperiled if we could not make that declaration as to the laws of the several States."[4]

The Pre-Marbury Precedents

The best-known American challenge to an act of Parliament came in 1761 when James Otis argued the Writs of Assistance Case in Boston. He claimed that British customs officials were not empowered by Parliament to use general search warrants. Even if Parliament had authorized the writs of assistance, Otis said that the statute would be "against the constitution," "against natural equity," and therefore void.[5] In 1766 a Virginia court held the Stamp Act unconstitutional. On the eve of the Declaration of Independence, Judge Cushing in Massachusetts instructed a jury that it should treat acts of Parliament in violation of fundamental law as "void" and "inoperative."[6]

The proposition that courts could void an act of Parliament appears in Chief Justice Coke's opinion in *Dr. Bonham's Case* (1610). He said that when an act of Parliament "is against common right and reason, or repugnant, or impossible to be performed, the common law will control it, and adjudge such Act to be void."[7] A few British judges in the seventeenth and eighteenth centuries cited Coke's argument, but the principle of judicial review never took root in English soil.[8] In 1884 the Supreme Court noted: "notwithstanding what was attributed to Lord Coke in *Bonham's Case* . . . the omnipotence of Parliament over the common law was absolute, even against common right and reason.[9]

For their understanding of British law the framers relied mainly on Blackstone's *Commentaries*, which stated the case for parliamentary supremacy with singular clarity. For those who believed that acts of Parliament contrary to reason were void, he offered this advice:

> But if the parliament will positively enact a thing to be done which is unreasonable, I know of no power that can control it: and the examples

---

4. Collected Legal Papers 295-96 (1920).
5. Edward S. Corwin, The Doctrine of Judicial Review 30 (1914).
6. Id. at 32.
7. 77 Eng. Rep. 646, 652 (1610).
8. Day v. Savadge, 80 Eng. Rep. 235, 237 (1614); The City of London v. Wood, 88 Eng. Rep. 1592, 1602 (1702).
9. Hurtado v. California, 110 U.S. 516, 531 (1884).

usually alleged in support of this sense of the rule do none of them prove, that, where the main object of a statute is unreasonable, the judges are at liberty to reject it; for that were to set the judicial power above that of the legislature, which would be subversive of all government.[10]

Although *Dr. Bonham's Case* provides inadequate support for the American concept of judicial review, it was accepted as good law and precedent by those who wanted to break with England. Intellectual justifications were needed to neutralize the appearance of impetuous and impulsive behavior. But "voiding" the acts of Parliament did not automatically deliver the power of judicial review to American courts, especially those at the national level.

From independence to the framing of the Constitution, some of the state judges challenged the acts of their legislatures. Scholars disagree on the strength of these precedents, but decisions providing support for the theory of judicial review were handed down by judges in Virginia, New Jersey, New York, Connecticut, Rhode Island, and North Carolina. The language used by these judges in holding state laws invalid was often more bold than the results they achieved.[11]

The Framer's Intent

By the time of the convention, some of the framers expected judicial review to be part of the new government. In reading their statements at the convention and during the ratification debates, it is important to keep their thoughts in context and recognize conflicting statements. The framers did not have a clear or fully developed theory of judicial review.

The farmers wanted to replace the Articles of Confederation to make the central government more effective. They worried that thirteen sets of state courts would announce contradictory rulings on matters of national concern. In *Federalist* No. 80, Hamilton said that thirteen independent courts of final jurisdiction "over the same causes, arising from the same laws, is a hydra in government from which nothing but contradiction and confusion can proceed." The convention resolved that problem by adopting the Supremacy Clause. Judicial review over Presidential and Congres-

---

10. William Blackstone, Commentaries on the Laws of England, Book One, sect. 3, at 91 (Oxford 1775).
11. Charles Groves Haines, The American Doctrine of Judicial Supremacy 88-120 (1932).

sional actions was a matter of much greater delicacy. By 1787 the framers had become alarmed about legislative overreaching. In *Federalist* No. 48, Madison wrote that the "legislative department is everywhere extending the sphere of its activity and drawing all power into its impetuous vortex." Several delegates to the Philadelphia Convention expressed the same concern.[12] But giving the courts the final say over Congressional acts was an extremely radical notion.

A common pastime of constitutional scholars is counting the heads of framers who favored judicial review. Depending on which year he wrote, Edward S. Corwin vacillated on the statistics, ranging from a high of seventeen framers to a low of five or six.[13] Other studies were also flavored by a crusading spirit, either to "prove" the legitimacy of judicial review[14] or to chop away at its foundations.[15] The issue remains unsettled, and this very ambiguity adds an inhibiting force to judicial activism.

Judicial review was discussed at the convention as a means of checking Congress and the states. The most important debate was over the veto of legislation passed by Congress. Randolph proposed a Council of Revision consisting of the "executive and a convenient number of the National Judiciary ... with authority to examine every act of the National Legislature before it shall operate, & every act of a particular Legislature before a Negative thereon shall be final; and that the dissent of the said Council shall amount to a rejection, unless the Act of the National Legislature be again passed . . . ."[16] Some commentators accept the elimination of the revisionary council as proof that the framers rejected judicial review. However, one of the arguments against the Council was the *availability* of judicial review. As reported by Madison: "Mr. Gerry doubts whether the Judiciary ought to form a part of it, as they will have a sufficient check agst. encroachments on their own department by their exposition of the laws, which involved a power of deciding on their Constitutionality. In some States the Judges had (actually) set aside laws as being agst. the Constitution. This was done too with general approbation."[17] King supported Gerry's argument after observing that the Justices of the Supreme Court

---

12. 1 Max Farrand, ed., Records of the Federal Convention 254 (Wilson); 2 Farrand 35 (Madison), 110 (Madison), and 288 (Mercer) (1937).
13. Leonard W. Levy, ed., Judicial Review and the Supreme Court 3-4 (1967).
14. Charles A. Beard, the Supreme Court and the Constitution (1912).
15. Louis B. Boudin, Government by Judiciary (1932) and William W. Crosskey, Politics and the Constitution (1953).
16. 1 Farrand 21.
17. Id. at 97.

"ought to be able to expound the law as it should come before them, free from the bias of having participated in its formation." This comment provides broad support for judicial review, whereas Gerry appeared to restrict it to legislative encroachments.

Also debated was the need for a Congressional veto over proposed state legislation. That idea was rejected for two reasons. The addition of the Supremacy Clause would presumably handle any conflicts between national law and state legislation. Moreover, the state courts could exercise judicial review to control legislative excesses. They "would not consider as valid any law contravening the Authority of the Union," and if such laws were not set aside by the judiciary they "may be repealed by a National law."[18] Madison later said that a law "violating a constitution established by the people themselves, would be considered by the Judges as null & void."[19] These statements were clearly limited to judicial review at the *state*, not the national, level. A year later, writing to Jefferson, Madison denied that the Constitution empowered the Court to strike down acts of Congress, for that would have made the judiciary "paramount in fact to the Legislature, which was never intended and can never be proper.[20]

The *Federalist Papers* include several essays that speak strongly for judicial review. The principal essay, Hamilton's *Federalist* No. 78, is designed partly to allay state fears about the power of the central government, but certainly he articulates a lucid case for judicial review. The restrictions that the Constitution places on the legislative authority, such as the prohibition on bills of attainder and ex post facto laws, "can be preserved in practice no other way than through the medium of courts of justice, whose duty it must be to declare all acts contrary to the manifest tenor of the Constitution void. Without this, all the reservations of particular rights or privileges would amount to nothing."

Hamilton denied that this power would "imply a superiority of the judiciary to the legislative power." His basic principle is that no authority

---

18. 2 Farrand 27-28 (Sherman and Morris).

19. Id. at 93.

20. 5 Writings of James Madison 294 (Hunt ed. 1904). Support for judicial review was also expressed by James Wilson at the Pennsylvania ratification convention (2 Jonathan Elliot, ed., Debates in the Several State Conventions on the Adoption of the Federal Constitution 445), by Oliver Ellsworth at the Connecticut ratification convention (id. at 196; see also Samuel Adams' comments in Massachusetts, id. at 131), and by John Marshall at the Virginia ratification convention (3 Elliot 553; see also George Nicholas, id. at 443).

can act in a manner contrary to the power delegated to it, for this would affirm "that the deputy is greater than his principal; that the servant is above his master; that the representatives of the people are superior to the people themselves; that men acting by virtue of powers, may do not only what their powers do not authorize, but what they forbid." To allow Congress to be the judge of its own powers would enable "the representatives of the people to substitute their *will* to that of their constituents." Hamilton dismissed the possibility that judges would abuse their powers and "substitute their own pleasure to the constitutional intentions of the legislature." As he noted earlier in the essay, the courts "may truly be said to have neither FORCE nor WILL, but merely judgment."

Hamilton's reasoning is not without its limitations. If Congress could not go beyond the power delegated to it without affirming that "the deputy is greater than his principal," how could the courts exercise the power of judicial review which is not, at least not expressly, delegated to it? If it is impermissible to let Congress be the judge of its own powers, for fear that the representatives will substitute "their *will* to that of their constituents," how will the courts be kept in check? Why should they be entrusted to be the judge of *their* powers? Is it realistic to expect courts to exercise only judgment and never will?

The arguments in *Federalist* No. 78 were later borrowed by John Marshall to buttress his *Marbury* opinion. Hamilton's enthusiasm for judicial review is somewhat suspect, since he appears to be a late convert to the cause. His plan of government presented to the 1787 convention did not grant this power to the judiciary.[21] State laws contrary to the Constitution would be "utterly void" but he did not identify the judiciary as the voiding agency.[22]

In the years between ratification and *Marbury v. Madison*, the issue of judicial review was debated often in Congress, but not necessarily with any consistency. When Madison introduced the Bill of Rights in the House of Representatives, he predicted that once they were incorporated into the Constitution, "independent tribunals of justice will consider themselves in a peculiar manner the guardians of those rights; they will be an impenetrable bulwark against every assumption of power in the Legislative or Executive."[23] But nine days later, during debate on the President's removal power, he denied that Congress should defer to the courts on this

---

21. 1 Farrand 282-283, 302-11; 3 Farrand 617-30.
22. 1 Farrand 293.
23. 1 Annals of Cong. 439 (June 8, 1789).

constitutional issue. He begged to know on what principle could it be contended "that any one department draws from the Constitution greater powers than another, in marking out the limits of the powers of the several departments?" If questions arose on the boundaries between the branches, he did not see "that any one of these independent departments has more right than another to declare their sentiments on that point.[24] In 1791, when proponents of a national bank cited judicial review as a possible check on unconstitutional legislation, Madison was unpersuaded and voted against the bank.[25]

The Road to Marbury

Federal courts reviewed both national and state legislation prior to *Marbury*. In *Hayburn's Case* (1792), three circuit courts held divergent views on an act of Congress that appointed federal judges to serve as commissioners for claims settlement. Their decisions could be set aside by the Secretary of War. One of the courts agreed to serve. The other two believed that the statute was "unwarranted" because it required federal judges to perform nonjudicial duties and to render what was essentially an advisory opinion. The Supreme Court postponed decision until the next term, and by that time Congress had repealed the offending sections and removed the Secretary's authority to veto decisions rendered by judges.[26] In 1794, a year after Congress repaired the statute, the Supreme Court decided that the original statute would have been unconstitutional if it sought to place nonjudicial powers on the circuit courts. Interestingly, this decision was not published until 1851.[27] The use of this 1794 case as a precedent for judicial review is rendered suspect by the fact that the statutory provision no longer existed.

Between 1791 and 1799, federal courts began to challenge and strike down a number of state laws.[28] With regard to national legislation, in *Hylton v. United States* (1796) the Supreme Court upheld the constitutionality of a Congressional statute that imposed a tax on carriages. If the Court had the authority to uphold an act of Congress, presumably it had the

---

24. Id. at 500 (June 17, 1789).
25. 12 Annals of Cong. 1978-79 (Feb. 4, 1791).
26. 2 Dall. 409 (1792). See 1 Stat. 243 (1792) and 1 Stat. 324 (1793).
27. United States v. Yale Todd, 13 How. 51.
28. 1 Charles Warren, The Supreme Court in United States History 65-69 (1937).

authority to strike one down. Otherwise, it would be engaged in a frivolous and idle enterprise. Justice Chase said it was unnecessary *"at this time, for me to determine, whether this court, constitutionally possesses the power to declare an act of Congress void* ... but if the court have such power, I am free to declare, that I will never exercise it, *but in a very clear case*."[29] Two years later the Court upheld the constitutionality of another Congressional act, this time involving the process of amending the Constitution.[30]

Three other cases between 1795 and 1800 explored the authority of federal judges to declare state acts unconstitutional. In the first case, a circuit court decided that a Pennsylvania law was unconstitutional and void.[31] In the second, Supreme Court Justices offered differing views on the existence and scope of judicial review.[32] In the third, Justice Chase said that even if it were agreed that a statute contrary to the Constitution would be void, "it still remains a question, where the power resides to declare it void." The "general opinion," he said, is that the Supreme Court could declare an act of Congress unconstitutional, "but there is no adjudication of the Supreme Court itself upon the point."[33]

From 1789 to 1802, eleven state judiciaries exercised judicial review over state statutes.[34] The assertion of power by the national judiciary was much more sensitive, and yet even the Jeffersonian Republicans rebuked the federal courts for not striking down the repressive Alien and Sedition Acts.[35] In that same year Jefferson looked to the courts to protect basic rights: "the laws of the land, administered by upright judges, would protect you from any exercise of power unauthorized by the Constitution of the United States."[36]

The election of 1800 marked a pivotal point for the nation. Although formally neutral between Britain and France, America was rapidly dividing into two warring camps. The Federalist Party was pro-British, while the Jeffersonian Republicans supported the French. Efforts by the Adams administration to limit Republican criticism led to the Alien and Sedition

---

29. 3 Dall. 171, 175 (1796) (emphasis in original).
30. Hollingsworth v. Virginia, 3 Dall. 378 (1798).
31. Vanhorne's Lessee v. Dorrance, 2 Dall. 304 (1795).
32. Calder v. Bull, 3 Dall. 386 (1798).
33. Cooper v. Telfair, 4 Dall. 14, 19 (1800).
34. Haines, supra note 10, at 148-64.
35. Warren, supra note 27, at 215.
36. 10 Writings of Thomas Jefferson 61 (Memorial ed. 1903). Letter to A. H. Rowan, Sept. 26, 1798.

Acts, further exacerbating partisan strife. When the Jeffersonians swept the elections of 1800, the Federalists looked for ways to salvage their dwindling political power.

Early in 1801, with a few weeks remaining of the Federalist Congress, two bills were passed to create a number of federal judges and D.C. justices of the peace.[37] Within a matter of days President Adams nominated Federalists to the new posts, much to the outrage of Republicans. John Marshall was at that point serving as Secretary of State, although he had already been appointed to the Supreme Court for the next term. The commissions of office were processed, sent to the Senate, and confirmed. Some of the commissions, William Marbury's among them, were never delivered.

Upon assuming the Presidency, Jefferson ordered that the commissions be withheld. The administration also urged Congress to repeal the Circuit Court Act (with its additional judgeships) and to block the anticipated 1802 term of the Supreme Court. Congress complied.[38] Partisan bitterness increased in the spring of 1801 when two Federalist judges instructed a district attorney to prosecute a newspaper which had published an attack on the judiciary. The jury refused to indict, but the Republicans saw this as additional evidence that the Federalists were engaged in a national conspiracy.[39] As part of a counterattack, the House of Representatives impeached District Judge John Pickering (a Federalist), contemplated the removal of Justice Chase from the Supreme Court, and planned the removal of other Federalist judges, including John Marshall.[40]

It was in this tense political climate that William Marbury brought his case directly to the Supreme Court under Section 13 of the Judiciary Act of 1789, which empowered the Court to issue writs of mandamus "in cases warranted by the principles and usages of law, to any courts appointed, or persons holding office, under the authority of the United States."[41] Marshall's options were circumscribed by one overpowering fact: whatever technical ground he used to rule against the administration, any order directing Madison to deliver the commissions was sure to be ignored. If the Court's order could be dismissed with impunity, the judiciary's power

---

37. 2 Stat. 89, 103 (1801).

38. Id. at 132, 156 (1802).

39. George Lee Haskins and Robert A. Johnson, 2 History of the Supreme Court of the United States: Foundations of Powers: John Marshall 1616-62 (1981).

40. Jerry W. Knudson, "The Jeffersonian Assault on the Federalist Judiciary, 1801-1805; Political Forces and Press Reaction," 14 Am. J. Leg. Hist. 55 (1970).

41. 1 Stat. 81 (1789).

and prestige would suffer greatly. Marshall chose a tactic he used in future years. He would appear to absorb a short-term defeat in exchange for a long-term victory. The decision has been called a "masterwork of indirection, a brilliant example of Marshall's capacity to sidestep danger while seeking to court it, to advance in one direction while his opponents are looking in another."[42]

The opinion acknowledged the merits of Marbury's case but denied that the Court had power to issue the mandamus. Through a strained reading, Marshall concluded that Section 13 expanded the original jurisdiction of the Court and thereby violated Article III of the Constitution. He maintained that Congress could alter the boundaries only of appellate jurisdiction. Announcing that the statute conflicted with the Constitution and that judges take an oath of office to support the Constitution, Marshall claimed that the power of constitutional interpretation was vested exclusively in the judiciary.[43]

The decision has its share of shortcomings. But Marshall, encircled by hostile political forces, decided that it was time to strike boldly for judicial independence. Instead of citing historical and legal precedents, all of which could have been challenged and picked apart by his opponents, Marshall reached to a higher plane and grounded his case on what appeared to be self-evident, universal principles. His decision seems to march logically and inexorably toward the only possible conclusion.

The power to strike down unconstitutional actions by coordinate branches of government was not used again until 1857, in *Dred Scott v. Sandford*.[44] Judicial review of state legislative actions was established in two decisions in 1809 and 1810. In the first, state officials in Pennsylvania attempted to resist a decree issued by a federal judge.[45] The state's resistance collapsed when President Madison lent his support to the execution of a decree sanctioned by the Supreme Court.[46] In 1810, the Court struck down an act of a state legislature as unconstitutional,[47] and two subsequent decisions established the Court's authority to review state court

---

42. Robert G. McCloskey, The American Supreme Court 40 (1960). For the evolution of judicial review prior to *Marbury*, see Julius Goebel, Jr., 1 History of the Supreme Court of the United States: Antecedents and Beginnings to 1801 (1971).

43. 5 U.S. (1 Cr.) 137 (1803).

44. 60 U.S. (19 How.) 393 (1857).

45. United States v. Peters, 9 U.S. (5 Cr.) 115 (1809).

46. Annals of Cong, 11th Cong. 2269. See Warren, supra note 27, at 382.

47. Fletcher v. Peck, 10 U.S. (6 Cr.) 87, 136-39 (1810).

decisions, not only in cases involving two private parties[48] but also where the state is a party.[49]

The Last-word Doctrine

Beginning with Chief Justice Marshall's declaration in *Marbury v. Madison* that "[it] is emphatically the province and duty of the judicial department to say what the law is,"[50] the Supreme Court has insisted that it alone delivers the "final word" on the meaning of the Constitution. According to a 1958 decision, *Marbury* "declared the basic principle that the federal judiciary is supreme in the exposition of the law of the Constitution . . . ."[51] The Court reasserted this principle in 1962. The exercise of constitutional interpretation "is a responsibility of this Court as ultimate interpreter of the Constitution."[52]

Being "ultimate interpreter" is not the same as being exclusive interpreter. The courts expect other branches of government to interpret the Constitution in their initial deliberations. "In the performance of assigned constitutional duties each branch of the Government must initially interpret the Constitution, and the interpretation of its powers by any branch is due great respect from the others."[53] Congressional interpretations are given substantial weight in some circumstances, even to the point of becoming the controlling factor.[54]

Congressional and executive practices over a number of years can be instrumental in fixing the meaning of the Constitution.[55] The Supreme

48. Martin v. Hunter's Lessee, 14 U.S. (1 Wheat.) 304 (1816).
49. Cohens v. Virginia, 6 Wheat. 264 (1821).
50. 5 U.S. (1 Cr.) 137, 177 (1803).
51. Cooper v. ron, 358 U.S. 1, 18 (1958).
52. Baker v. Carr, 369 U.S. 186, 211 (1962). The notion that the Supreme Court is the "ultimate interpreter" was repeated in Powell v. McCormack, 395 U.S. 486, 549 (1969).
53. United States v. Nixon, 418 U.S. 683, 703 (1974).
54. *See* Rostker v. Goldberg, 453 U.S. 57, 64 (1981). (In the context of a challenge to male-only registration for military service, the Court noted: "The customary deference accorded the judgments of Congress is certainly appropriate when, as here, Congress specifically considered the Act's constitutionality.")
55. *See* Stuart v. Laird, 5 U.S. (1 Cr.) 299, 309 (1803). (Dismissing a challenge that the Judiciary Act of 1789 was unconstitutional, the Court stated that "practice, and acquiescence under it, for a period of several years, commencing with the organization of the judicial system, affords an irresistible answer, and has indeed fixed the construction. It is a contemporary interpretation of the most forcible nature.")

Court, upholding the President's removal power in 1903, based its ruling largely on the "universal practice of the government for over a century."[56] Presidential action in which Congress acquiesced can become a justification for the exercise of power.[57] The cumulative force of these customs has transformed the Constitution over time.[58]

Inviting a Challenge on Finality

In a sentence rendered almost hypnotic by its elegance, Justice Jackson said that decisions by the Supreme Court "are not final because we are infallible, but we are infallible only because we are final."[59] The historical record amply proves that the Court is neither final nor infallible. Judicial decisions rest undisturbed only to the extent that Congress, the President, and the general public find the decisions convincing, reasonable, and acceptable. Otherwise, the debate on constitutional principles will continue.

Being "ultimate interpreter" does not grant the judiciary superiority in the sense that final judgments are unreviewable. Eight years before writing *Dred Scott*, Chief Justice Taney wrote a dissenting opinion in which he noted that the Court's opinion "upon the construction of the Constitution is always open to discussion when it is supposed to have been founded in error, and that its judicial authority should hereafter depend altogether on the force of the reasoning by which it is supported."[60] Referring to Taney's dissent, Justice Frankfurter spoke about the need for "judicial exegesis" in interpreting broadly phrased charters like the Constitution. To Frankfurter, "the ultimate touchstone of constitutionality is the Constitution itself and not what we have said about it."[61]

---

56. Shurtleff v. United States, 189 U.S. 311, 316 (1903).

57. *See* United States v. Midwest Oil Co., 236 U.S. 459, 474 (1915). (Presidential decisions over a period of years "clearly indicate that the long-continued practice, known to and acquiesced in by Congress, would raise a presumption that the withdrawals had been made in pursuance of its consent or of a recognized administrative power of the Executive in the management of the public lands.")

58. For an effective critique of court doctrines on custom and acquiescence, see Michael J. Glennon, "The Use of Custom in Resolving Separation of Powers Disputes," 64 B.U.L. Rev. 109 (1984).

59. Brown v. Allen, 344 U.S. 443, 540 (1953) (Jackson, J., concurring).

60. The Passenger Cases, 48 U.S. (7 How.) 283, 470 (1849) (Taney, C. J., dissenting).

61. Graves v. New York ex rel. O'Keefe, 306 U.S. 466, 491-92 (1939).

What is "final" at one stage of our political development may be reopened at some later date, leading to fresh interpretation and overruling of past judicial doctrines. Courts are the ultimate interpreter of a particular case, but not of the larger issue of which that case is a part. Consequently, they signal their willingness at times to review previous decisions and perhaps overturn them.

A good example of this attitude occurred during the 1930s and 1940s. After Congress and the Court had gone back and forth on a tax issue, the Court invited Congress to pass legislation and challenge previous rulings:

> There is no reason to doubt that this Court may fall into error as may other branches of the Government. Nothing in the history or attitude of this Court should give rise to legislative embarrassment if in the performance of its duty a legislative body feels impelled to enact laws which may require the Court to reexamine its previous judgment or doctrine.[62]

The Court admitted that it is less able than other branches "to extricate itself from error. It can reconsider a matter only when it is again properly brought before it as a case or controversy."[63] Statutory action is often necessary to permit the Court to review and possibly overturn its previous holdings. Congress may feel that it is not only its right but its duty to present a question once more to the Court, hoping to elicit a more favorable ruling.[64] By overruling itself, the Court admits its ability on an earlier occasion to commit error.

A type of implicit invitation appeared in *Leisy v. Hardin* (1900). Building on the "original package" doctrine of *Brown v. Maryland* (1827),[65] the Court ruled that a state's prohibition of intoxicating liquors could not be applied to original packages or kegs. Only after the original package was broken into smaller packages could the state exercise control. The Court qualified its opinion by saying that the states could not exclude incoming articles "without Congressional permission."[66]

As a result of the Court's decision, imaginative entrepreneurs opened up "original-package saloons" making it impossible for the states to exercise any control. Brewers and distillers from outside the state could pack-

---

62. Helvering v. Griffiths, 318 U.S. 371, 400-401 (1943).
63. Id. at 401.
64. Compare Ashton v. Cameron County Dist., 298 U.S. 513 (1936), striking down sections of the Bankruptcy Act of 1934, and United States v. Bekins, 304 U.S. 27, 33 (1938), sustaining Chapter X of the Bankruptcy Act of 1937.
65. 25 U.S. (12 Wheat.) 419, 441 (1827).
66. Leisy v. Hardin, 135 U.S. 100, 125 (1890).

age their goods "even in the shape of a vial containing a single drink."[67] Within a matter of months Congress was considering legislation to over-turn the decision. The feisty attitude in Congress is reflected in remarks by Senator George Edmunds of Vermont. The opinions of the Supreme Court regarding Congress "are of no more value to us than ours are to it. We are just as independent of the Supreme Court of the United States as it is of us, and every judge will admit it." If members of Congress con-cluded that the Court had made an error "are we to stop and say that is the end of the law and the mission of civilization in the United States for that reason? I take it not." Further consideration by the Court might produce a different result: "as they have often done, it may be their mission next year to change their opinion and say that the rule ought to be the other way."[68]

Congress quickly overturned the decision by passing legislation that made intoxicating liquors, upon their arrival in a state or territory, subject to the police powers "to the same extent and in the same manner as though such liquids or liquors had been produced in such State or Terri-tory, and shall not be exempt therefrom by reason of being introduced therein in original packages or otherwise."[69] The Supreme Court upheld the constitutionality of this statute.[70]

Uninvited Collisions

After courts hand down a decision, a disappointed Congress may decide to test the firmness of the Court's conclusion by passing new legislation and provoking further litigation. The history of child labor legislation offers a striking example. The first child labor law passed by Congress in 1916 was based on the commerce power. The Supreme Court invalidated that statute in 1918,[71] Congress bounced back a year later with another statute on child labor, this time based on the taxing power. The Court struck it down in 1922.[72] Undaunted, Congress passed a constitu-tional amendment in 1924 to give it the power to regulate child labor.[73] By 1937, however, only twenty-eight of the necessary thirty-six states had

---

67. 21 Cong. Rec. 4954 (1890).
68. Id. at 4964.
69. 26 Stat. 313 (1890).
70. In re Rahrer, 140 U.S. 545 (1891).
71. Hammer v. Dagenhart, 247 U.S. 251 (1918).
72. Bailey v. Drexel Furniture Co., 259 U.S. 20 (1922).
73. 65 Cong. Rec. 7295, 10142 (1924).

ratified the amendment. On its final effort, Congress returned to the commerce power by including a child labor provision in the Fair Labor Standards Acts of 1938.[74] This time a unanimous Court upheld the statute.[75]

In 1956 the Supreme Court invalidated a state sedition law because the Smith Act, passed by Congress, regulated the same subject. The Court concluded that it had been the intent of Congress to occupy the whole field of sedition.[76] The author of the Smith Act promptly denied that he ever intended the result reached by the Court. Congressional committees reported legislation to permit Federal-state concurrent jurisdiction in the area of sedition and subversion, and to prohibit courts from using intent or implication to decide questions of federal preemption over state activities. X These bills were never enacted.[77] In 1959, however, while these bills were still under consideration, the Court held that a state could investigate subversive activities against itself. To this extent state and federal sedition laws could coexist.[78] The decision in 1959 satisfied Congressional critics who thought the preemption doctrine announced by the Court in 1956 intruded upon state sovereignty.

In 1983 the Supreme Court struck down all forms of the legislative veto, which had served to accommodate legislative and executive interests ever since 1932.[79] There has been no head-on collision between Congress and the courts on the legislative veto, but the record since 1983 is filled with instances in which Congressional committees continue to exercise a veto over agency actions, not only indirectly but directly.[80] The "last word" in this area is somewhere between what the Court said and what Congress does.

---

74. 52 Stat. 1060, 1067 (1938).
75. United States v. Darby, 312 U.S. 100 (1941).
76. Pennsylvania v. Nelson, 350 U.S. 497, 504 (1956).
77. H. Rept. No. 2576, 84th Cong., 2d Sess. (1956); S. Rept. No. 2117, 84th Cong., 2d Sess. (1956); S. Rept. No. 2230, 84th Cong., 2d Sess. (1956); H. Rept. No. 1878, 85th Cong., 2d Sess. (1958); 104 Cong. Rec. 13844-65, 13993-14023, 14138-62 (1958); H. Rept. No. 422, 86th Cong., 1st Sess. (1959); 105 Cong. Rec. 11486-508, 11625-67, 11789-808 (1959).
78. Uphaus v. Wyman, 360 U.S. 72 (1959).
79. INS v. Chadha, 462 U.S. 919 (1983).
80. Louis Fisher, "Judicial Misjudgments About the Lawmaking Process: The Legislative Veto Case," 45 Pub. Adm Rev. 705 (Special Issue, November 1985).

On some constitutional issues the Court not only lacks the last word but has no word at all. When the judiciary refuses to decide a case because it falls within the category of "political question," Members of Congress and executive officials must dispose of the issue. Courts have stated their reluctance to decide an issue when there has been "a textually demonstrable constitutional commitment . . . to a coordinate political department."[81] The Constitution empowers Congress "[t]o provide for organizing, arming, and disciplining the Militia, and for governing such part of them as may be employed in the Service of the United States, reserving to the State respectively, the Appointment of the Offices, and the Authority of training the Militia according to the discipline prescribed by Congress."[82] When this clause was interpreted in the Kent State University decision, the Supreme Court regarded the supervision of the National Guard as a matter vested solely in Congress. The Court noted that "it is difficult to conceive of an area of governmental activity in which the courts have less competence."[83]

Courts also defer to Congress in cases that lack "judicially discoverable and manageable standards for resolving" a dispute.[84] Is thirteen years too long a time to allow states to ratify a constitutional amendment? The Supreme Court decided that it lacked statutory and constitutional criteria for a judicial determination of this issue. The question of a reasonable time involved "an appraisal of a great variety of relevant conditions, political, social and economic, which can hardly be said to be within the appropriate range of evidence receivable in a court of justice . . . ."[85]

Courts are loath to adjudicate when it is impossible to decide a controversy "without an initial policy determination of a kind clearly for nonjudicial discretion."[86] Did President Reagan violate the War Powers Resolution by sending military advisers to El Salvador? The fact-finding necessary to resolve this dispute rendered the case nonjusticiable because that question was "appropriate for Congressional, not judicial, investigation and determination."[87]

---

81. Baker v. Carr, 369 U.S. 186, 217 (1962).
82. U.S. Const., art. I, sect. 8, cl. 16.
83. Gilligan v. Morgan, 413 U.S. 1, 10 (1973).
84. Baker v. Carr, 369 U.S. at 217.
85. Coleman v. Miller, 307 U.S. 433, 453 (1939) (the number of years needed to ratify the Child Labor Amendment).
86. Baker v. Carr, 369 U.S. at 217.
87. Crockett v. Reagan, 558 F.Supp. 893, 898 (D.D.C. 1982), aff'd, 720 F.2d 1355 (D.C. Cir. 1983).

Other constitutional questions are denied judicial resolution because the plaintiffs are unable to establish standing. The Constitution provides an explicit safeguard for financial accountability: "[A] regular Statement and Account of the Receipts and Expenditures of all public Money shall be published from time to time."[88] A legal challenge to the CIA's covert spending ended with a Supreme Court decision stating that the plaintiff lacked standing to maintain his suit.[89] The interpretation of the Statement and Account Clause therefore is left to Congress. Thus far, Congress has concluded that publication of the expenditures of the intelligence community, even in aggregate, poses too much risk to national security.[90]

Standing also has barred adjudication of the Incompatibility Clause, which states that no officer of the United States, "shall be a Member of either House during his Continuance in Office,"[91] and the Inelligibility Clause, which prohibits Senators and Representatives from being appointed "to any civil Office under the Authority of the United States, which shall have been created, or the Emoluments whereof shall have been increased during such time."[92]

Protecting Legislative Prerogatives

On occasion there have been direct confrontations to prevent courts from deciding issues considered within the institutional prerogatives of Congress. An example occurred in 1970 when the House Committee on Internal Security released a report on "Limited Survey of Honoraria Given Guest Speakers for Engagements at Colleges and Universities." The report included the names of leftist or antiwar speakers and the amounts they received. The American Civil Liberties Union obtained a copy of the galleys and asked for an injunction. District Judge Gesell agreed that the report served no legislative purpose and was issued solely for the sake of

88. U.S. Const., art. I, sect. 9, cl. 17.
89. United States v. Richardson, 418 U.S. 166 (1974).
90. Louis Fisher, Constitutional Conflicts Between Congress and the President 249-51 (1985).
91. U.S. Const., art. I, sect. 6, cl. 2; Schlesinger v. Reservists Comm. to Stop the War, 418 U.S. 208 (1974) (class action challenging the Reserve membership of members of Congress as violating the Incompatibility Clause dismissed for lack of standing).
92. U.S. Const., art. I, sect. 6, cl. 2. See Ex parte Levitt, 302 U.S. 633 (1937); 42 Op. Att'y Gen. 381 (1969); 33 Op. Att'y Gen. 88 (1922); McClure v. Carter, 513 F.Supp. 265 (d. Idaho), aff'd sub nom. McClure v. Reagan, 454 U.S. 1025 (1981).

exposure or intimidation. He ordered the Public Printer and the Superintendent of Documents not to print the report "or any portion, restatement or facsimile thereof," with the possible exception of placing the report in the *Congressional Record*.[93]

On December 14, 1970, the House of Representatives passed a resolution that told the courts, in essence, to step back. During the course of the debate, it was explained that it was not the practice of the House to print committee reports in the *Congressional Record*.[94] Moreover, Judge Gesell's order "runs afoul not only of the speech and debate clause—article I, section 6—of the Constitution, but obstructs the execution of other constitutional commitments to the House as well, including article I, section 5, which authorizes each House to determine the rules of its proceedings, and requires each House to publish its proceedings."[95] The resolution passed by a large bipartisan margin of 302-54.[96] The new committee report, which was a "restatement" of the previous one, was printed without any further interference from the judiciary.[97]

A similar confrontation occurred in the 1980's. The dispute began with an investigation by the House Select Committee on Aging into abuses in the sale of supplemental health insurance to the elderly. Without the knowledge of George H. Benford, an independent agent of the American Family Life Assurance Company, the committee videotaped a meeting at which Benford advised two women (who had volunteered for the committee) of the company's cancer policy. Portions of the tapes were broadcast within a few weeks on the ABC Nightly News. Benford filed suit, claiming that the taping and broadcasting violated his constitutional rights. In a series of rulings a federal district court rejected the claim that televising a portion of the taped meeting was a legitimate part of the "informing function" of Congress, and held that it had inherent power to serve a subpoena duces tecum upon the Clerk of the House, requesting certain documents related to the case.[98]

The House of Representatives passed a resolution which denied the district court the documents it sought. Voting with bipartisan strength (386-22), the House regarded the court's subpoena as "an unwarranted

---

93. Hentoff v. Ichord, 318 F.Supp. 1175, 1183 (D.D.C. 1970).
94. 116 Cong. Rec. 41358 (1970).
95. Id.
96. Id. at 41373.
97. H. Rept. No. 1732, 91st Cong., 2d Sess. (1970).
98. Benford v. American Broadcasting Companies, 502 F.Supp. 1148 (D. Md. 1980); Benford v. American Broadcasting Companies, Inc., 98 F.R.D. 40 (D. Md. 1983).

and unconstitutional invasion of its Congressional prerogative to determine which of its proceedings shall be made public, and in direct contravention of the constitutional protection for Congressional investigative activity . . . ."[99] The district court upped the ante by holding the Clerk of the House in contempt.[100] The Fourth Circuit reversed that holding and quashed the district court's subpoena for lack of proper service.[101] In 1986 the suit against the Congressional defendants was dismissed.[102]

Conflicting Constitutional Values

The Supreme Court's claim that it is the exclusive or at least the final interpreter of the Constitution is especially difficult to assert when it construes not merely a particular section but balances that section against another. Although there may be some legitimate grounds, such as the framer's intent, when interpreting one section of the Constitution, there are no such guidelines for balancing competing and conflicting sections. With what interpretive tools does the Court balance individual liberties against the President's claims of national security? When must the rights of a free press yield to the interests of a fair trial? On what grounds should law enforcement prevail over a person's right to privacy? Answering these questions can resemble a quasi-legislative activity and invite Congress to step in and participate.

A 1978 decision by the Supreme Court involved a police search of a student newspaper, *The Stanford Daily*, which had taken photographs of a clash between demonstrators and police. A search warrant was issued to obtain the photographs and discover the identities of those who had assaulted police officers. The Supreme Court held that a state is not prevented from issuing a search warrant simply because the owner of a place is not reasonably suspected of criminal involvement.[103] In upholding the right of third-party searches, the Court invited the other two branches to participate by noting that the Fourth Amendment "does not prevent or advise against legislative or executive efforts to establish non-

---

99. 129 Cong. Rec. H2450 (daily ed. April 28, 1983).
100. Benford v. American Broadcasting Companies, Inc., 565 F.Supp. 139 (D. Md. 1983).
101. In re Guthrie, 733 F.2d 634 (4th Cir. 1984).
102. For further details, see Louis Fisher, "Congress and the Fourth Amendments," to be published in a special symposium issue in 1987 in *Georgia Law Review*.
103. Zucher v. Stanford Daily, 436 U.S. 547, 560 (1978).

constitutional protections against possible abuses of the search warrant procedure . . . ."[104]

The decision was promptly denounced by newspapers as a first step toward a police state. Although Congress could not pass legislation to weaken the Fourth Amendment, it could act to strengthen its protection.[105] Congress passed legislation in 1980 to place limits on newsroom searches. With certain exceptions, it required the use of a subpoena instead of a search warrant to obtain documentary materials from those who disseminate newspapers, books, broadcasts, or other similar forms of public communication.[106]

A second example of a Congressional-judicial dialogue involves the privacy rights of bank depositors. In 1972 agents from the Treasury Department's Alcohol, Tobacco, and Firearms Bureau presented grand jury subpoenas to two banks in which a suspect maintained accounts. Without advising the depositor that subpoenas had been served, the banks supplied the government with microfilms of checks, deposit slips, and other records. The Supreme Court held that a Fourth Amendment interest could not be vindicated in court by challenging such a subpoena. The Court treated the materials as business records of a bank, not private papers of a persons.[107]

Congress responded by passing the Right to Financial Privacy Act of 1978.[108] Congressman Charles Whalen explained that the primary purpose of the statute was to prevent warrantless Government searches of bank and credit records that reveal the nature of one's private affairs. The Government should not have access "except with the knowledge of the subject individual or else with the supervision of the courts."[109]

Procedural Rules vs. Constitutional Interpretation

Many decisions handed down by the courts are presented as "rules" of criminal procedure, even when constitutional questions are present. This approach allows the executive and legislative branches to exercise a coor-

---

103. Id. at 567.
104. S. Rept. No. 874, 96th Cong., 2d Sess. 4 (1980).
105. 94 Stat. 1879 (1980).
106. United States v. Miller, 425 U.S. 435, 438 (1976).
107. 92 Stat. 3617 (1978).
108. 124 Cong. Rec. 33310 (1978).

dinate role. For example, Title II of the Omnibus Crime Control and Safe Streets Act of 1968 modified three controversial Supreme Court rulings on criminal procedures. The first, *Mallory v. United States* (1957), held that suspects must be taken before a magistrate for arraignment as quickly as possible.[110] Admissions obtained from the suspect during illegal detainment could not be used against him. The Court made room for Congressional involvement by basing its decision partly on the Federal Rules of Criminal Procedure enacted by Congress.[110] The decision thus invited Congress to enter the arena and modify those rules. Congress did so: Title II established six hours as a reasonable period before arraignment.

In the second case, *Miranda v. Arizona* (1966), the Court held that confessions by criminal suspects could not be used unless the suspects had been informed of their rights by law enforcement officers.[112] The opinion discussed constitutional principles but also referred to the Federal Rules of Criminal Procedure, thus inviting Congress to contribute its own handiwork.[113] Congress did so again: Title II allowed for the admissibility of confessions if voluntarily given.[114] Trial judges would determine the issue of voluntariness after taking into consideration all the circumstances surrounding the confession, including five elements identified by Congress.[115]

In the third case, *United States v. Wade* (1967), the Court decided that if an accused was denied the right to counsel during a police lineup, the identification would be inadmissible unless the in-court identifications had an independent source or the introduction of the evidence would be harmless error.[116] The Court stated that "[l]egislative or other regulations, such as those developed by the local police departments, [might] eliminate the risks of abuse and unintentional suggestion at lineup proceedings," but that "neither Congress nor the Federal authorities have seen fit to provide a solution."[117] Title II provided that eyewitness testimony would be admissible as evidenced in any criminal prosecution, regardless of whether the accused had an attorney present at the lineup.[118]

---

109. 354 U.S. 449, 454 (1957).
110. Id. at 451.
111. 384 U.S. 436, 467-79 (1966).
112. Id. at 439-44, 445, 463, 467, 490.
113. 18 U.S.C. sect. 3501(a) (1982).
114. Id. sect. 3501(b)
115. 388 U.S. 218, 239-42 (1967).
116. Id. at 239.
117. 18 U.S.C. sect. 3502 (1982).

Thus, what appears to be constitutional interpretation by the courts is sometimes "a substructure of substantive, procedural, and remedial rules drawing their inspiration and authority from, but not required by, various constitutional provisions; in short, a constitutional common law subject to amendment, modification, or even reversal by Congress."[119]

Enforcement of the Civil War Amendments

The Thirteenth, Fourteenth, and Fifteenth Amendments give Congress the power to enforce the amendments "by appropriate legislation." In 1966 the Supreme Court adopted a broad interpretation of the power to enforce the provisions of the Fourteenth Amendment. At issue in *Katzenbach v. Morgan* was the power of Congress to prohibit New York's requirement for literacy in English as a condition for voting. Section 4(e) of the Voting Rights Act of 1965 provided that no person who had completed the sixth grade in Puerto Rico, with the language of instruction other than English, could be denied the right to vote in any election because of an inability to read or write in English. Although important constitutional issues of federalism were at stake, the Court regarded section 4(e) as a "proper exercise" of the powers granted to Congress to enforce the Fourteenth Amendment.[120] Fact-finding was a legislative, not a judicial responsibility: "It was for Congress, as the branch that made this judgment, to assess and weigh the various conflicting considerations . . . . It is not for us to review the Congressional resolution of these factors. It is enough that we be able to perceive a basis upon which the Congress might resolve the conflict as it did."[121]

One commentator claimed that the *Morgan* decision suggested that, "to some extent at least," the power of Congress to enforce the Fourteenth Amendment exempted that amendment "from the principle of Court-Congress relationships expressed by *Marbury v. Madison*, that the judiciary is the final arbiter of the meaning of the Constitution."[122] This assertion goes too far. The Court added qualifications to *Morgan*[123] and in 1970

---

118. Henry P. Monaghan, "The Supreme Court 1975 Term—Foreword: Constitutional Common Law," 89 Harv. L. Rev. 1, 2-3 (1975).

119. 384 U.S. 641, 646 (1966).

120. Id. at 653.

121. Robert A. Burt, "Miranda and Title II: A Morganatic Marriage," 1969 Sup. Ct. Rev. 81, 84.

122. 384 U.S. 653, 651-52 n. 10 (1966).

ruled that the power of Congress to enforce the Fourteenth Amendment did not allow it to lower the voting age to eighteen in state elections.[124] Nonetheless, the application of the Equal Protection Clause or the Due Process Clause in the Fourteenth Amendment depends heavily on Congressional fact-finding and judgments.

Similarly, Congress has ample powers to enforce the provisions of the Fifteenth Amendment. The Supreme Court has deferred to Congressional interpretations so long as Congress uses "any rational means to effectuate the constitutional prohibition of racial discrimination in voting."[125] Congress is "chiefly responsible" for implementing the rights created in the Fifteenth Amendment.[126] Under its enforcement powers, Congress may prohibit practices that "in and of themselves" do not violate the Fifteenth Amendment "so long as the prohibitions attacking racial discrimination in voting are 'appropriate' . . . ."[127]

Conclusions

No single institution, including the judiciary, has the final word on constitutional questions. The courts find themselves engaged in what Alexander Bickel once called a "continuing colloquy" with political institutions and society at large, a process in which constitutional principle is "evolved conversationally and not perfected unilaterally."[128] It is this process of give and take and mutual respect that permits the unelected Court to function in a democratic society.

At times the Court will admit its errors of constitutional interpretation and reverse a previous decision. Some members of the Court have the intellectual integrity to adopt Justice Jackson's attitude: "I see no reason why I should be consciously wrong today because I was unconsciously wrong yesterday."[129] Others, under the spell of stare decisis, will stick doggedly to errors of the past. It is particularly at such times that Congress, the President, and the public have a duty to prevail upon the Court to revisit and rethink anachronistic holdings.

---

123. Oregon v. Mitchell, 400 U.S. 112 (1970).
124. South Carolina v. Katzenbach, 383 U.S. 301, 324 (1966).
125. Id. at 327.
126. Rome v. United States, 446 U.S. 156, 177 (1980).
127. Alexander M. Bickel, The Least Dangerous Branch 240, 244 (1962). See Louis Fisher, "Constitutional Interpretation by Members of Congress," 63 N.C.L. Rev. 707 (1985).
128. Massachusetts v. United States, 333 U.S. 611, 639-40 (1948) (dissenting opinion).

The Judiciary: Supreme Interpreter of the Constitution?

There is no justification for deferring automatically to the judiciary because of its technical skills and political independence. Each decision by a court is subject to scrutiny and rejection by private citizens and public officials. What is "final" at one stage of our political development may be reopened at some later date, leading to revisions, fresh interpretations, and reversals of Court doctrines. Through this process of interaction among the branches, all three institutions are able to expose weaknesses, hold excesses in check, and gradually forge a consensus on constitutional issues. Also through that process, the public has an opportunity to add a legitimacy and a meaning to what might otherwise be an alien and short-lived document.

The Constitution and the Courts

Gary L. McDowell

There was a time not so long ago when constitutional interpretation was understood to move between the poles of "strict construction" and "loose construction," between what was then known as a Jeffersonian view and a Hamiltonian view .[1] That time has passed. Now constitutional interpretation is understood to move between the poles of "interpretation" and "non-interpretation." In the older jurisprudence the issue was *how* to read the Constitution; in the new, the issue is *whether* to read the Constitution. To say the very least, constitutional theory, not unlike the old gray mare, just ain't what she used to be.

The question is obvious: how did this happen? The answer is probably equally obvious: as a result of the revolution in rights spawned by the Supreme Court under Chief Justice Earl Warren. To say the least, the Warren Court administered a resounding jolt to the course of American politics. In a series of cases the Warren Court transformed the structure and processes of the federal government and, to an even greater degree, the political processes within the states. Longstanding principles such as federalism and separation of powers were no match for the Court's zeal to do justice.

But whatever effect the Warren Court had on the institutional contrivances (as Madison called them) of the Constitution, its true legacy has proved to be far more pervasive and far more problematic. As Judge J. Skelly Wright once put it in a famous article, the greatest legacy of Earl Warren's Supreme Court has been its "revolutionary influence" on the thinking of several generations of law students, students who are now professors and judges. The deepest lesson these legal scholars learned was that, in Warren's view, there need be "no theoretical gulf between law and morality."

To say that the Warren Court found an appreciative audience in the legal academy is to sorely understate the case. Accepting as an unchallenged maxim Ronald Dworkin's curious view that rights cannot be taken seriously until there has been a "fusion of constitutional law and moral

---

1. This essay is a transcript of the remarks delivered at the conference. It presents the views of the author and not necessarily those of the U. S. Department of Justice.

theory," the current generation of legal scholars has made a veritable industry of constitutional theorizing. But the new constitutional theorizing is largely aconstitutional. On the whole, these new theories have little to do with the Constitution itself, either its text (including subsequent amendments) or the intentions of those who wrote, proposed, and ratified that text. They are merely ideological justifications for a textually unmoored and historically questionable exercise of judicial power. The various theories seem to be, as Leonard Levy has said, "concocted to rationalize a growing satisfaction with judicial review among the liberal intellectuals and scholars."

Judge Robert Bork has summed up the situation this way:

> Never has so much professional talent been devoted to general theories about the role of the court under the Constitution. Surely, one might think, this is a cause of optimism, a sign of renewed vigor in American constitutionalism and scholarship . . . [But] a more pessimistic outlook may be appropriate.

As Judge Bork concludes:

> Self-confident legal institutions do not require much talking about. If this is so, then this sudden flood of innovative theories signifies not the health of scholarship and constitutionalism but is instead a sign of malaise and, quite possibly, deterioration.

The greatest tragedy of the current state of constitutional theorizing goes beyond its explicit rejection of what Attorney General Meese has called a jurisprudence of original intention. The deeper problem lies in the implicit rejection of our entire legal tradition and the ultimate abandonment of the sturdy foundation of common sense upon which that tradition was built.

I

For much of our history—certainly in the Eighteenth and throughout the Nineteenth and into the Twentieth Centuries—it was common sense to embrace the proposition that the Constitution as our fundamental law is a document with a discoverable meaning, one found in the words of the text as illuminated by the intentions of those who framed, proposed, and ratified it. This common sense approach did not involve specific results in cases or controversies; rather, it was a mode of analysis that took the written Constitution seriously. This was the mainstream of legal and constitutional thinking from 1789 into the middle part of this century.

James Madison and Alexander Hamilton, Thomas Jefferson and Edmund Randolph, John Marshall and Joseph Story, Felix Frankfurter and Robert Jackson—these are among the greatest of our statesmen, lawyers, and justices who took this approach to our Constitution and who understood that all branches of our government stood under it. And this view of the Constitution and its limiting character was assumed by judges, if not explicitly argued for, during most of our judicial history. In constitutional cases judges began by seeking to discern the original meaning of the text. In other words, they assumed its fundamental intelligibility. They understood the Constitution as law—a law that was understood to bind judges no less than anyone else.

James Madison expressed the consensus on this matter almost two centuries ago. "[If] the sense in which the Constitution was accepted and ratified by the nation," he wrote, "be not the guide in expounding it, there can be no security for a consistent and stable government, more than for a faithful exercise of its powers." This was the common sense of what legal interpretation was all about. Finding the sense or meaning of the Constitution as it was accepted and ratified by the nation, as Madison had said, required serious consideration of the words in their general and popular usage. Beyond the obvious meaning, the words had to be read in the context in which they were written; attention had to be paid to their intended effects and consequences, to the spirit or reason of the law. This mode of analysis that looked to the intention of the lawgiver as expressed in the words of the law was widely accepted. It was, in short, so common as to be second nature.

So it was that Chief Justice Marshall, writing in 1819 under the fitting pseudonym, "Friend of the Constitution," in a defense of his controversial opinion in *McCulloch v. Maryland*, stated that "the most complete evidence [is] that *intention* is the most sacred rule of interpretation." In this Marshall was merely reiterating the understanding voiced at least as long ago as 1615 by Sir Edward Coke that "in acts of parliament which are to be construed according to the intent and meaning of the makers of them, the original intent and meaning is to be observed." As the example of Marshall makes clear, when the Americans parted from England, they did not abandon this bit of juridical wisdom.

As the early Americans moved from colonies to nation and framed and ratified the Constitution, they continued to understand that the text, as illuminated by intention, was the only legitimate means of interpretation. And they had, it was generally agreed, a solid scourcebook—*The Federalist*. Even Jefferson, one of the most consistent critics of Federalists Hamilton and Marshall, embraced this celebrated work as an essential guide to sound interpretation. *The Federalist*, he wrote, is properly received "as evidence of the general opinion of those who framed, and of those who accepted the Constitution ... on questions as to its genuine meaning." Since that time nearly every sitting justice has relied on this work that Jefferson would further describe as the best exposition of the Constitution available.

This is not to suggest that constitutional interpretation was or should be easy or simple. Neither is it to say that everyone in Madison's or any other time came to the same answers. Interpretation can be and often is a difficult intellectual task and conscientious Americans have reached different, even contrary, conclusions about the meaning of certain provisions. Hamilton and Jefferson, for example, differed on the constitutionality of a National Bank. So did Marshall and President Andrew Jackson. But the fact that two people conclude differently after a serious interpretive effort does not mean that there is no correct interpretation, and certainly not that the effort to construe the Constitution according to the sense in which it was ratified and accepted by the Nation should be abandoned.

Some interpretations are straightforward: there can be no religious test for office. Some are less so. Others are difficult: some provisions are ambiguous. But it was understood from the beginning of our tradition of a written Constitution binding on us all that we must take it seriously by conscientiously seeking its original intention. As one of the first Justices, James Wilson, said: "The first and governing maxim in the interpretation of [law] ... is to discover the meaning of those who made it." A much later, 20th Century Justice, the famous Oliver Wendell Holmes, Jr., put it much the same way. A constitutional amendment, he wrote, should be read in a "sense most obvious to the common understanding at the time of its adoption."

This common sense approach to interpretation constituted the received *tradition* of our commitment to the idea of the rule of law. It was not deemed quaint or archaic to suggest that the Constitution was law limiting all governmental power, including judicial power. Indeed, to have argued otherwise would have been considered bizarre. But as I have said, during the past thirty years or so a radically new view of the Constitution has appeared. This new and radical approach holds that the Constitution's original meaning either cannot be discerned or, if discerned, cannot—more accurately, should not—be applied today. The general belief is that "judicial decisions should be gauged by their results and not by ...

their coincidence with a set of allegedly consistent doctrinal principles." This new jurisprudence argues that judges act properly when they seek to infuse the Constitution with new meanings derived from their perceptions of contemporary morality. It is only a matter of allowing judges to pour fresh ideological wine into the old constitutional bottle.

The major source of this new jurisprudence has been the law schools. In recent decades we have seen, as Judge Bork has put it, a "torrent of constitutional theorizing . . . pouring from America's law schools." Consider this new approach to the Constitution as expressed by three leading scholars. One has argued that:

> Courts . . . should work out principles of legality, equality, and the rest, revise those principles from time to time in the light of what seems to the Court *fresh moral insight*, and judge the acts of Congress, the states, and the president accordingly.

Another has suggested that:

> The Constitution is an intentionally incomplete, often deliberately indeterminate structure for the participatory evolution of political ideals and governmental practices . . . . The structural norms through which a substantive value is best preserved may be expected to vary over time and from one setting to the next.

The last of this trio has said that:

> constitutional decisionmaking has . . . an expressive function . . . . The Constitution is our Mona Lisa, our Eiffel Tower, our Marseillaise. . . . [I]f we accept the expressive function of the Court, then it must sometimes be in advance of and even in contrast to, the largely inchoate notions of the people generally.

However poetic these formulations, we must recognize that to view the Constitution as infinitely mutable and to place such a soft wax in judges' hands is to deny the document's substance and lasting power. Ultimately, this new jurisprudence denigrates the Constitution's status as law.

It is hard to imagine Madison or Hamilton discoursing about the Constitution as our Mona Lisa or referring to the "inchoate notions of the people." For they believed—and with considerable evidence—that they had crafted a document that would well serve the ordinary and competent free people who would live under it.

Yet not only is the modern theorizing at odds with our past—both the intentions of the Founders and the legal tradition that came to be built upon that sturdy foundation of common-sense—more importantly it is a jurisprudence that cannot be reconciled with the fundamental precepts of a democratic society. Our Constitution gives judges only the authority to interpret the text. And, as Justice Hugo Black once said, to interpret means to explain and expound, not to amend "the fundamental law." Such an awesome authority can lie only in the people themselves. In our form of government the people rule; and the judicial power assumed by too many legal scholars and presumed by too many judges today, violates this most sacred maxim of popular government.

Stuart Taylor of the *New York Times*, writing in *The New Republic*, has put it most accurately. "[J]udicial legislation," he has pointed out,

> erodes democratic self government. It converts judges into an unelected and illegitimate policy-making elite. Indeed, its most radical exponents evince a deep antipathy for the democratic process . . . . The urge to do good is powerful, the urge to court greatness is intoxicating. Judges should resist the sincere but arrogant assumption that they know best.

II

This is not simply a disease that infects the liberal left. Indeed, there is today a pernicious movement afoot in the often tangled underworld of jurisprudence. This new movement portends an even more egregious assault on the Constitution than we have yet seen. This new assault is the bastard child of a most unholy coupling. For the liberal left now finds itself being nuzzled up to by the economic libertarians on the right. Though their purposes differ, their premises are the same: to achieve desired results, it is necessary to free ourselves from the stifling clutch of the cold dead hand of the Founders and their theory of politics—a theory that lies at the heart of our written Constitution's delicate balance of institutional arrangements.

What is at play here is what can only be called a result-oriented jurisprudence. On the left, there are those who seek a certain and rather well-known social agenda. Their tactics come down in principle to the idea of an extraconstitutional set of rights—"penumbras formed by emanations" from the text, as Justice Douglas famously put it. The right to privacy and the right to abortion and other such rights are the hallmarks of their juridical agenda. But this view goes deeper. As its foremost judicial proponent, Justice William J. Brennan has put it, it involves constantly evolving moral values that may range from abortion to equal rights for those workers displaced by the technological revolution. The result this group seeks is personal or human rights with an ideological vengeance.

On the other side one finds the economic libertarians. Now, while all libertarians are much concerned with limiting the reach and power of government in favor of personal autonomy and privacy, the libertarian right has a more specific agenda. The object here is, in effect, to resuscitate the old—and until recently, largely discredited—doctrine of substantive due process for judicial application in the economic realm. This effort is aimed at recovering what *Locher v. New York* once gave: an extraconstitutional doctrine that seeks the preservation of certain economic liberties in the opinions of like-minded judges.

In fact the proponents of this new approach are quite explicit. The problem is not that the "Old Men" of the *Lochner* era were wrong in going outside the Constitution to find fundamental economic liberties; they erred only in not going far enough and protecting such noneconomic liberties as freedom of speech. The modern Court in similar fashion also errs only in not going far enough and thereby "arbitrarily neglecting values that have a high place in the Constitution's scheme of values." In this case, those values allegedly being neglected are economic rights. In a nutshell, the Constitution itself is deemed an insufficient guard to rights. The new libertarian quest is for a "principled activism" in the courts in behalf of "individual rights both personal and economic."

In rejecting a jurisprudence of original intention in favor of a more freewheeling judicial power, Stephen Macedo has argued that such a jurisprudence of original intention ultimately presents a "narrow interpretation of individual rights . . . supported not by the Constitution but by an ideology of majoritarianism and moral skepticism that is deeply at odds with the Constitution." He suggests the need for a principled activism born of the fusion of "constitutional interpretation and moral theory" in order to vindicate "the Constitution's authority by establishing its rightness." He goes even further:

> [T]he best reason for even acknowledging the supremacy of the Constitution is the document's conformity with our best understanding of justice. By engaging in moral reflection rather than historical research to complete the meaning of the Constitution's difficult passages, judges help justify and vindicate the Constitution's moral supremacy, help to realize the Constitution's moral aspirations, and help to ensure that we will be governed by more than the will and preferences of the most powerful [the majority].

He concludes that:

> [B]oth the text, especially the preamble and the Ninth Amendment, and our tradition direct us beyond the rights explicitly stated in the document so it is not possible to dispense with an understanding of the morality of individual rights.

At a minimum, this allegedly "higher law" tradition, this concern for extraconstitutional moral principles, extends to a concern for "judicially protected economic liberties." For from this perspective, the "Constitution lends explicit support to the values of economic freedom, private security, property rights, and liberty of contract . . . . Personal security and privacy are . . . clearly linked with property ownership." The need, he concludes, "is for conscientious interpreters of the Constitution to correct, not abandon, judicial activism."

What is interesting about this new-found fondness between the advocates of extraconstitutional property rights and the advocates of extraconstitutional personal rights is the degree to which they are willing to join ranks to undermine the true tradition of American constitutionalism —the tradition that is rooted in the firm ground of a jurisprudence of original intention. By seeking to discredit the idea that rights, to be constitutional rights, must be textually explicit, both camps expect to further their cause. The obvious discrepancy between the two will not go away—that is a battle that will remain to be fought. And it will be fought, but in the courtrooms of this nation as judges seek to determine questions of policy across the board.

The result of this strange union of conflicting theories of rights goes beyond anything seen before. Substantive Due Process in league with the new Substantive Equal Protection promises not only government by judiciary but government exclusively by judiciary. For both efforts undermine the constitutional structures that grant legitimacy to the popular branches of government. Each seeks to erode any belief in the power of legislatures to govern decently. Each has a greater confidence in the arguments of advocates than in the opinions of the people. In the end they both seek to weaken the public confidence in the institutional design which has sustained this nation as the most free and the most prosperous.

III

That the various devices of constitutional restraint are severely threatened today by a judiciary that has been encouraged to arrogate unto itself the primary responsibility for declaring fundamental values external to the Constitution's text and original intention, is increasingly obvious. There is a growing awareness that a constitution deemed nothing more than what the judges say it is is no constitution at all—it is merely a vehicle for judicial whim and personal predilection. But this is precisely what the new constitutionalism is. Call it what they will—"non-interpretivism," "ethical arguments," "result-oriented jurisprudence" or even the more highfalutin' "moral philosophy"—the fact is that this is no longer constitutionalism in any politically safe and democratically responsible sense.

In closing let me repeat James Madison's long ago warning: "If the sense in which the Constitution was accepted and ratified by the nation ... be not the guide in expounding it, there can be no security for a consistent and stable, more than for a faithful, exercise of its powers." Ultimately, this is, I suggest, the lesson of the Founders we most need to recover today if constitutionalism as a vital force in a world still all-too-prone to tyranny is to be maintained. For in the end, a constitutionalism bereft of the Constitution is not constitutionalism at all.

Is the Supreme Court the Ultimate Interpreter of the Constitution?

Lino A. Graglia

In *Cooper v. Aaron*,[1] the famous Little Rock, Arkansas case, the Supreme Court held, unsurprisingly, that a state official, Governor Orval Faubus, could not prevent the carrying out of a federal court order—in that case a district court order requiring the Little Rock School Board to begin to end school racial segregation. This was all that was necessary for the decision of the case, as the Court itself explicitly stated, but the time was one of high drama and uncertainty and the Court sought to bolster its position by every available means. There was a real question whether the President would support the Court's prohibition of segregation by enforcing the so far unenforced *Brown v. Board of Education*[2] decision of four years earlier. The Court considered it necessary or useful to state that the three justices who had joined the Court since *Brown* supported that decision and that it was therefore "unanimously reaffirmed."[3] For the first and only time in the Court's history, the opinion was signed by each of the nine justices, and near the end it contained the following passage in which the Court apparently asserted an authority for its decisions that it had never asserted before:

> Article VI of the Constitution makes the Constitution the 'supreme Law of the Land.' In 1803, Chief Justice Marshall, speaking for a unanimous Court, referring to the Constitution as 'the fundamental and paramount law of the nation,' declared in the notable case of *Marbury v. Madison*, I Cranch 137, 177, that 'it is emphatically the province and duty of the judicial department to say what the law is.' This decision declared the basic principle that the federal judiciary is supreme in the exposition of the law of the Constitution, and that principle has ever since been respected by this Court and the Country as a permanent and indispensable feature of our constitutional system. It follows that the interpretation of the Fourteenth Amendment enunciated by this Court in the *Brown* case is the supreme law of the land. . . .[4]

---

1. 358 U.S. 1 (1958).
2. 347 U.S. 483 (1954).
3. Cooper v. Aaron, 358 U.S. at 19.
4. *Id.* at 18.

This passage has been the subject of much scholarly comment. In *Marbury v. Madison*[5] the Court asserted and exercised the power to determine whether a federal statute involved in a case properly before the Court was inconsistent with the Constitution and, if found to be so, to refuse to give effect to the statue. The Court did state, as *Cooper* notes, that "it is emphatically the province and duty of the judicial department to say what the law is," but the Court was not understood to assert judicial supremacy in the interpretation of the Constitution, that is, that its interpretation was the only "authoritative" one and "binding" on all others. Indeed, many of our strongest Presidents and Congressional leaders,

---

5. Wl Cranch 137 (1803).
6. "You seem [to] consider the judges as the ultimate arbiters of all constitutional questions: a very dangerous doctrine indeed, and one which would place us under the despotism of an oligarchy. [The] constitution has erected no such single tribunal, knowing that to whatever hands confided, with the corruptions of time and party, its members would become despots. It has more wisely made all the departments co-equal and co-sovereign within themselves."
Letter to William C. Jarvis, Sept. 28, 1820, *The Writings of Thomas Jefferson*, ed. Ford (1899), vol. 10, p. 160.
"You seem to think it devolved on the judges to decide on the validity of the sedition law. But nothing in the Constitution has given them a right to decide for the Executive, more than to the Executive to decide for them . . . .[The Constitution] meant that its co-ordinate branches should be checks on each other. But the opinion which gives to the judges the right to decide what laws are constitutional, and what not, not only for themselves in their own spheres of action, but for the Legislature & Executive also, in their spheres, would make the judiciary a despotic branch."
Letter to Abigail Adams, September 11, 1804, *The Writings of Thomas Jefferson*, ed. Ford (1897), vol. 8, p. 310.
7. "I acknowledge, in the ordinary course of Government, that the exposition of the laws and constitution devolves upon the Judiciary. But I beg to know, upon what principle it can be contended, that any one department draws from the Constitution greater powers than another, in marking out the limits of the powers of the several departments?" *Annals of Congress* vol. I, pp. 519-21 (June 17, 1789).

including Jefferson,[6] Madison,[7] Jackson,[8] and Lincoln,[9] although they recognized the Court's authority to interpret the Constitution in cases properly before it, insisted that the other departments of government were also authorized to interpret the Constitution in performing their functions and were by no means bound by the Court's interpretation.

The question arises, therefore, as to how, if at all, the Court's assertion of interpretational supremacy in *Cooper*, repeated in several later cases,[10] changes the situation and whether it, in effect, puts the Court above the Constitution. The answer is that the Court's assertion changes the situation very little if at all, because as a practical matter the Court has been above the Constitution since the advent of judicial review.

No one is any less free after *Cooper* than he was before to act on his own interpretation of the Constitution, regardless of the Supreme Court's interpretation. For example, a Congressman can still vote against pro-

---

8. "The Congress, the Executive, and the Court must each for itself be guided by its own opinion of the Constitution. Each public officer who takes an oath to support the Constitution swears that he will support it as he understands it, and not as it is understood by others. It is as much the duty of the House of Representatives, of the Senate, and of the President to decide upon the constitutionality of any bill or resolution which may be presented to them for passage or approval as it is of the supreme judges when it may be brought before them for judicial decision. The opinion of the judges has no more authority over Congress than the opinion of Congress has over the judges, and on that point the President is independent of both. The authority of the Supreme Court must not, therefore, be permitted to control the Congress or the Executive when acting in their legislative capacities, but to have only such influence as the force of their reasoning may deserve." Andrew Jackson—Veto Message, July 10, 1832, *Messages and Papers of the Presidents* ed. Richardson, (1896) vol. 2 pp. 576, 581-583.

9. "I do not forget the position assumed by some that constitutional questions are to be decided by the Supreme Court, nor do I deny that such decisions must be binding in any case upon the parties to a suit as to the object of that suit, while they are also entitled to very high respect and consideration in all parallel cases by all other departments of the Government .... At the same time, the candid citizen must confess that if the policy of the Government upon vital questions affecting the whole people is to be irrevocably fixed by decisions of the Supreme Court, the instant they are made in ordinary litigation between parties in personal actions, the people will have ceased to be their own rulers, having to that extent practically resigned their Government into the hands of that eminent tribunal."
First Inaugural Address, March 4, 1861, *Messages and Papers of the Presidents*, ed. Richardson (1897) vol. 6, pp. 5, 9-10.

10. *E.g.*, Baker v. Carr, 369 U.S. 186 (1962); Powell v. McCormack, 395 U.S. 486 (1969); United States v. Nixon, 418 U.S. 683 (1974).

posed legislation and a President can veto proposed legislation or grant a pardon to persons convicted under a statute on the ground that he considers it unconstitutional even though the Supreme Court has or clearly would hold that the law is constitutional. When one is free to act for any reason, he is certainly free to act on the basis of his constitutional views. *Cooper* makes it possible for someone to object that constitutional views contrary to those expressed in a Supreme Court decision are necessarily invalid, but one can always respond, in the words of Lincoln, that "it is obviously possible that such a decision may be erroneous."[11]

What a Congressman or President cannot do, but also could not do before *Cooper*, is effectively take a view of the Constitution that is less restrictive than the Court's view. He may not, for example, take the view that a law is not unconstitutional despite a Supreme Court's ruling that it is. Insofar as the effectuation of such a view by the application and enforcement of a law requires the participation of the courts, as it ordinarily does, it is the Court's view that will prevail. As Madison pointed out even before the adoption of the Constitution, "as the courts are generally the last in making the decision, it results to them by refusing or not refusing to execute a law, to stamp it with its final character." He recognized that "this makes the Judiciary Department paramount in fact to the Legislature," even though he went on to object that this "was never intended and can never be proper."[12]

It is often said that a Supreme Court decision interpreting the Constitution is not itself "law," because it binds only the parties to the case. On closer examination, however, the difference between a Supreme Court decision and other legal pronouncements is seen to be less than might at first appear. What would the practical difference have been, one can ask, in terms of anyone's legal rights and obligations if school racial segregation had been prohibited by a constitutional amendment in 1854 instead of by the *Brown* decision? Unless it entertained the possibility that the Court might overrule *Brown* or that Congress might act to restrain the Court, the position of a school board practicing school segregation would have been much the same as it was after *Brown*. Supreme Court constitutional rulings do not enforce themselves, but neither do statutes, and failure to comply with the Supreme Court's announcements of the law

---

11. First Inaugural Address, March 4, 1881, *Messages and Papers of the Presidents* vol. 6, pp. 9-10.
12. Letter to John Brown, October 12, 1788, *The Writings of James Madison* (New York: Putnams' Sons, 1904), vol. V, pp. 292-294.

can, like failure to comply with a statue, lead to fines, damages, and other adverse legal consequences as well as to a suit to compel compliance.[13]

The finality and legal effectiveness of the Court's constitutional interpretations mean that the Supreme Court is indeed the "ultimate" interpreter of the Constitution in a practical sense, even though of course nothing is absolute and everything is subject to change. This is not the result of *Cooper v. Aaron*, but as Madison recognized, of judicial review. And the fact that the Supreme Court is the ultimate interpreter of the Constitution in turn means that it is also true that the Court is above the Constitution. The simple fact of the matter, as unpalatable as it may be and should be, is that it is not the Constitution but the Supreme Court's interpretations of the Constitution that constitute our highest law, the law that is in fact enforced and that determines our legal rights and obligations.

The only thing surprising to me in all of this is that any knowledgeable person should consider these conclusions surprising—evidence, I think, of the strength of our desire to believe that we live, in Chief Justice Marshall's words, "under a government of laws, and not of men."[14] To say that it is not the Constitution but the Court's interpretation of the Constitution that is our highest law is, after all, only to repeat Charles Evan Hughes' famous statement that "we are under a Constitution, but the Constitution is what the judges say it is";[15] which is to say, of course, that we are under the Supreme Court. It is also only to repeat the even earlier and also well-known statement of Bishop Hoadly in a sermon to the King in 1717: "Who ever hath an absolute authority to interpret any written or spoken laws, it is he who is truly the lawgiver, to all intents and purposes, and not the person who first spoke or wrote them."[16]

Of course Bishop Hoadly is correct that absolute authority to interpret the law makes one the true lawgiver, but one might ask, does the Supreme Court really have such authority, are there in fact no limits on what the Supreme Court can say the Constitution means? This question can only be answered by looking at what the Court has actually done in the name of interpreting the Constitution and by considering the possible ways in which the representative institutions of government can change what the

---

13. See Farber, "The Supreme Court and the Rule of Law; Cooper v. Aaron Revisited," *University of Illinois Law Review*, 1982, p. 387.

14. Marbury v. Madison, 1 Cranch at 163.

15. Speech, 1907, quoted in Lockhard, Kamisar, Choper, and Shiffrin, *Constitutional Law*, 6th ed., vol. 8 (1986).

16. *Id.* 1.

Court has done. It is not possible to review the work of the Court over the past three decades without concluding that the limits on the Court's power are indeed exceedingly remote.

That the Supreme Court's ability to say what the Constitution means is effectively unlimited, that the Constitution in fact has little or nothing to do with constitutional law, can be easily seen by considering the Court's decision in almost any area of constitutional law. The history of the law of school segregation, for example, provides an almost scientific demonstration of the irrelevance of the Constitution to the making of constitutional law. There was a time when the Constitution, we were told, permitted racial discrimination in the assignment of children to school;[17] there then came a time when the Constitution prohibited such discrimination, as the Court announced in *Brown* in 1954;[18] there then came a time, the present, when the Constitution often requires such discrimination.[19] In all this time, the Constitution was not changed in any relevant respect. The independent variable, a scientific investigator might say, that produced this full range of possible results is obviously something other than the Constitution. All that changed and all that had to change, of course, was the identity of the persons doing the constitutional "interpretation."

To take another example from the same area of law, in *Brown* the Supreme Court said that school racial segregation was unconstitutional because prohibited by the equal protection clause of the Fourteenth Amendment. On the same day, however, the Court considered the question of the constitutionality of school racial segregation in the District of Columbia, to which the Fourteenth Amendment, applicable by its terms only to states, does not apply. The unavailability of the equal protection clause, it turned out, made not the slightest difference in the result that the Court reached. School racial segregation was also prohibited by the Constitution in the District of Columbia, the Court said, only now it was prohibited by the due process clause of the Fifth Amendment, which does apply to the federal government.[20] The fact that the Fifth Amendment was adopted in 1791 as part of a Constitution that explicitly recognized the institution of slavery was not seen as an impediment to this "interpretation."

---

17. Plessy v. Ferguson, 163 U.S. 537 (1896).
18. Brown v. Board of Education, 347 U.S. 483 (1954).
19. *E.g.*, Green v. County School Board of New Kent County, 391 U.S. 430 (1968); Swann v. Charlotte-Mecklenburg Bd. of Educ., 402 U.S. 1 (1971). See, Graglia, *Disaster by Decree: The Supreme Court Decisions on Race and the Schools* (1976).
20. Bolling v. Sharpe, 347 U.S. 497 (1954).

The unconstitutionality of legal distinctions on the basis of legitimacy provides another interesting illustration of the interpretive techniques available to the Court. Such distinctions go back to the beginning of Anglo-American law, but it was not known that they were frowned upon by the Constitution until Justice Douglas suddenly so announced in an opinion for the Court in 1968.[21] In the absence of other precedent, Justice Douglas, known for his direct approach to constitutional law, found it entirely sufficient to cite *King Lear* and quote the speech of Edmund the Bastard in which he asks why he should not be considered as good as "honest madam's issue."[22]

In an even more famous and important exhibition of interpretive skill, Justice Douglas decided that constitutional prohibitions may be found not only in the Constitution's actual provisions, but also in "the penumbras, formed by emanations" from those provisions.[23] Justice Douglas' "reasoning" can hardly be related in public without causing snickering, and it would certainly be amusing enough except for the fact that the result was to create a so-called right of privacy that has proved to be an important additional limitation on the right of self-government. It has led, for example, to the decision that the states are virtually powerless to make public policy on the issue of abortion and to the Court's institution of a regime of virtual abortion on demand.[24] Finally, that constitutional law, not only need not be related to, but can be directly contrary to the Constitution, is illustrated by the insistence by Justices Brennan and Marshall that the Constitution prohibits capital punishment[25] despite the fact that several constitutional provisions explicitly recognize the taking of life as a punishment for crime.[26]

The Court's position as ultimate interpreter of the Constitution and apparently limitless ability to say what the Constitution means has made it arguably the most important institution of American government for the past three decades, the source of nearly every important change in the basic social policies that determine the nature and quality of a society. During this time it has been a majority of the nine justices of the Court, not the electorally accountable representatives of the people, that have determined public policy for the nation as a whole on such issues as

---

21. Levy v. Louisiana, 391 U.S. 68 (1968).
22. *Id.* at 72 n. 6.
23. Griswold v. Connecticut, 381 U.S. 479, 484 (1965).
24. See, *e.g.*, Roe v. Wade, 410 U.S. 113 (1973); Doe v. Bolton, 410 U.S. 179 (1973).
25. See, *e.g.*, Furman v. Georgia, 408 U.S. 238, 257, 314 (1972).
26. U.S. Const. Amends. V, XIV.

abortion,[27] capital punishment,[28] compulsory school racial integration,[29] prayer in the schools,[30] government aid to religious schools,[31] criminal procedure,[32] pornography,[33] control of street demonstrations[34] and vagrancy,[35] and the permissibility of legal distinctions on the basis of sex,[36] alienage,[37] and legitimacy.[38] That these decisions have been made and are regularly enforced surely puts beyond doubt that it is not the Constitution but the Supreme Court's putative interpretations of the Constitution that are the supreme law of the land. The only real question, therefore, is what if anything, is it that the Supreme Court cannot do, what are the actual practical limits on the Court's power? The answer is that there are several potential means of checking the Court's power, but that as a matter of history and practice we have now arrived at a position where they are more theoretical than real.

The most obvious means available to limit the Court's policy-making power is the adoption of constitutional amendments overturning disapproved Court decisions. Constitutional amendments, of course, become part of the Constitution and are therefore themselves subject to the Court's interpretation, and the Court has in fact largely read out of the Constitution one amendment, the Eleventh, that was adopted to overturn a Court decision.[39] Nevertheless, if a group should actually succeed in mobilizing the enormous political power needed to obtain a constitutional amendment, the Court would likely be impressed and, at least for a while, treat the amendment with respect; the next amendment, after all, might deal with judicial tenure or with judicial review itself. Constitutional amendments, however, are extremely difficult to obtain, requiring proposal by two-thirds of each house of Congress or two-thirds of the states and ratification by three-quarters of the states.[40] A negative vote in

27. Note 24, *supra.*
28. Note 25, *supra.*
29. Note 19, *supra.*
30. Engel v. Vitale, 370 U.S. 421 (1962).
31. *E.g.,* Wolman v. Walters, 433 U.S. 229 (1977).
32. *E.g.,* Miranda v. Arizona, 384 U.S. 111 (1966).
33. *E.g.,* Memoirs v. Massachusetts, 383 U.S. 413 (1966)
34. *E.g.,* Gregory v. Chicago, 384 U.S. 111 (1969).
35. *E.g.,* Papachristou v. Jacksonville, 405 U.S. 155 (1972).
36. *E.g.,* Craig v.Boren, 429 U.S. 190 (1976).
37. *E.g.,* Graham v. Richardson, 403 U.S. 365 (1971).
38. Note 21, *supra.*
39. The Eleventh Amendment, adopted to overturn Chisholm v. Georgia, 2 Dall. 419 (1793), which permitted a suit against a state, was very much limited in effect, to say the least, by the Court's holding that a suit against a state official for acts performed in his official capacity is not necessarily a suit against the state. Ex parte Young, 209 U.S. 123 (1908).
40. U.S. Const. Amend. V.

one legislative chamber in as few as thirteen states can defeat an amend-ment. Nonetheless, it might have been possible to develop a tradition of readily adopting constitutional amendments to overturn unwanted Supreme Court decisions, and this could have become a very real limit on the Court's power. We have, however, apparently developed a contrary tradition that constitutional amendments overturning Supreme Court decisions are somehow inappropriate; in any event, a legion of constitu-tional law professors has been willing to troop to Congress to so testify whenever such an amendment has been proposed in recent times. The result is that as a practical matter the amendment route is almost totally foreclosed as a check on the Court's power.

Another potentially important check on the Court is the clear power of Congress to limit the Court's appellate jurisdiction.[41] Here one faces the "Catch 22" situation that a statute limiting the Court's jurisdiction will effectively restrain the Court only if the Court first agrees that it has been effectively restrained. Even if this difficulty can be overcome, as I think it often can, depriving the Court of jurisdiction in some area in which it has made an unwanted decision would have the effect of leaving that decision in force to be followed and applied by lower federal courts and state courts. Even more important, it is not politically attractive to obtain a result only by foreclosing constitutional challenge, leaving opponents to claim that the result obtained is clearly unconstitutional nonetheless.[42] For these and other reasons, control of the Court's jurisdiction has not proven to be an effective means of imposing restraints.

Finally, Alexander Hamilton argued that judicial review presented no danger of judicial usurpation of legislative power because impeachment would be readily available as a corrective.[43] President Jefferson's unsuc-cessful attempt to impeach Justice Samuel Chase, however, led him to conclude, correctly, that impeachment was "not even a scare-crow."[44] Having permitted if not encouraged judicial policy-making for several decades, we are not now in a position to declare that judicial eagerness for the task is an impeachable offense. Our judges well know that they have nothing to fear from impeachment, just as they know they have very little

---

41. U.S. Const. Art. III, Sec. 2. See, Graglia, "The Power of Congress to Limit Supreme Court Jurisdiction," 7 *Harvard Journal of Law and Public Policy* (1984), p. 23.
42. See, Graglia, "Constitutional Mysticism: The Aspirational Defense of Judicial Review," 98 *Harvard Law Review* (1985), pp. 1331, 1341.
43. *The Federalist Papers*, ed. C. Rossiter (Mentor Books, 1961), No. 79.
44. Quoted in Gunther, *Constitutional Law*, 11th ed. (1985), p. 12.

to fear from either the possibility of a constitutional amendment or jurisdiction-limiting legislation.

The only real possibility, therefore, it seems, for diminishing the policy-making role the Supreme Court has assumed in our system of government in the last several decades is by the appointment of new justices more willing to confine themselves to the judicial function of applying rather than making the law. The growing rarity of voluntary resignations from a Supreme Court seat, combined with advances in medical science—requiring, in my opinion, a rethinking of lifetime judicial tenure—however, have made opportunities for appointments infrequent occurrences. President Carter had no appointments during his term and President Reagan only one during his first term. Further, the country has apparently become so accustomed to having basic policy issues decided by the Supreme Court, and the practice is so strongly defended and encouraged by a large majority of our most eminent legal scholars that it is doubtful that even new appointments will bring about a significant change. Nothing has been more surprising or more disappointing to me than how little difference six consecutive appointments by Republican Presidents supposedly committed to judicial restraint have made; none of the Warren Court's surprising innovations have been overruled and some even more surprising innovations, such as the busing and abortion decisions, have occurred.

The Supreme Court is indeed the ultimate interpreter of the Constitution. The unrestrained judicial policy-making that has resulted in the past three decades has become, I believe, a virus in the body of the American democratic political system, and there is no guarantee that we will find a cure. If our achievement of a uniquely free and prosperous society should come to an end in the near future, it will be, I believe, because we have so largely abandoned the system of self-government through elected representatives that made the achievement possible, in favor of government by a committee of nine lawyers unelected by and unanswerable to the people whose lives they govern.

Judicial Review, Democracy, and the Rule of Law

Glen E. Thurow

In looking at the judiciary we note this paradox: it is the branch of government most distant from the American people and yet it also seems to be the branch which most reflects that people's high aspiration to achieve a rule of law. Are democracy and the rule of law incompatible?

The distance is brought out most forcefully in these essays by Lino Graglia. Do we have a democratic government, he asks, if the most important issues affecting our common lives are made by nine unelected judges? If these unelected, but scarcely Platonic, guardians are to decide whether our children are to be bused across the city, whether fathers may have any say in aborting their offspring, whether criminals are to be free to roam the streets because of crowded jails, whether Darwinism or Creationism can or must be taught in our schools, can we still say that the American people govern themselves?

The aspiration is noted by Louis Fisher and stressed by Grant Mindle. The power and prestige of the judiciary, they suggest, reflect our attachment to the constituted principles of republican government and civil and religious liberty. Neither majorities nor minorities are free to do anything they may happen to desire, but must conform to the Constitution. Does not a court independent of the partisan fray reveal to all the limits of the "raw force of politics," as Fisher says, and rest upon our dedication to the rule of law, as Mindle argues?

The exercise of judicial review by the Supreme Court has been a recurring constitutional issue since the founding of the country. As Mindle shows for the judiciary debate of 1802, what has appeared to one party as admirable independence for the purpose of guarding the rule of law has appeared to another to be outrageous partisanship designed to thwart the democratic will. Does the obvious partisanship of both supporters and defenders of the Court show that the aspiration to a non-partisan rule of law superior to the partisan rule offered by Congressional majorities is simply a "noble lie," as it was called at the conference? Is our true choice the partisan rule of the elected representatives of the majority or the partisan rule of unelected judges? The deepest dispute in these papers concerns whether and how judicial review contributes to reconciling democratic government and the rule of law.

Glen E. Thurow

The Traditional Understanding and Today's

The classic defense of judicial review, found in *Federalist #78* and *Marbury v. Madison*, sought to minimize the tension between judicial review and democracy by noting that the Court upholds the fundamental will of the people by upholding the ratified Constitution. By distinguishing between the people's temporary, passionate, or ill-considered will and their long run, dispassionate, and considered will found in the Constitution, judicial review could be united with democracy understood as the rule of the reasonable will of the people. To refuse to enforce a law of Congress would not usurp the people's power if judges relied on standards set by the Constitution. The people and their fundamental law would rule even those judges who declare unconstitutional the laws passed by the people's representatives.

This reconciliation of democracy and judicial power made two important demands upon judges. The first was that they correctly interpret the Constitution. This meant that judges had to be people with deep loyalty to, and disciplined understanding of, the Constitution. The second requirement was that they act as judges rather than as legislators or executives. Judges had to recognize, or to be brought to recognize, limits to their powers. Both requirements were seen to be necessary in order that judges would uphold the people's will rather than their own and serve the rule of law rather than their own passions.

Although the contemporary dispute over judicial review contains elements that have characterized such disputes since the founding of the country, the central issues at stake in the contemporary debate are fundamentally different from those of the past. It is sometimes said that the issue is judicial activism. But activist courts have existed since the time of John Marshall, and there is little in the original defense of judicial review that would suggest that courts should not actively uphold the Constitution. The unique circumstance today is not so much the activism of courts, or even the degree of their failure in practice to interpret the Constitution correctly or to remain within proper judicial boundaries. Rather, it is found in the extent to which the traditional justification of judicial review and the limits it places upon judges has been abandoned as a standard. Throughout our history judges have sometimes misinterpreted the Constitution and forgotten their own limits, but everyone acknowledged that they should correctly interpret the Constitution and should remember that they are judges, not legislators. Today it is commonly denied that judges can be distinguished from legislators and often maintained that judges should find their standards outside the written Constitution.

This change is described and deplored in Gary McDowell's paper. As he notes, jurists and legal scholars no longer debate whether the words of the Constitution should be given a loose or a strict construction. Rather, today's issue is between interpretavists and noninterpretavists. Instead of debating *how* to interpret the Constitution, scholars now debate *whether* to interpret the Constitution. The present Court's majority, in McDowell's view, takes the noninterpretavist view. Without the constraints of the words of the Constitution and the intention of its authors, the Court has been free to indulge in arbitrary and undemocratic opinions of what is right and just.

Lino Graglia regards the traditional argument reconciling judicial review with democracy as a myth. He agrees with McDowell that the decisions of the contemporary Court cannot be justified as correct interpretations of the Constitution. He also agrees that its decisions must therefore be seen as arbitrary and undemocratic. But he disagrees with McDowell's view that this state of affairs is due to the unique failure of today's Court to adhere to the traditional standard. Rather he believes it is due to the very notion of judicial review itself. Judicial review makes the Court the ultimate interpreter of our highest law and therefore the ultimate authority determining the nature of our society. The view expressed in *Cooper v. Aaron* that the decisions of the Court are the supreme law of the land (or, in effect, that the Court is the Constitution) is not a contemporary invention, but the reality implicit in judicial review from the beginning. Graglia further denies that any of the traditional restraints on judicial power have much effectiveness. Court decisions on busing, abortion, and criminal rights reveal how much the Court can defy popular judgments on matters of importance with how little constitutional warrant or fear of reprisal. We are ruled, he concludes, by an undemocratic Court.

Revealingly, none of the defenders of the Court at the conference did so in terms of the traditional defense of judicial review. None argued that the Warren and post-Warren Court decisions are fundamentally faithful to the written Constitution. Rather the Court's defenders implicitly agreed with its detractors that it could not be defended by the arguments of Hamilton and Marshall. They suggested instead a more indirect justification for the power of the Court.

Neil Cogan of Southern Methodist University, one of the commentators on these papers, tried to mollify the conservatives present by arguing that the Court has made many opinions they should like, just as it has made many liberals like. This effort seemed unpersuasive partly because the conservative arithmetic differed from his (How many *Browns* are worth how many *Wades?*). More importantly, a calculus of mutual partisan advantage cannot conclude in a nonpartisan justification for the Court. Two robbers do not equal one judge.

Clovis Morrisson of North Texas State University, the other commentator, acknowledged that the Court could not be defended as being in some way uniquely faithful to the Constitution. Rather he implicitly attacked the traditional defense of judicial review by denying that there is any distinction in principle between judicial and legislative power: just as the legislature makes its political and partisan judgments, so do the judges as well. Yet this does not mean that the Constitution is overthrown through the operation of judicial power. The government as a whole, he maintained, can be understood as a continual power struggle in which one branch or another may get the upper hand, but only temporarily. The genius of the system is to be found in the continual check to power it provides. The result of this struggle, he believes, is the preservation of the principles of 1787.

This view seems to rest upon a rather extraordinary faith: that the blind competition of three groups seeking their partisan advantage will result in upholding the Constitution. Can we, by forgetting the Constitution, preserve it? Were the founders so skillful that future generations would uphold their principles without even their highest defenders having to think of them? Or is there no principle in the Constitution other than that of not letting anyone get too much? It is cheering, but perhaps naive, to think that it does not matter whether Supreme Court Justices are faithful to the Constitution because the Constitution will prevail even if they are not.

Louis Fisher's essay seeks to defend the Court against the charge of being arbitrary or undemocratic, again not by revealing its faithfulness to the Constitution, but by arguing that the Supreme Court does not have the final say on the meaning of the Constitution. He saves the Court by denying its power. The Constitution's meaning is determined, as he sees it, by a dynamic process in which some issues of constitutional interpretation are decided by the other branches and never get to the Court, some interpretations made by the other branches are simply accepted by the Court, and interpretations by the Court itself are overturned by a persistent Congress utilizing the various weapons it has at its command. In yet other cases the Court shows restraint through respect for the legislature or by recognizing that some questions are political in character and beyond its proper ken. The true operation of the Court must be understood as part of a dialogue with the other branches. Dialogue—not confrontation and authority—marks the character of the Court's determination of the meaning of the Constitution.

Fisher's view does seem to describe some important elements of the Court's work. One might see the death penalty decisions—in which the Court seemed to be deflected from its path of holding the death penalty unconstitutional—to have been influenced by the debate and reaction of state legislatures to its original holding. And one might argue that its decision in *Brown* reflected, as well as led, changes in how segregation of the races was regarded by other institutions of government and the American people generally. Indeed, in the light of Grant Mindle's analysis of the inherent weakness of the Court, one might conclude that the apparently tremendous power of the Court is something of a mirage made possible by the lassitude of the legislature rather than by the indomitable strength of the judiciary.

However, one can easily push this view too far. Fisher perhaps underestimates the degree to which the Court is not merely a member of a debating society, but engaged in definitively determining the meaning of the law. After all, it does not say, "Here is my view, what do you think?", but "This is the law. Obey!" Would a national dialogue have resulted in the same decisions on busing, on abortion, or on the meaning of the religious clauses of the First Amendment? The Supreme Court has undoubtedly taken many issues out of the hands of the majority and their elected representatives. However much we can diminish the threatening size of the Court's apparent power by noting the degree to which it shares power with others, that power is still great enough that we cannot defend it solely by denying that it rules.

Grant Mindle's analysis of the 1802 debate suggests that the Court is weak when measured by the powers given it by the Constitution. He shows that a determined Congress has the means at its disposal to curb the courts, as it did in 1802. The current Court's evident strength, on the other hand, comes from the deference the other branches are willing to extend to it. The other branches are willing to defer, he argues, because of their belief that the independence of the Court is vital to the preservation of the rule of law. He concludes that it is essential for the Court not to act in so arbitrary a manner that it becomes implausible to think that the independence of the Court is vital to the rule of law.

Mindle's essay usefully reminds us that it is not realistic to forget that men's beliefs shape their actions. But does the power of the contemporary Court come from the general respect people have for the rule of law, or does it come from the fact that the direction in which the Court is heading is supported by the most articulate and powerful segments of the community? It may be true that many decisions of the Court have not had the support of the majority of the American people, but the direction set by the Warren Court has clearly been supported by such groups as the media, the academic community, and the legal profession. These groups do not support the Court out of a general respect for the rule of law, but because they can achieve the triumph of their opinions through the rule of judges even when they fail to achieve their goals through elected representatives. If the educated opinion of America supported the rule of law, would it not decry every attempt at judicial lawmaking? Instead, whether liberal or conservative, it only decries those it dislikes.

As for Congress, while it would not have made law the busing, abortion, criminal rights, and other decisions of the Court, it is restrained from trying to reverse them by the fact that large numbers of its members agree with the decisions and many others do not want the political risk involved in trying to overturn the *faits accomplis* against the wishes of the media and other leading segments of the population.

The Rule of Law and the Power of the Court

Mindle to the contrary, perhaps support for the contemporary Court comes not because people believe in the rule of law, but because belief in the rule of law has eroded in America. To be ruled by law means to be ruled by general rules not fashioned simply for the immediate parties in dispute. It is precisely a characteristic of judicial power that it rules in immediate cases before it. Judicial law-making is therefore particularly dangerous to the rule of law, and proper judicial power requires that the discretion of judges be reduced as much as possible. Judges must follow laws made by others because of the great temptation in a situation of judging to judge in behalf of the person or group one prefers.

The danger of judicial rule is seen in the current Court's interpretation of the Fourteenth Amendment. In holding that some classes of people— those who are discrete and insular minorities—have rights and privileges other people do not have, the Court has yielded to the temptation to twist the Constitution (which guarantees to all persons the equal protection of the laws) to favor the groups it thinks most deserving. This is the typical evil of judicial rule.

The rule of law in the United States requires the supremacy of the written Constitution in determining the fundamental law, the supremacy of Congress in making ordinary law, and the subordination of the Court to both these laws. A Congress that legislates by making general rules, and that refrains from the execution of the laws, is the keystone to the rule of law. We could have a rule of law without the power of judicial review; we could not have such a rule without the supremacy of Congress in lawmaking. In order for judicial review to be compatible with a rule of law, judges must declare laws invalid only when they are contrary to the Constitution, and there must be a clear distinction between judicial and legislative power. But these are precisely the two injunctions of the traditional defense of judicial review. In abandoning that defense contemporary opinion is also abandoning the premises of a rule of law.

The Justice of the Constitution

However, it is not sufficient to say that we ought to be ruled by general laws rather than judicial fiat. A rule of law is not good if the content of the laws is bad. A rule of Nazi laws ought to be overthrown. It is important that we be governed by general rules, but it is even more important what those general rules are. Laws are made by men who have particular outlooks and understandings. Whose law is, or ought to be, ruling us?

One answer is that of the framers of the Constitution. It is often alleged that it is impossible for us to be ruled by the principles of the framers. The Constitution they wrote contains too many vague phrases and inconsistencies for us to follow its words by themselves. And the intention behind the Constitution cannot be discovered because it was made by many people with differing motives a long time ago. There was no single intention, and if there was, time has blotted it out.

Gary McDowell tries to counter this view by arguing that we know quite well what the intentions were. There was, he believes, a common understanding among the founders of what the provisions of the Constitution meant, even though that sense might have to be made more specific and refined in order to understand its injunctions for any particular issue. The framing did not occur in some prehistoric past, but at a period of time we know quite well. Information about the founding is fulsome. The problem with modern constitutional interpretation, he believes, is that judges have abandoned the known original intentions of the framers in order to rely upon some "higher law." This "higher law" is simply a cover leaving the judges free to follow their subjective opinions.

Common sense tells us that we can determine the meaning of much of the Constitution simply by reading it, and we can tell more by studying it and its formation. The traditional defense of judicial review would maintain that if there are passages whose meaning cannot be determined, they do not properly bind judges. Judges can enforce only laws that can be known. The argument that the Constitution has passages whose meaning cannot be determined does not constitute an objection to the traditional view of judicial review, but merely suggests that there are fewer cases in which judicial review can be properly applied. But perhaps the issue of whether it is possible to conform to the Constitution is a red herring. The real issue is not the possibility but the desirability of conforming to the Constitution.

Although the Constitution is rarely attacked openly or in public, it is difficult to escape the impression that the traditional defense of judicial review is being abandoned in contemporary America because many now doubt that the Constitution as written is just. It is commonly said by those who wish to be kind that it is outmoded and might have been suitable for the 18th century, but not for the 20th. Recently these reservations have received a blunter expression. In a noted speech, no less than a Justice of the Supreme Court, Thurgood Marshall, celebrated its Bicentennial by attacking the Constitution,[1] The Constitution, in his view, is both racist and sexist. (What indictment could be worse in 1987?) The good we now have, he says, is the direct result of the willingness of people to abandon the original Constitution and its principles. At best, the Constitution was enlightened for its day, but fatally flawed to guide the future development of the country. We ought to celebrate those who have deviated from the Constitution (including Justice Marshall?) rather than the Constitution itself or those who have been loyal to it.

It is the measure of the state of the Constitution today that it was not considered astounding that a man who has sworn to be one of the chief defenders of the Constitution should regard it as unjust and despicable in principle. To the contrary, Marshall's view was greeted with a visible sigh of relief in many quarters: at last someone has spoken the truth about the Constitution. The Emperor *has* no clothes.

---

1. Remarks of Thurgood Marshall at the Annual Seminar of the San Francisco Patent and Tradesmark Law Association in Maui, Hawaii, May 6, 1987.

Justice Marshall's attack makes it clear why it is insufficient for the defenders of the Constitution to say that we should follow the intentions of its framers in determining its meaning. This is not because it is impossible to determine those intentions; it is rather because men will not follow the intentions of the founders unless they believe them to be good. As we might learn from *Federalist* 51:

> Justice is the end of government. It is the end of civil society. It ever has been, and ever will be pursued, until it be obtained, or until liberty be lost in the pursuit.

Or, we might add, "until the Constitution be lost in the pursuit." If men do not believe the Constitution to be just, they will not obey it, even—or perhaps especially—if they are Justices of the Supreme Court. But the Constitution can only be understood to be just by reference to a standard not determined by the Constitution itself. The defenders of the Constitution in our time, contrary to McDowell, cannot avoid resort to a higher law.

In interpreting the Constitution in his Bicentennial speech, Justice Marshall relies upon the authority of Chief Justice Taney in the *Dred Scott* case. (It is hard to escape the irony that the Court's first black Justice should regard Taney as the authoritative interpreter of the Constitution.) Marshall would do well to consider the argument of Taney's great opponent, Abraham Lincoln. In response to the interpretation of the Constitution offered in the *Dred Scott* case, Lincoln argued that the founders had formed a Constitution to embody the principles of the Declaration of Independence. Noting that, contrary to Taney's opinion, there was nothing in the Constitution that endorsed the principle of slavery, Lincoln argued that the compromises of the Convention did not compromise the principle of human equality, but simply recognized that it was not possible to fully implement the principle immediately.

Whether Abraham Lincoln, or Thurgood Marshall, is right is not difficult to decide. But in order to see this it is necessary to be clear about the relationship of the Constitution to principle and to practice. The Constitution is not simply a document of philosophic principle; neither is it simply a document encoding the existing practices of our country.

The rule of law in general in our democracy has a dual character. It must have such a character if it is to be compatible with democracy. On the one hand it means that a higher standard than simple partisanship will guide us. The rules laid down are not simply rules the majority thinks will result in its advantage in the particular instant at hand, but have been formed at times when reason and principle, rather than passion and narrow interest, may have some say in their formulation. On the other hand, these are rules made by our own representatives, not by some body alien to us. Since they are made by our representatives, they will be suitable for us, reflecting our interests and empowered by our consent.

Our written Constitution reflects this dual character of the rule of law in democracy. It means to guide the country towards the fulfillment of those principles that ought to rule us. Yet it also means to fashion a rule that will acknowledge our interests and gain our consent.

If one regards the Constitution as simply an 18th century document reflecting the practice of the 18th century, as does Justice Marshall, then one will not pause to read it carefully. The compromises regarding slavery will be taken as an endorsement of the principle of slavery. It will not be noticed that the Constitution never mentions slavery, the principle of slavery, or any racial distinction, and thus cannot possibly be held to have endorsed the principle that one man may justly be made the property of another, much less that one race has rights not possessed by another. One will not pause to distinguish between the principles the Constitution endorses and the compromises of practice it makes to maintain government by consent of the governed.

The problem is not the introduction of higher law into constitutional deliberation; the problem is the failure to discern the natural law incorporated in the Constitution itself, and to recognize the imperfect embodiment of higher law possible in a political society based upon the consent of the governed. The Constitution can only have the dual character of being at once a practical guide and a goal which we have yet to fulfill completely. Judicial review may contribute to such a Constitution, but if and only if our judges remain loyal to the Constitution and never forget that they are not our rulers, but only our judges.

Chapter Five

Federalism and Freedom

Tocqueville wrote: "Local institutions are to liberty what primary schools are to science; they put it within the people's reach." Is local autonomy, as Tocqueville thought, necessary for the development of a citizenry suitable for free, democratic government, or are freedom and equality threatened by local prejudice and the states?

Freedom, Pluralism, and Federalism:
An Enigmatic Trio?

James L. Gibson

Introduction

Classical American democratic thought argues that democracy is best protected through pluralism. Madison's dictum to "set faction against faction" is perhaps one of the most notable statements of this position. Modern theories are of a similar view.[1] Only through fairly unrestrained competition among a wide spectrum of political groups can the abuses so threatening to the freedom necessary for democracy be avoided.

The basic structure of the American national government (e.g., separation of powers) reflects this view. So too does the federal structure of the United States. Federalism is thought to enhance democracy because it provides a restraining check on the national government. Those who favor democracy frequently exhibit a basic antipathy to unitary government.

Yet federalism may itself be one of the most significant institutional structures that limits freedom and endangers democracy. To the extent that there is insufficient competition for political power within the states —to the extent that there is no *subnational pluralism*—democracy and freedom may be threatened. Especially in light of evidence of the fairly widespread and basic political intolerance of the American people,[2] the failure of pluralism to insulate state politics from antidemocratic majorities is terribly important.

In this essay, I address the basic problem of pluralism and freedom in the states of the United States. I begin by analyzing the theoretical connections among freedom, pluralism, and federalism. I next examine

---

1. e.g., Robert A. Dahl, *Polyarchy: Participation and Opposition* (New Haven: Yale University Press, 1971); *Dilemmas of Pluralist Democracy* (New Haven: Yale University Press, 1982).

2. Samuel A. Stouffer, *Communism, Conformity and Civil Liberties* (Garden City: Doubleday, 1955); John L. Sullivan, James Piereson, and George E. Marcus, *Political Tolerance and American Democracy* (Chicago: University of Chicago Press, 1982).

empirical evidence on the interrelationships among the concepts. Research examining the degree to which states have protected the rights of unpopular political minorities to compete for political power is considered as well. A specific conflict over political freedom for unpopular minorities—in particular, political repression of communists during the Truman/McCarthy era—is analyzed, with the objective of explaining how the federal structure of the United States affects the outcomes of such disputes.

Finally, I conclude this essay with a discussion of diversity and democracy. The classical assertion that democracy is enhanced by smallness is challenged. Instead, I argue (with Madison) that the essential ingredient of democracy is size. Only with large size is there the cultural and political diversity that is essential to democracy. Though cultural and political pluralism themselves generate certain problems for the political system, the future of American democracy is best protected through the promotion of political differences.

The Function of Federalism in Democratic Polities

Perhaps the most clearly articulated framework for analyzing freedom and democracy has been developed by Robert Dahl. Dahl asserts that democracy (or "polyarchy") is a political system that requires unimpaired opportunities for all full citizens:

1. to formulate their preferences

2. to signify their preferences to their fellow citizens and the government by individual and collective action

3. to have their preferences weighed equally in the conduct of the government, that is, weighted with no discrimination because of the content or source of the preference.[3]

Democracies need not allow all political interests equal influence over public policies, but they must allow all political interests equal opportunity to compete for the control of public policies. Thus, for Dahl, opportunities for everyone to compete for political power, to contest the political status quo, are essential. On ordinary policy issues, the majority should

---

3. Dahl, 1971, pp. 1, 2.

prevail, but a democracy cannot allow the rights of minorities to compete for political power to be subject to majority preferences. Instead, there must be institutionalized guarantees of these rights.

Dahl provides a compelling analysis of the conditions conducive to the development of a democratic regime. For instance, he considers the effects of levels of economic development and decentralization, as well as social pluralism. His scheme is essentially designed to account for the democratization of polities that are dominated by non-competitive monarchs or oligarchs.

Just as difficult is the issue of how democracies maintain democracy. Democracies seem to contain the seeds of their own destruction. Democracy as a system of majority rule may provide an opportunity for destroying democracy as a system of equal opportunity to compete for political power. The implementation of majority rule is not too difficult to achieve; the implementation of schemes for protecting against majority tyranny is exceedingly difficult.

The framers of the American political system recognized full-well the dangers of majority tyranny. Madison, for instance, admitted the legitimacy of the following lamentation:

> Complaints are everywhere heard from our most considerate and virtuous citizens, equally the friends of public and private faith and public and personal liberty, that our governments are too unstable, that the public good is disregarded in the conflicts of rival parties, and *that measures are too often decided, not according to the rules of justice and the rights of the minor party, but by the superior force of an interested and overbearing majority.*[4]

Their solution for curing the evils of majority factions were largely structural. The political system ought to be configured so that if factious majorities were to form, they would be neutralized.[5] Political structures should promote size and diversity:

> The smaller the society, the fewer probably will be the distinct parties and interests composing it; the fewer the distinct parties and interests, the more frequently will a majority be found of the same party; and the smaller the number of individuals composing a majority, and the

---

4. Alexander Hamilton, James Madison, and John Jay, *The Federalist Papers* (New York: New American Library, 1961), *Federalist* #10, p. 77, emphasis added.

5. Madison defined factions as "a number of citizens, whether amounting to a majority or minority of the whole, who are united and actuated by some common impulse of passion, or of interest, adverse to the rights of other citizens, or to the permanent and aggregate interests of the community." *Federalist* #10, p. 78.

smaller the compass within which they are placed, the more easily will they concert and execute their plans of oppression. Extend the sphere and you take in a greater variety of parties and interests; you make it less probable that a majority of the whole will have a common motive to invade the rights of other citizens; or if such a common motive exists, it will be more difficult for all who feel it to discover their own strength and to act in unison with each other.[6]

Though he was sanguine about the prospects of an abusive majority forming—"in the extended republic of the United States, and among the great variety of interests, parties, and sects which it embraces, a coalition of a majority of the whole society could seldom take place on any other principles than those of justice and the general good. . . ."[7] —Madison's simple hypothesis was that size is associated with diversity and that diversity blocks repression.

The dangers inherent in the creation of a strong federal government were minimized by the greater size and diversity of the Union. At the national level, unlike politics at the state level, faction was likely to be set against faction.

The influence of factious leaders may kindle a flame within their particular states but will be unable to spread a general conflagration through the other States. . . . A rage for paper money, for an abolition of debts, for an equal division of property, or for any other improper or wicked project, will be less apt to pervade the whole body of the Union than a particular member of it, in the same proportion as such a malady is more likely to taint a particular county or district than an entire State. . . . In the extent and proper structure of the Union, therefore, we behold a republican remedy for the diseases most incident to republican government.[8]

Even within the context of majority rule, pluralism was thought to protect political minorities.

This idea has recently been given new emphasis in the work of Sullivan, Piereson, and Marcus.[9] These authors argue that a diversity of interests among citizens of the United States has been instrumental in protecting the rights of political minorities. It is, however, a sort of perverse diversity. Beginning with a host of empirical research portraying widespread intolerance among the mass public in the United States, Sullivan, Piereson, and Marcus argue that it is the inability of the majority to agree upon the

---

6. *Federalist* #10, p. 83.
7. *Federalist* #51, p. 325.
8. *Federalist* #10, p. 84.
9. Sullivan, Piereson, and Marcus (1982).

particular political minorities that are worthy of political repression that serves to block repression and preserve freedom. They term this a "federalist theory of tolerance":

> A federalist theory of tolerance requires only that the targets of whatever intolerance does exist should be diverse. In other words, although a significant portion of the mass public may be intolerant of some ideas or groups, citizen hostility ought not to concentrate on particular groups or ideas. When citizen hostility is dispersed, ordinary politics will moderate mass sentiments of intolerance, given the practical necessity to forge a majority on other issues. If intolerance is directed at many targets, the federal constitutional order will protect the civil liberties of all. The same logic applies to political elites, who need not adopt the norms of tolerance, so long as they are unable to reach agreement about whom to repress.[10]

Thus, intolerant factions get set against opposing intolerant factions.

In addition to these system-level arguments about diversity and freedom, there is a body of literature at the micro- or individual-level that links exposure to diversity with political tolerance.[11] As individuals confront alternative, even threatening social and political points of view, they generally become less threatened by political differences, and consequently become more tolerant of them.[12] Homogeneity is thus the enemy of willingness to put up with one's political opponents. While the processes are quite different, social pluralism creates more tolerant individuals, just as it creates a more tolerant polity.

Thus, there is widespread agreement that heterogeneity and social pluralism enhance freedom and democracy. Structural arrangements can be devised—such as federalism—that enhance heterogeneity. Heterogeneity also contributes to the political tolerance of individual citizens within the polity.

---

10. Sullivan, Piereson, and Marcus, 1982, p. 22.
11. See for examples Stouffer, 1955; Sullivan, Piereson, and Marcus, 1982; and Clyde Z. Nunn, Harry J. Crockett, Jr., and J. Allen Williams, Jr., *Tolerance for Nonconformity* (San Francisco: Jossey-Bass, 1978).
12. Differences in exposure to diversity may be one of the variables that accounts for the typical finding that elites are more tolerant than masses. See James L. Gibson and Richard D. Bingham, *Civil Liberties and the Nazis: The Skokie Free-Speech Controversy* (New York: Praeger, 1985).

James L. Gibson

The Limits of Federalism

The arguments of the federalists were largely developed to justify the transfer of political power from the states to the national government. Madison and the other framers of the Constitution were interested in justifying the creation of a strong national government. Consequently, many of their arguments were cast in terms of structures and processes for keeping the federal government from becoming abusive. Much less attention was devoted to political repression in the states, even though political repression was widespread in the states at the time the adoption of the United States Constitution.[13] Though they obviously feared abusive majorities in the states, the relationship of federalism and democracy at the subnational level was not their primary political concern.

The very arguments used by the Federalists to allay fears of federal repression can be levied against the states themselves. Madison feared the political homogeneity of the American states. He wrote:

> In a free government, the security for civil rights must be the same as for religious rights. It consists in the one case in the multiplicity of interests, and in the other, in the multiplicity of sects. The degree of security in both cases will depend on the number of interests and sects; and this may be presumed to depend on the extent of the country and the number of people comprehended under the same government. This view of the subject must particularly recommend a proper federal system to all the sincere and considerate friends of republican government, since it shows that in exact proportion as the territory of the union may be formed into more circumscribed Confederacies, or States, oppressive combinations of a majority will be facilitated; the best security, under the republican forms, for the rights of every class of citizen, will be diminished . . . ."[14]

The essential ingredients of democracy at the national level were sorely missing in the politics of many of the American states.

Sullivan, Pierson, and Marcus are also a bit troubled about the implications of federalism for their theory. For instance, they assert:

> The fact that we have shown a great deal of diversity at the national level does not preclude the possibility that a more powerful potential for repression exists locally. It may merely be the case that local majorities are different and cancel one another out when aggregated nationally. For instance, one community may agree that the group to suppress is

---

13. E.g., seditious libel; see Leonard W. Levy, ed., *Freedom of Speech and Press in Early American History: Legacy of Suppression* (New York: Harper and Row, 1963).

14. *Federalist* #51, p. 324.

the communists, while another agrees that it is the fascists or Nazis. In the aggregate it appears that there is little consensus, when in fact there are a series of local consensus situations.[15]

Thus, the processes operative at the national level to preserve democracy may not be operative at the state level. The very arguments used by the federalists to justify the sharing of power with the national government can be marshaled to question the degree to which democracy is secure in the states.

Several specific questions concerning federalism and democracy must be addressed. First, what evidence is there of political repression at the state level in the United States? Second, how much pluralism—social or political—can be found in the states of the United States? Third, is the degree of social pluralism connected to the degree of political pluralism or democracy? These questions require an empirical analysis of politics in the American states. I shall begin with a consideration of political repression by the states of the United States.

The States and Political Repression

For my limited purposes, an assessment of political repression within the states of the United States need not survey comprehensively the whole of American history.[16] The issue is not whether (or what proportion of the time) the states have engaged in political repression. It is instead whether the states have been able to withstand the demands of repressive majorities *when they arise*. Thus, even if political repression is atypical in American state politics, an examination of repressive eras can lead to insights about the relationship of freedom and federalism. I shall therefore examine repression from the perspective of the "Red Scare" following World War II. An understanding of the relationship between pluralism and repression in the states of the United States during this era may shed some light on the role of federalism in democracies.

---

15. Sullivan, Piereson, and Marcus, 1982, pp. 86-87.
16. For an excellent, comprehensive consideration of political repression in the United States at both the state and national levels see Robert Justin Goldstein, *Political Repression in Modern America* (Cambridge: Schenkman, 1978). For a review of repression in the late 18th century, see Levy, 1963.

Conceptualization of State Political Repression

Many observers of American democracy assume that public policy in the United States is quite tolerant. From the system or macroscopic view, the United States does indeed appear to be fairly tolerant, though it is far from being the most tolerant country in the world.[17] Compared to most countries, political minorities have considerable political freedom.

From an historical perspective, however, glaring and recurrent instances of political repression can be found. The Alien and Sedition Act of 1798, a host of repressive measures adopted during the Civil War, and the two "Red Scares" of the 20th century are just the most well-known testaments to the capacity of the American system for political repression.[18] No rigorous, scientific studies of the amount of political repression have been conducted previously, but vivid exemplars of the systemic intolerance of unpopular political minorities are easy to find.

Conceptually, I define repressive public policy as policy that places restrictions on oppositionist political activity—by which is meant activities through which citizens, individually or in groups compete for political

---

17. For instance, Dahl provides system scores on one of his main dimensions of polyarchy for 114 countries for approximately 1969. In terms of opportunities for political opposition, the United States lagged behind 8 other countries, and was tied with Chile, Iceland,and Israel (Dahl, 1971, p.232). See also John F. O. Bilson, "Civil Liberty: An Econometric Investigation," *Kyklos*, 35 (1982), pp. 94-114. In terms of intolerance in mass opinion, Americans are far less willing to tolerate unpopular political minorities than are New Zealanders—see John L. Sullivan, Michal Shamir, Patrick Walsh, and Nigel S. Roberts, *Political Tolerance in Context: Support for Unpopular Minorities in Israel, New Zealand, and the United States,* (Boulder: Westview Press, Inc., 1985)—although they are more tolerant than Israelis: see also Michal Shamir and John L. Sullivan, "The Political Context of Tolerance: The United States and Israel," *American Political Science Review* 77 (1983), pp. 911-28. Shamir and Sullivan found similar levels of intolerance in the United States and Israel, though the intolerance of Israelis was thought to be more menacing because it was more focused. Dan Caspi and Mitchell A. Seligson, "Toward an Empirical Theory of Tolerance: Radical Groups in Israel and Costa Rica," *Comparative Political Studies* 15 (1983), pp. 385-404, report that residents of San Jose, Costa Rica, are more tolerant than residents of New York City. James L. Gibson and Peter J. Van Koppen, "Political Tolerance in the Netherlands and the United States," Paper delivered at the 1986 Annual Meeting of the Law and Society Association, Chicago, Illinois, found that American college students are roughly as intolerant as are Dutch college students, although the breadth of groups not tolerated is wider in the United States.
18. E.g., Goldstein, 1978; Caute, David, *The Great Fear* (New York: Simon and Schuster, 1978).

power[19]—upon some competitors for power but not on all competitors.[20] For example, policy outlawing a political party would be considered repressive, just as would policy that requires the members of some political parties to register with the government while not placing similar requirements on members of other political parties. Though there are some significant limitations to this definition, there is utility in considering the absence of political repression (political freedom) as including unimpaired opportunities for all full citizens to compete for political power. This is the working definition to be used in this research.

Political repression may come about through "democratic" means. That is, the majority may adopt repressive legislation through proper and legitimate means. Because democracy is a sort of government requiring certain procedures (majority rule) *as well as* substantive policies (protection of the right of all to compete for political power), such action must be considered anti-democratic. Democracies must restrain intolerant and repressive factions, even if they are majority factions. Indeed, this may be the "principal task of modern legislation."[21] Whatever the procedures of adoption, then, repressive public policies are inimical to democracy.

Operationalizing Political Repression—1950s

Political repression during the Truman/McCarthy era is here measured by an index that indicates the degree of restraint on the political activities of the Communist Party and its members during the late 1940s and

---

19. E.g., Goldstein, 1978; Caute, David, *The Great Fear* (New York: Simon and Schuster, 1978).
20. This is similar to Goldstein's definition: "Political repression consists of government action which grossly discriminates against persons or organizations viewed as presenting a fundamental challenge to existing power relationships or key governmental policies, because of their perceived political beliefs." Goldstein, 1978, p. xvi, emphasis removed.
21. *Federalist* #10, p. 79.

1950s.[22] A host of actions against communists was taken by the American states, including denying communists public employment (including teaching positions in public schools), denying them access to the ballot as candidates and prohibiting them from serving in public office even if legally elected, requiring communists to register with the government, and outright bans on the Party. Thus the repression ranged from prohibiting those predisposed toward communist ideology from (1) organizing political parties, to (2) running candidates for office, to (3) holding non-elective public offices. Forced registration was a means toward achieving these ends.

Of the 50 American states, 25 took none of these actions against

---

22. Some might object that the repression of communists, though it is clearly repression within the context of the definition proffered above, is not necessarily "antidemocratic" because the objects of the repression are themselves "antidemocrats." To repress communists is to preserve democracy, it might be argued. Several retorts to this position can be formulated. First, for democracies to preserve democracy through non-democratic means is illogical because democracy refers to, as much as anything else, a set of means, as well as ends—e.g. Joseph Schumpeter, *Capitalism, Socialism, and Democracy* (New York: Harper & Row, 1950); Robert A. Dahl, *A Preface to Democratic Theory*, (Chicago: University of Chicago Press, 1956), *Who Governs?* (New Haven: Yale University Press, 1961), and *Polyarchy*, 1971; and V. O. Key, *Public Opinion and American Democracy*, (New York: Alfred A. Knopf, 1961). The means argument can also be judged in terms of the necessity of the means. At least in retrospect (but probably otherwise as well), it is difficult to make the argument that the degree of threat to the polity from communists in the 1940's and 1950's in any degree paralleled the degree of political repression (e.g. Goldstein, 1978). Second, the assumption that communists and other objects of political repression are "anti-democratic" must be considered as an empirical question itself in need of systematic investigation. As a first consideration, it is necessary to specify which communists are being considered inasmuch as the diversity among those adopting—or being assigned—the label is tremendous. Merely to postulate that communists are anti-democratic is inadequate. Third, the repression of communists no doubt has a chilling effect on those who, while not communists, oppose the political status quo. In recognizing the coercive power of the state and its willingness to direct that power against those who dissent, the effect of repressive public policy extends far beyond the target group.

communists.[23] (It should be noted that following World War I, most states adopted criminal syndicalism statutes that could be relatively easily applied to subversive activities by communists in the 1940s and 1950s.[24]) Two states—Arkansas and Texas—banned communists from the ballot and from public employment, as well as banning the party and requiring that communists register with the government. Another 9 states took all three measures against the communists, but did not require that they register with the government. The remaining 14 states took some, but not all, actions against the communists.

From these data, a simple index of political repression against communists has been calculated. The index indicates the level of political repression against communists and ranges from those states that took no action to those banning communists from public employment, to those banning communists from running candidates and holding public office, to those completely banning communists and the Communist Party. A "bonus"

---

23. The source for these data is a 1965 study requested by a subcommittee of the Committee on the Judiciary in the United States Senate. The Subcommittee to Investigate the Administration of the Internal Security Act and other Internal Security Laws had data compiled on seven categories of statutes: (1) criminal and unlawful advocacy statutes (statutes making it a crime to advocate the overthrow of the government by force or violence or other unlawful means); (2) statutes requiring the registration of particular political organizations; (3) statutes outlawing subversive organizations; (4) statutes concerning the loyalty of public officers and employees and teachers; (5) statutes and other administrative rules governing admission to and exclusion from the bar; (6) statutes providing for the denial of incidental benefits to subversive persons or subversive organizations; and (7) a miscellaneous category. See Library of Congress, Legislative Reference Service, The American Law Division, *Internal Security and Subversion: Principal State Laws and Cases. A study prepared for the Subcommittee to Investigate the Administration of the Internal Security Act and Other Internal Security Laws of the Committee on the Judiciary, United States Senate,* (Washington, D.C.: U.S. Government Printing Office, 1965), Prepared by Raymond J. Celada. See also Gellhorn, 1952; and William B. Prendergast, "State Legislatures and Communism: The Current Scene," *American Political Science Review* 44 (1950), pp. 556-74.

24. For example, the statue adopted by California shortly after World War I defined the

Table 1. Political Repression of Communists by American State Governments

State	Banned From Public Employment	Banned From Politics	Banned Outright	Scale Score[a]
Arkansas	Yes	Yes	Yes	3.5
Texas	Yes	Yes	Yes	3.5
Arizona	Yes	Yes	Yes	3.0
Indiana	Yes	Yes	Yes	3.0
Massachusetts	Yes	Yes	Yes	3.0
Nebraska	Yes	Yes	Yes	3.0
Oklahoma	Yes	Yes	Yes	3.0
Pennsylvania	No	Yes	Yes	3.0
Tennessee	No	Yes	Yes	3.0
Virginia	No	No	Yes	3.0
Washington	No	Yes	Yes	3.0
Alabama	Yes	Yes	No	2.5
Louisiana	Yes	Yes	No	2.5
Michigan	Yes	Yes	No	2.5
Wyoming	Yes	Yes	No	2.5
Florida	Yes	Yes	No	2.0
Georgia	Yes	Yes	No	2.0
Illinois	Yes	Yes	No	2.0
Kansas	No	Yes	No	2.0
Wisconsin	No	Yes	No	2.0
California	Yes	No	No	1.0
New York	Yes	No	No	1.0
Delaware	No	No	No	0.5
Mississippi	No	No	No	0.5
New Mexico	No	No	No	0.5
Alaska	No	No	No	0.0
Colorado	No	No	No	0.0
Connecticut	No	No	No	0.0
Hawaii	No	No	No	0.0
Iowa	No	No	No	0.0
Idaho	No	No	No	0.0
Kentucky	No	No	No	0.0
Maryland	No	No	No	0.0
Maine	No	No	No	0.0
Minnesota	No	No	No	0.0
Missouri	No	No	No	0.0
Montana	No	No	No	0.0
North Carolina	No	No	No	0.0
North Dakota	No	No	No	0.0
New Hampshire	No	No	No	0.0
New Jersey	No	No	No	0.0
Nevada	No	No	No	0.0
Ohio	No	No	No	0.0
Oregon	No	No	No	0.0
Rhode Island	No	No	No	0.0
South Carolina	No	No	No	0.0
South Dakota	No	No	No	0.0
Utah	No	No	No	0.0
Vermont	No	No	No	0.0
West Virginia	No	No	No	0.0

a. A "bonus" of 0.5 was added to the scale score if the state also required that communists register with the government.

score of + .5 was given to those states requiring that communists register with the government.[25] Table 1 shows the scores of the individual states. This measure can rightly be considered to be a valid indicator of political repression by the states. In asserting this I do not gainsay that the state has the right—indeed, the obligation—to provide for its internal security. Consequently, statutes that prohibit such actions as insurrection

---

crime as:

> any doctrine or precept advocating, teaching or aiding and abetting the commission of crime, sabotage (which word is hereby defined as meaning willful and malicious physical damage or injury to physical property), or unlawful acts of force and violence or unlawful methods of terrorism as a means of accomplishing a change in industrial ownership or control, or effecting any political change —California General Laws Annotated. act 9428 (Deering), quoted in Carol E. Jenson, *The Network of Control: State Supreme Courts and State Security Statutes, 1920-1970* (Westport: Greenwood Press, 1982), p. 25.

Between 1917 and 1920, 24 states adopted criminal syndicalism statutes. By 1937, 3 states had repealed their statutes, although one of these—Arizona— apparently did so inadvertently during recodification. As of 1981, 7 of these states still had the statutes on their books, and one additional state—Mississippi —had passed such legislation. See Eldridge Dowell, *A History of Criminal Syndicalism Legislation in the United States* (New York: Da Capo Press, 1969; Originally published by Johns Hopkins University Press, 1939); Walter Gellhorn, *The States and Subversion* (Ithaca: Cornell University Press, 1952); Zechariah Chafee, Jr., *Free Speech in the United States* (Cambridge: Harvard University Press, 1967); and Jenson, 1982, pp. 167-75.

There is a reasonably strong relationship between adoption of criminal syndicalism laws following World War I and the passage of legislation following World War II repressing communists (gamma = -.39). However, the relationship is not as expected. Only one third of the states with criminal syndicalism statutes passed new legislation restricting communists, while nearly two-thirds of the states without such legislation adopted anti-communist statutes. The explanation may be that many states with existing laws against syndicalism found it unnecessary to adopt new legislation repressing communist. Existing laws could be mobilized for that purpose. Thus, most states had one sort of law or the other, but not both.

25. It should be noted that these three items scale in the Guttman sense. That is, nearly all of the states outlawing the Communist Party also denied it access to the ballot and public employment. Nearly all of the states that denied Communists access to the ballot also made them ineligible for public employment. The registration variable does not, however, exhibit this pattern of cumulativeness. Registration seems to be a means of enforcing a policy goal such as banning membership in the Party. Because registration raises Fifth Amendment self-incrimination issues, some states chose not to require it. Statutes requiring registration are treated for measurement purposes as representing a greater degree of commitment to political repression of the communists, and for that reason the "bonus" points were added to the basic repression score.

do not necessarily constitute political repression. However, as the action prohibited moves beyond a specific, criminal behavior, the line between repressive and non-repressive legislation becomes less clear. Commenting in 1936 about sedition and criminal syndicalism, the University of Pennsylvania Law Review asserted:

> The concept of the state carries with it the right to punish those who would overthrow it. But the nature of the democratic state is such that encroachment by statute on the free expression of ideas, though aimed at a revolutionary movement, inevitably discourages those who would peacefully reform. Militancy of language should not thus be allowed to be confused with advocacy of violence. If one believes with Mr. Justice Holmes that "the best test of truth is the power of the thought to get itself accepted in the competition of the market," and that the American way of life has been to allow even the most inflammatory words to circulate freely, these statutes are not a legitimate exercise of the police power but an unwarranted stifling of freedom of expression .... Faith in democracy would allow all dangerous political ideas to reach the eyes and ears of all, trusting in their repudiation by the ultimate governing body, the electorate.[26]

Gellhorn has identified another major defect in such statutes:

> Traditionally the criminal law has dealt with the malefactor, the one who himself committed an offense. Departing from this tradition is the recent tendency to ascribe criminal potentialities to a body of persons (usually, though not invariably, the Communists) and to lay restraints upon any individual who can be linked with the group. This, of course, greatly widens the concept of subversive activities, because it results, in truth, in forgetting about activities altogether. It substitutes associations as the objects of the law's impact. Any attempt to define subversion as used in modern statutes must therefore refer to the mere possibility of activity as well as to present lawlessness.[27]

There is also widespread evidence that the American states have used state security statutes as a means of repressing legitimate political opposition. For instance, in one of the earliest disputes of this century the state of Minnesota used a sedition law enacted in 1917 as a tool to repulse the Nonpartisan League's challenge to the Republican establishment in the state.[28] Similarly, Carleton (1985) convincingly shows that political repression in Houston and Texas was directed as much against organized labor,

---

26. "Legislation: State Control of Political Thought," *University of Pennsylvania Law Review* 84 (January, 1936), pp. 398-99.
27. Gellhorn, 1952, p. 360.
28. Jenson, 1982, p. 16.

those advocating progressive education, etc., as it was against communists and miscellaneous revolutionaries.[29]

Some might also argue that such legislation is of little consequence unless it is actively enforced. Such a position is tantamount to asserting that the effectiveness of criminal laws can be adequately measured by the number of prosecutions. American judges have directly confronted the issue of whether unenforced dormant statutes are of any consequence. For instance, the United States Court of Appeals, Second Circuit, addressed this issue in a ruling concerning the disclosure requirements of the election campaign committee of the Communist candidates for President and Vice-President (Hall-Tyner).[30] The court asserted:

> These laws, drafted by Congress and the legislatures of the various states, are an ever-present threat of reprisal to those who contribute to the Committee. It is of little moment that prosecutions under these laws are rare and that these statutes may currently lie dormant. This misses the point for three reasons. First, these statutes are significant as a reflection of popular will and therefore evidence popular animus against the Communist Party. Second, many of these statutes have not been declared unconstitutional and may be used in the future by a zealous prosecutor. The right of free speech can be trampled or chilled even if convictions are never obtained. Finally, the statutes may be reinterpreted to avoid the direct constitutional infirmity. Surely, it is not inconceivable that a statute long ignored may suddenly be resurrected and employed in a criminal prosecution. Moreover, although a penal statute may not be enforced, First Amendment freedoms may still suffer from its lingering presence.[31]

Thus, the passage of such laws is itself a significant policy output, irrespective of the degree to which such laws are strictly enforced.

Moreover, some such laws have indeed been enforced in the past:

> Many states that passed criminal syndicalism statutes in the aftermath of World War I did not enforce them to any degree, but this was not the policy in California. Between 1919 and 1924 the state arrested 504 persons and tried 264 of them. Thirty-four of these cases went on to

---

29. Donald E. Carleton, *Red Scare!* (Austin: Texas Monthly Press, 1985).
30. The court reasoned that since undisputed evidence established a reasonable probability that compelled disclosure of names of contributors to the Party would subject the contributors to threats, harassment, or reprisals from either governmental officials or private parties, the communist candidates were exempt from the disclosure and record keeping requirements of the Federal Election Campaign Act.
31. Federal Election Commission v. Hall-Tyner Election Campaign Committee, 678 Federal Reporter, 2d Series, 416 (1982), citations omitted, emphasis added.

appellate courts, and these proceedings served to silence much IWW activity except for legal defense and amnesty campaigns. As a result between 1924 and 1930 the state prosecuted no one under the statute because IWW activity was at such a low ebb.[32]

Dowell states that by 1932 California had imprisoned 135 people for violations of its Criminal Syndicalism Act.[33]

It has also been estimated that of the workforce of 65 million Americans, 13.5 million were affected by loyalty and security programs during the Truman/McCarthy era.[34] Brown calculates that over 11,000 individuals were fired as a result of government and private loyalty programs. Over 100 people were convicted under the federal Smith Act, and 135 people were cited for contempt by the House Unamerican Activities Committee. Nearly one-half of the social science professors teaching in universities at the time expressed medium or high apprehension about possible adverse repercussions to them as a result of their political beliefs and activities.[35] The "Silent Generation" that emerged from McCarthyism is testimony enough to the widespread effects—direct and indirect—of the political repression of the era.[36]

Thus, political repression in the states of the United States during the Truman/McCarthy era was fairly widespread. One-half of the states took direct statutory action limiting the right of communists to compete for political power. To determine whether the repression was related to the degree of pluralism in the states requires that pluralism be given more rigorous attention.

Pluralism in the States of the United States

The levels of pluralism in the American states are not easy to measure. At a minimum, however, pluralism probably requires that there be a diversity of opinions within the state. I shall begin this investigation of pluralism by examining political intolerance in the opinions of masses and elites in the states.

Political philosophers have long recognized that one of the most signifi-

---

32. Jenson, 1982, p. 25, citing Chafee, 1967, p. 327.
33. Dowell (1939, 1969, p. 122 in note 46).
34. Ralph S. Brown, *Loyalty and Security* (New Haven: Yale University Press, 1958).
35. Paul Lazarsfeld and Wagner Thielens, Jr., *The Academic Mind* (Glencoe: Free Press, 1958).
36. Goldstein provides extensive documentation of the wide variety of effects of the repression (1978; pp. 369-96).

cant threats to democracy is the intolerance of the majority. Though the classical dilemma of government has been that of controlling abusive rulers, the dilemma of democracy is to control majorities that become abusive and tyrannical.

Just how committed to democratic values are the peoples of the American states? Little is currently known about the distribution of public opinion in the states, largely due to the difficulties and costs of conducting state by state surveys. Yet the pluralism thesis is perhaps best tested in the context of the opinions of elites and masses in the states. Where opinion is intolerant and concentrated, we would expect to find the least amount of freedom. To the extent that opinion is divided, abusive majorities are less likely to form.

Table 2 reports data on the willingness of citizens to support the political repression of admitted communists. The subjects were asked whether an admitted communist should be jailed. The data are taken from a national survey conducted in 1954 by Samuel Stouffer.[37] Though there are very substantial limitations associated with aggregating national surveys by state,[38] these data do provide some clues to the nature of opinion in the American states.

Several aspects of the data in this table are important. First, though a slim majority of Americans supported the jailing of communists,[39] there is a great deal of variability among the states in the proportions supporting the repression of communists. The range is from barely more than a quarter of the population of Missouri supporting such a proposal to near unanimity in Arkansas. Indeed, in five states there is a consensus among the mass public that communists ought to be jailed, and no states in which there is a consensus that communists ought not to be jailed.[40] Thus,

---

37. Stouffer actually conducted two independent surveys, one through AIPO and the other through NORC. The data reported here are drawn from the NORC portion of the survey because the states of residence of subjects in the AIPO survey are unknown (Stouffer, 1955). For additional details see James L. Gibson, "Political Repression in the American States," Paper delivered at the 1986 Annual Meeting of the Law and Society Association; and "The Policy Consequences of Political Tolerance," Paper delivered at the 1986 Annual Meeting of the American Political Science Association.

38. For a thorough discussion of these issues, as well as evidence on the validity of the aggregated scores, see Gibson, 1986.

39. Of those with opinions on the issue, 59.0 percent would jail admitted communists.

40. This assertion is based on 70 percent agreement as evidence of consensus. If we were to consider only the proportion of the population with opinions on the question, there are 13 states in which there is an anti-communist consensus, but still no states in which there is a pro-liberty consensus.

though there may be sufficient diversity of opinion in many states to block the political repression of communists, in many states there is not.

Table 2 also reports elite opinion on exactly the same question.[41] Considerable variability in elite opinion is also observed, ranging from the very intolerant elites of North Carolina to the very tolerant elites of Missouri and New Hampshire. Though the number of elite interviews conducted within each state is small, there is a strong relationship between elite and mass opinion (r = .71). This in part reflects the influence of the political culture of the state in that both elite opinion and mass opinion are strongly correlated with political culture.[42] There is much less support among the elites for repression of communists—in only Kentucky and North Carolina do a majority of the elites support jailing admitted communists. Generally, the elites of southern states are considerably more intolerant than elites in other regions of the country. Though the elites are not generally intolerant, in seven states at least a significant minority of the elites support political repression.

The close connection of elite and mass opinion suggests that elites do not necessarily constrain the intolerant masses as is commonly suggested by elitist theories of politics.[43] Though there is not a single state in which the elites appear to be more intolerant than the masses, where elites are relatively more intolerant, so too are the masses. This again points to the political culture as a possible source of intolerance and political repression.

We have seen that at the national level, the American people were fairly divided on the question of jailing communists. A proposal to do so would have generated considerable support, but it also would have generated considerable opposition. A similar sort of division of opinion could not

41. Stouffer defined "elites" as those who held certain positions of influence and potential influence in local politics, including Community Chest chairmen; school board presidents, library committee chairmen, Republican and Democratic county chairmen, American Legion commanders, Bar Association presidents, Chamber of Commerce presidents, P.T.A. presidents, women's club presidents, D.A.R. regents, newspaper publishers, and labor union leaders.

42. The correlation of the Elazar measure of political culture—Daniel Elazar, *American Federalism: A View from the States*, 2nd ed. (New York: Harper & Row, 1972) as slightly modified by Gibson, "Policy Consequences," note 26, p. 17—and mass opinion is .62; the correlation with elite opinion is .60. When mass opinion is regressed on elite opinion and political culture, elite opinion has the greatest impact, though the effect of political culture is not reduced to insignificance.

43. E.g. Bernard R. Berelson, Paul F. Lazarsfeld, and William N. McPhee, *Voting* (Chicago: University of Chicago Press, 1954).

Table 2. Support for Jailing Admitted Communists—1954

	Percent Supporting Jailing Admitted Communists	
State	Mass Public	Elites
Arkansas	94.7 (19)	—
Kentucky	86.4 (22)	50.0 (26)
North Carolina	81.5 (65)	70.0 (10)
Alabama	75.7 (37)	44.4 (27)
Tennessee	72.7 (44)	—
Texas	67.3 (156)	47.5 (40)
West Virginia	65.5 (29)	—
Indiana	62.8 (129)	38.9 (36)
Kansas	62.7 (59)	—
Florida	61.9 (84)	41.7 (24)
Georgia	60.0 (50)	—
Illinois	59.3 (86)	35.9 (39)
Oklahoma	58.2 (67)	23.1 (13)
Nevada	58.1 (31)	—
Michigan	54.0 (163)	31.6 (38)
Oregon	53.3 (15)	—
Virginia	53.3 (15)	—
Connecticut	52.9 (17)	25.0 (12)
Louisiana	50.0 (13)	41.7 (12)
Pennsylvania	49.2 (179)	27.9 (43)
Iowa	47.8 (23)	—
New Hampshire	47.4 (19)	0.0 (11)
Washington	46.2 (52)	14.3 (14)
Wisconsin	43.9 (41)	4.0 (25)
Nebraska	43.8 (16)	40.0 (10)
Ohio	43.7 (103)	24.1 (54)
Minnesota	42.2 (64)	18.5 (27)
Idaho	40.9 (22)	38.5 (13)
Massachusetts	40.7 (81)	26.8 (41)
Maryland	35.3 (51)	—
New York	35.2 (273)	27.2 (81)
California	35.1 (174)	15.4 (65)
Colorado	34.8 (23)	14.3 (14)
North Dakota	34.1 (41)	33.3 (12)
New Jersey	31.1 (61)	25.0 (60)
Missouri	27.8 (18)	0.0 (11)
United States	50.6 (2448)	28.8 (758)

Note: Figures in parentheses are numbers of respondents within the state. Percentages are of all respondents, including those without an opinion on the subject. Dashes indicate that no interviews were conducted in the state.

Table 3. The Effects of Elite and Mass Intolerance on Political Repression in the States of the United States

Percent Supporting Jailing Communists

Percent Repressing Communists	⟨40%	40-50%	50-60%	⟩60%
Mass Opinion				
	28.6	50.0	62.5	72.7
	(7)	(10)	(8)	(11)
Elite Opinion				
	55.0	100.0	.0	—
	(20)	( )	(2)	(0)

be found in some of the states. In some areas, opinion was too homogeneous for opposition to materialize. In some states, opinion pluralism was sorely lacking.

Opinion Pluralism and Political Repression

It has been shown that many of the states took significant action to repress communists seeking to compete legally for political power. We can now consider whether this political repression during the Truman/McCarthy era was associated with the degree of opinion pluralism in the states.

Table 3 reports the relationship between the political repression of communists and elite and mass opinion in the states. The table reveals a fairly strong relationship between mass opinion and repression, with nearly three-fourths of those states with a strongly intolerant mass public engaging in repression, in contrast to only one-fourth of the states with a fairly tolerant mass public. The effect of elite opinion on policy is much more limited, largely because most states had relatively tolerant elites. However, it should be noted that even where elite opinion was relatively tolerant, mass opinion had a substantial effect on public policy. Thus, we see strong evidence here that opinion makes a difference for levels of freedom.

Conclusions

Political repression during the Truman/McCarthy era of American politics was far from universal. In some states majority opinion favored freedom for all political groups; in other states, there was a pluralism of opinion. But where a strong, anti-democratic majority formed, political repression resulted. To the extent that federalism creates states that are homogeneous and small, pluralism is threatened and the likelihood of majority tyranny increases.

Others have recognized that federalism can be inimical to freedom and democracy. Sullivan, Piereson, and Marcus summarized their position on the issue as follows:

> The weakest link in the federal model's solution is its assumption that most controversy is supra-local. Certainly as conflict grows, participants are usually forced to moderate their views to deal effectively with those who are apathetic or opposed to them. But at the local level, there may not be sufficient protection for the rights of the minority, particularly on issues that do not generate national or regional attention.[44]

To the extent that rights conflicts become nationalized, the possibility exists that a variety of differing political interests will become mobilized and, consequently, that the rights of political minorities will be protected. To the extent that rights disputes are managed at the state or local levels, the likelihood that a homogeneous majority will be able to impose a solution without accommodation and compromise increases significantly. The key issue is whether the dispute receives national attention.[45] Thus, it appears that the arguments made by federalists in defense of a strong national government may have some validity. To the extent that the polity encompasses a broad diversity of political interests, factions—even major-

---

44. Sullivan, Piereson, and Marcus, 1982, p. 22.
45. This idea has been applied to the dispute in Skokie, Illinois, over the rights of Nazis to hold a demonstration in the predominantly Jewish community. See Gibson and Bingham, 1985, and David G. Barnum, "Decision Making in a Constitutional Democracy: Policy Formation in the Skokie Free Speech Controversy," *Journal of Politics* 44 (1982), pp. 480-508.

ity factions—are unable to control the government for the purposes of repressing unpopular political minorities.[46]

Many of the American states are of sufficient size and diversity that it is possible for pluralist processes to be effective. Many of the states are not, however. Some states are characterized by highly intolerant mass publics, reinforced by the political culture, with elites who are not capable of neutralizing the policy effects of the intolerance. Interest groups do not serve to protect unpopular political minorities—indeed, those most in need of protection through interest groups are the least likely to have their interests represented. Nor do political parties ameliorate majority tyranny. As an unpopular political minority becomes salient enough to attract the attention of the majority, repression is likely to result. The culprit in the process is homogeneity.

Some have recently argued for a reorganization of the American states, rationalizing boundaries along the lines of commonality of interests. From the standpoint of protecting the rights of political minorities, it may instead be preferable to reorganize the states so as to minimize the commonality of interests of the citizens. To the extent that heterogeneity is related to size—as it surely is—this would require a reduction, rather than an increase, in the number of states. For faction to neutralize faction, a diversity of competitive interests, not a commonality of interests, is required.

Some observers have also recently expressed concern about the influx of immigrants to the United States. Among the concerns is the fear that cultural heterogeneity will intensify political conflict, perhaps even to the point that accommodation, negotiation, and compromise will be impossible. While such a level of political conflict would certainly be undesirable, one of the by-products of the heterogeneity may well be a socio-political pluralism that contributes to much greater tolerance and political freedom.

Federalism may well have served a useful purpose throughout the 200 years of the United States. As beneficial as it may have been for solving certain political problems, the price of federalism may be measured in

---

46. This is not to deny that significant political repression occurred at the national level during the Truman/McCarthy era. Indeed, much of the legislation adopted by the states imitated federal legislation. Perhaps the significant point is, however, that abusive majorities are more easily combated at the federal level due to the diversity of interests that can be mobilized. The demise of the Red Scare certainly began at the national level. In any event, I only argue that it is easier for repressive majorities to form at the state level than at the national level, not that they never from at the national level.

terms of freedom lost. Federalism, pluralism and freedom are indeed an enigmatic trio.

Partisans of Federalism

David Broyles

Each member [of a political confederacy] will be more devoted in their attachments and obedience to their own particular governments, than to that of the union.

Hamilton, *The Continentalist*

If, having regulated the great interests of the country, [the directing power of the American communities] could descend to the circle of individual interests, freedom would soon be banished from the New World.

Tocqueville, *Democracy* 1.16

Most Americans seem to agree, without reaching any great precision about the matter, that state and local governments are important. They implement community decisions about a variety of common concerns, from schools to health. Such decisions should be made locally, it is felt, to accommodate locally varying views on religion, morals, and related concerns. There are other matters, however, of greater urgency and dignity, that require action in Washington. The more weighty matters, the ones handled by the union, will attract citizen loyalty with less force, just as Alexander Hamilton said when he spoke as *The Continentalist*.

This commonsense perspective on federalism is increasingly ignored, however, by those who are supposed to know most about public life. And there can be only one result of the public's relying on opinion leaders who do not share their commonsense viewpoint: Ordinary citizens remain uninformed and are less capable of grasping serious issues. They are therefore less competent to decide how to govern themselves.

The public particularly needs certain questions aired. The institution of federalism gives rise to these questions in America, because it has been made constitutional. They are about fundamental differences between local and national politics—questions like the following, which agitated the Founders and their Antifederalist opponents: Are local activities of higher dignity than the national, or vice versa? Is the nation meant to regulate the affairs of local units so that they can survive and live by their own lights? Or, is the nation meant to superintend the local units so that they can achieve a better life than they would if left on their own to judge what constitutes their welfare? Such questions were raised at the Constitutional Convention when it became necessary to modify Virginia's first plan for a strictly national government. They suggest the possibility that the union can develop a wholesome interplay between competing national and local "sovereignties." They suggest, in the words of *The Federalist*'s Publius, that "the [American] Constitution ... is in strictness neither a national nor a federal constitution; but a composition of both" (39,195).[1]

On these matters partisan feeling runs high today, just as it has historically. Today's partisanship is denied, however. Instead of admitting its partisanship, the dominant camp insists that federalism be refused constitutional status. It insists that it is unnecessary to decide between competing claims of the states and the nation. The difference between them is only one of scale, it says, and both ought to stand opposed to "individual interests," as Alexis de Tocqueville said in his great work, *Democracy In America*. This is said to be so, because the nation and states generally cooperate for common purposes which are widely approved.

What is left unattended by this claim, however, is that the supposed purposes are not shared by the opposing partisan camp. Nor are they the traditional ones which are most important to the general public. America's opinion leaders, it turns out, are waging partisan war against both their ideological opponents and the general public. They suppress issues of federalism, because they do not want their political program challenged.

Notwithstanding the lack of discussion, the fact is that the states and the national government do regularly divide jurisdictions, even now. But they do so in violation of the Constitution. There are matters where, by traditional constitutional principle, the states ought to have the final say, but where they are now regularly overruled, even in defiance of the Founders'

---

1. References within parentheses have been used to direct attention to pertinent passages of *The Federalist*. In the parentheses, the number of the paper is given first, and then the number of the page, if this is included. Page numbers are from the edition published by Bantam Books (New York, 1982) and introduced by Garry Wills. The text of the Wills edition is taken from the authoritative J. E. Cooke edition (Middletown: Wesleyan University Press, 1961). A useful companion reference work is *The FEDERALIST Concordance* (Wesleyan University Press, 1980), edited by Thomas S. Engeman, Edward J. Erler and Thomas B. Hofeller.

dictum that the national powers are limited to certain specified purposes. Schools are an example, and family policy. On the other hand, the national government defers to the states now where it ought to have the final say. Licensing of economic activity for interstate commerce is an obvious example. Ensuring that a republican standard of decency is maintained by the states is another one, although this traditional national power has been almost forgotten since it was chosen as a special target of attack by the Supreme Court.

Should the older constitutional division of jurisdictions be given new recognition? Only the public can decide. But it can do so, it would seem, only on a solid foundation. It can do so only on a foundation of revitalized debate about what was once America's most contested constitutional feature, federalism.

Tocqueville's Participatory Localism

It is difficult to reach the constitutional questions about federalism, partly because they are hard to discern among the great variety of issues put forth for public attention. They are obscured in a haze created by an intoxicating fervor for citizens to participate—participate in everything. In the confusion, it is forgotten that America is not one of those unstable and oft-tyrannized "pure democracies" of the Greek past, but a constitutional democracy instead.[2] It is forgotten that liberties are protected best when citizens make certain critical decisions only, and accept constitutional restraints against wanton dabbling in others.

In this environment of total participation, the tough questions about constitutional federalism are forgotten, replaced by what appears to be a bland observation that it energizes democratic participation. Tocqueville is often quoted to lend respectability to this interpretation of federalism. In a well known comment, he says, "local institutions are to liberty what primary schools are to science; they put it within the people's reach." Tocqueville voices an opinion which is now widely held, one which is also shared by another highly respected observer of America, Harvard's James Q. Wilson. In the language of today, Wilson gives it as his textbook

---

2. Paul Eidelberg, *The Philosophy of the American Constitution* (Lanham: University Press of America, 1986), p. 217-18 and *passim*.

judgment that "[federalism's] most obvious effect has been to facilitate the mobilization of political activity."[3]

There can be little doubt about the truth of these observations. But no responsible person of our century, a century which has witnessed Hitler's Nuremberg rallies and the many repetitions of these under Communist "Peoples' Republics," should be willing to support the proposition that just any kind of participation in politics is good. Hysterical rallies are not proper participation, and neither is voting, when there is only one candidate. Experience with such things, with "totalitarian participation" at home as well as abroad, is a sobering reminder. It cautions Americans to revive the same questions about so-called democratic participation that agitated the Founders.

The Founders knew what today's opinion pollsters seem often to forget, that the best participation is participation through constitutional channels. Their work has made us raise questions about these channels. In particular, is the quality of participation improved by federalism as well as by separated powers? That is, is participation improved by including local "sovereignties" as organic parts of a constitutional system? Does such a system perform as the Founders promised, and does it give voice to the peoples' deepest concerns for justice and the common good? To such questions, the Founders and succeeding generations, as well, who were schooled by fiery public debates about federalism would have responded with firm convictions, for the most part giving a firm, yes.

These days, the questions might be too unfamiliar to evoke a response. Because he is so often made an authority, it is useful to trace this omission to Tocqueville as one very important source. His America is before the eyes of contemporary leaders more than the Founders'. And in his—*Democracy*—Tocqueville omits to discuss the contest between local and national politics that the Founders thought was so important.[4] Nor does he take seriously the Founders' views that the difference might be described as one between limited national powers and unlimited local ones. Instead of confronting such problems as these, Tocqueville encourages complacency in the view that participation in peaceful local societies is good in itself, regardless of whether the societies pursue proper or improper purposes. His fears about democracy going astray are confined to the possibility that national powers, not local ones, will be misused.

---

3. *American Government: Institutions & Policies*, 3rd Edition (Lexington: D. C. Heath and Company, 1986), p. 51.

4. *Democracy In America*, ed. J. P. Mayer (Garden City: Doubleday & Company, Inc., 1969), 1.1.8.

Tocqueville, it will be recalled, understands democratic man as alternating between "privatism" and altruism. He praises peaceful local societies indiscriminately, because they are supposed to employ artifice to gently wean man from his natural tendency, which is towards privatism and self-interested idiosyncrasy. Local societies are the means for developing gregarious sentiments and also foresight. Cooperating in them for mutual advantage, men develop a sophisticated version of self-interest, one which continues throughout life to encourage a sense of public duty. A kind of "caring" sentiment towards others would thrive there, Tocqueville thought, as it would even more in the family, where the binding forces arising out of natural affections could aid those generated by cooperative labor.[5] Such a sentiment would be innocent, Tocqueville seems to say, because it would be devoid of egoistic desires to dominate others. It would be devoid, that is, of privatism turned to vanity.

Because he saw democratic man by the lights of modern political philosophy, saw him as precariously balanced between selfishness and altruism, what Tocqueville feared most was a "soft despotism." Such a despotism encourages a perverted equality of materialism, in which a government of administrators, rather than statesmen, "invades the circle of individual interests" to minister to a citizen body which has been softened by everyday comforts and which values them above all else. Citizens must only forget their "manly self-reliance" and "freedom" in exchange for the beneficence of these administrators. It was to rescue men from this despotism that Tocqueville recommended schools for democracy: like juries, town council meetings, and participatory groups of all kinds.

In Tocqueville's thought, such groups appear as the only alternative in a world which, many readers agree, is portrayed as providentially moving towards catastrophe. Participatory groups emerge as the best hope in a world threatened by despotism, and thus they tend to assume for students of Tocqueville the character of ends in themselves. For these students, it is not easy to think that a proper combination of local and national powers achieves constitutional government, because Tocqueville's local governments have become in all ways preferable to the national regime of the Founders.

---

5. *Democracy* 2.3.8-12.

Federalism and Freedom

Liberal and Conservative Federalism

Liberal and conservative ideologies also constitute authorities for modern leaders, and like Tocqueville, they contribute to the haze obscuring constitutional federalism. At first glance, the conservatives seem to approve tradition and to agree with the Founders that federalism is a vital constitutional principle, not just an uninteresting mechanical feature of the system. But on further investigation, it becomes clear that conservatives have their own understanding of federalism. Some conservatives, those particularly interested in economics, simply turn away from politics to libertarian anarchy; but for others, republicanism pursues such ends as justice and charity, and these are realized at the local level, they believe, not the national.[6] Furthermore, they believe, federalism was understood best by the Antifederalists who opposed the original Constitution and by later opponents of it, like John C. Calhoun.

Often conservatives simply disdain the contribution of the Founders and attribute American liberties to British tradition.[7] The Founders, it appears from these writings, are often to be understood as unfortunate impediments to history's flow. But they sometimes argue differently, that constitutionalism has been transformed into its present bad condition by later statesmen like Lincoln. Professor Felix Morley concludes his book in which he describes this transformation as the triumph of "democracy" over republicanism, as follows. He speaks with characteristic conservative dismay:

> When Caesar stood on the banks of the Rubicon, deciding whether or not to strike down the sadly corrupted Roman Republic, he argued to himself that the issue was really already settled. "It is nothing," he said, "to be a republic, now a mere name without substance or character."

---

6. Conservatives often confuse their substantive aims for local government, here summarized as "justice and charity," with freedom. In their formulation, justice is sometimes also understood not as an ally of charity, but as a constraint on freedom, and this constraint appears to be enforced at the national level. The Antifederalists often used the same formulation. Their understanding was that freedom was realized in diverse localities, each of which gained the voluntary attachment of its citizens because, on the one hand, it was responsible, and on the other, they were virtuous. This is their "small republic" theory recapitulated by Professors Herbert J. Storing and Murray Dry. See Storing and Dry, *What the Anti-Federalists Were For* (Chicago: The University of Chicago Press, 1981), p. 16.

7. Russell Kirk is surely the most persistent exponent of this view. For a recent summary of his views, see "Edmund Burke and the Constitution," *The Intercollegiate Review*, Vol. 21, No. 2 (Winter 1985-86).

If that is the way we have come to feel about federalism, then is our Republic also, in less than two centuries of history, on the way out.[8]

Morley's judgment is typical of conservative writers who complain of today's centralized state that it pursues social engineering and in doing so gives expression to Jacobinism. The great danger is misapplied theory, these conservatives argue—theory which wrenches men from their concrete surroundings and prescriptive rights to satisfy democracy's tyrants with their secular science of human nature.[9] This danger is to be avoided, conservatives typically recommend, in one of two ways, neither of which raises constitutional questions about federalism: by a libertarian retrenchment of all government from the sphere of privacy, or as in Morley's case, by returning to a federalism which encourages vigorous local pursuit of justice and charity.[10]

Whereas conservatives generally despise the national government for what they see as its Jacobin purposes, liberals praise it. They regard it as the source of morally responsible policies to solve problems which the Founders had blocked out of national life by means of their mutually checking institutions, especially the institution of federalism. Liberals propose to overcome this checking by the unifying effect of parties. A kind of parliamentary democracy can be realized, they hope, that will work together with a neutral administrative apparatus. These new institutions, they expect, will overcome poverty, ignorance, and despair among the citizenry. More fundamentally, liberals expect to overcome impediments to realizing a new freedom where men can engage in creative self-realization.

If the liberal is less alarmed than the conservative about the present state of federalism, it is because he is quite satisfied with what they deplore. He borrows freely from Tocqueville to make a distinction between materialist "privatism" and non-materialist altruism, and he is satisfied that altruism is now permanently nationalized. Secure in this

---

8. *Freedom and Federalism* (Chicago: Henry Regnery Company, 1959), p. 276.

9. See Joseph Sobran's recent sentimentalized elaboration of this theme in *National Review* Vol. XXXVII, No. 25 (December, 1985), pp. 23-58.

10. Morley's is a non-elitist rendition of the conservative position. For an elitist interpretation, see Martin Diamond, "Conservatives, Liberals, and the Constitution," in *Left, Right and Center*, ed. Robert A. Goldwin (Chicago: Rand McNally & Co., 1965). Diamond argues the conservatives are oligarchic, and want to block majority rule by clever use of the separation of powers. His version of the conservative position corresponds to the liberal perspective on it, rather than to the way conservatives see themselves.

opinion, the liberal is usually quite willing to leave it to local jurisdictions to exercise independent control over those matters remaining to them, although he often favors national standards and the creation of administrative units which are more efficient than the states. He does not believe that serious constitutional issues are raised by his opinions.

Surface disagreements between liberals and conservatives about the relative merits of national and local government obscure the fact that there is an agreement between them on the fundamentals of republicanism. They agree, in the first place, that the Founders' original Constitution is irrelevant to today's world. And this agreement holds fast even as they disagree about what the Constitution was originally intended to do. As a consequence, neither liberals nor conservatives take seriously the Founders' understanding of federalism. Their views of the Constitution rest on Antifederalist inspired Amendments to it more than on the Constitution itself. This is because they both disdain the Founders' understanding of political life.[11]

The agreement between liberals and conservatives is most evident when both are seen to mistrust all political power. They believe that power moves irresistibly towards a Tocquevillian despotism, because men are fatally infected by materialism and vanity. They agree on this diagnosis, and they imagine that a utopian remedy is possible, even though they disagree on the specifics of the remedy. Conservatives expect to overcome the problem by resort to revitalized localism, and liberals by resort to beneficent nationalism. Rather than take seriously the Founders' federalism, they prefer to intellectualize, instead, about an idyllic associative activity, local or national.

The Study of Federalism

Whether they are avowedly partisan or not, the views of opinion leaders are acquired from a common source, the intellectuals of today's academy. The political science discipline of federalism is the most immediate source, although it appears not to be at first, because it claims to have become professionalized. (At the same time it has become lackluster, even by the standards of political science.) The great bulk of the studies it

---

11. For an extended discussion of this matter, see David B. Broyles, "Federalism and Political Life" in Charles Kesler, ed. *Saving the Republic: The Federalist Papers and the American Founding* (New York: The Free Press, 1986).

supports purport to be "managerial" or "financial," and not political at all. They purport only to eliminate inefficiency.

Students may be introduced to the subject by a melancholy review of the worst examples of inefficiency—overlapping jurisdictions that have unavoidably grown up in America. Cook County, Illinois, has been a good place to start. Around Chicago, it has been possible to live under many different local "governments" at the same time, most of them having taxing and police powers appropriate to their specialized purposes. Such "worst case" examples of wasteful duplication are said to illustrate the workings of American federalism, which, unlike unitary democracies such as England, must make provisions for a polyglot of ethnic groups. The existence of such groups is said to illustrate the working of necessity, not of good government. England's situation is much to be preferred.

The political scientist, now turned financial or managerial professional, takes a stand of knowing disinterest towards political developments. And when a politician such as President Nixon or Reagan stirs up an attempt to "do something" about federalism, he is shown that his efforts were nugatory in the greater context of necessarily increasing bureaucratic centralization. The analyst's disdain for the political controversy is quite evident in the delight he takes in demonstrating that the politician's effort was naive.[12]

As might be expected, a like contempt for political controversy over federalism is given a more general statement in the less professionally minded textbooks of American Government. The national government is taken as the focus of attention in most of these texts, and this is given as the reason for a lack of interest in local matters. In fact, though, the states are slighted more than would be necessitated by space requirements. Occasionally, a paternalistic concession is made to the rule of local authority when the states are praised, as Justice Brandeis praised them, for being "laboratories" of democracy. But, for the most part, state activities are regarded as lacking dignity. Regularly omitted is any extended treatment of such things as health services, family law, criminal justice, or public education.

While local protest—such as is lodged, for example, against "secular humanism" in schools—is peremptorily dismissed by scholars as interference with progress, national and local units are declared to be cooperative, not competitive, and what used to be called federalism is renamed

---

12. See, for example, Richard P. Nathan and Fred C. Doolittle, "The Untold Story of Reagan's 'New Federalism'," *The Public Interest* No. 77 (Fall, 1984), pp. 96-105.

"intergovernmental relations."[13] The only respectable question is said to be a technical one: which unit can do the job most efficiently? On the whole, defense is accomplished best nationally, it is generally agreed, and also gaining rights for disadvantaged classes. Garbage collection, on the other hand, is more a local matter. Between the two extremes, programs like public education are said to benefit from a mixture of authorities. The metaphor which became popular in the years following World War II was that of Professor Morton Grodzins' marble cake, and the proportion of federal, state or local activity to be found in the layers of any given slice of the cake is said to vary with the program that the slice represents.[14] In recent years the metaphor has been modified, but not abandoned, to account for a welcomed increase of federal control by means of category grants and performance standards.

Meanwhile, debate continues over the history, but not the present significance, of constitutional questions posed by federalism from its inception. Results of these debates are not very satisfying, though, because while one side demonstrates that strict constructionism is not defensible as an interpretation of the letter of the Constitution, the other side relies upon evidence from a different source to prove the opposite. Today's strict constructionism relies on its reading of the spirit behind the Constitution and especially on the circumstances of its ratification.[15]

Common to both sides of this debate is a corrosive fear that, anyway, the questions under discussion have become irrelevant to today's industrial world.[16] This concession to the possibility that federalism may be moot

---

13. The older conflict phase of federalism is attributed to the progeny of the Supreme Court's decision in *McCulloch v. Maryland*. Now, cooperation means that there are no clear boundaries between functions of the state and the nation. See Deil S. Wright, *Understanding Intergovernmental Relations* (North Scituate, Mass: Duxbury Press, 1978), p. 42. Also, Morton Grodzins, "Centralization and Decentralization In the American Federal System" in Robert A. Goldwin, ed. *A Nation of States: Essays on the American Federal System* (Chicago: Rand-McNally & Company, 1961), p. 23.

14. "The Federal System" in *Goals For Americans: Report of the President's Commission on National Goals and Chapters Submitted For the Consideration of the Commission* (New York: Prentice-Hall, 1960), pp. 265-282.

15. The best examples are those of James J. Kilpatrick, "The Case For 'States' Rights'" and Harry V. Jaffa, "'Partly Federal And Partly National': On the Political Theory of the Civil War," both in *A Nation of States*.

16. This is argued by William Riker, *Federalism: Origin, Operation, Significance* (Boston: Little Brown and Co., 1974). Not surprisingly, since he disregards its distinctive origins in the thought of the American Founders, Riker argues that federalism is common to all "empire" nations.

"civilizes" the debate for the academy by making it easy for the left-liberal partisans who dominate the campuses to ignore the whole matter. Their program requires an "updated" constitutional theory. Various forms of updated constitutional theory, revised policy agendas, etc. are indeed entertained. They lend support to the partisans' proposition (usually tacit) that recently evolved national purposes are far superior to state concerns.

Any controversy over federalism is usually muffled in this environment, but this is not the whole story. Some academically based conservatives are directing attention once again to the importance of states' programs. They wish to affect the national environment by beginning at the state level with such programs as tax reform. They also resist judicial governing of public schools. Revitalization of the separated powers is the aim of a general attack on federal judicial elitism, which is also underway. These initiatives are especially noteworthy because they show that, as the Founders foresaw they might, citizens can come to have more confidence in states than in a national government which is poorly administered.[17]

A side glance at disciplines other than federalism shows relevant controversy still to be alive there, also. Stronger parties are sometimes defended as means to inhibit the local responsiveness and patrimony which are typically excused in studies of federalism. Parties, it is said, provide the means by which self-interest may be subordinated to national altruism, even though such parties can only be gotten by disciplining local idiosyncrasies. Such views hark back to a more strongly held view of only a few years ago. Then, states' rights were regarded with open hostility. They were seen as devices for conservatives to promote unbridled capitalism and racism—devices for liberals to attack in the name of humanitarian economics and civil rights.[18] The decay of liberals' alarm over these concerns is an indication of increased confidence that their program is well entrenched.

There is also more controversy in new, state-of-the-art federalism stud-

---

17. A preference for the national government will only ensue upon its showing "good administration." Publius says: "I believe it may be laid down as a general rule, that [the peoples'] confidence in and obedience to a government, will commonly be proportioned to the goodness or badness of its administration" (27,174).

18. The best known statement of this position is that of James MacGregor Burns, *The Deadlock of Democracy: Four-Party Politics in America* (Englewood Cliffs: Prentice-Hall, Inc., 1963). Virginia's Representative Howard Smith was Burns' whipping boy. pp. 311-14. See also, Terry Sanford, *Storm Over the States* (New York: McGraw-Hill Book Company, 1967).

ies. Surprisingly, they take a turn to preferring local governments over the national.[19] An idyllic "unitary" democracy is said to be possible locally. In unitary democracy, direct participation replaces the representative principle and the separated powers. As a result, such democracies, according to the title of a recent popular work on the subject, go *Beyond Adversary Democracy*.[20] They encourage innocent cooperation and fraternalism among citizens whose common goals consist of satisfying the kind of needs which are seen by participants as clear, urgent, and undisputed. Needless to say, these needs are undisputed because they correspond to those respected by the academy's partisans.

The new theory points to something beyond the merely technical purposes usually announced openly by today's federalism studies. The preference for idealized local democracies is really a preference for a certain kind of politics, and only secondarily is it of concern whether it is practiced locally, nationally, or even internationally. Still, there are good reasons for calling it a local politics, even when it is urged on the national government, since it ministers best to the more tangible, bodily needs which stimulate strong universal recognition and support among men generally, just as partisan purposes stimulate such recognition among partisans. Thus, Professor Pranger describes today's federalism studies appropriately as an effort to impose local politics on the national government. He says:

> In a word, the national government has declined from its ideal representation as the center for the public good, to the position as the ultimate center for local power; the public good has become domesticated.[21]

---

19. It also favors a new international order. It does not, however, suggest a developed theory of international government, except such as is implied by the methodologies of comparative government and international relations studies.

20. Jane J. Mansbridge (New York: Basic Books, Inc., 1980). Samuel H. Beer speaks for the profession when he approves (with qualifications about localism) such projects as that of Mansbridge. He comments that they are "appealing both as means of enhancing democracy and of reducing conflict. But," he goes on, "it is hard in this day of increasing interdependence to identify functions of government whose impact is so limited geographically as to justify their control being entrusted to small jurisdictions." See "The Modernization of American Federalism," *Publius* Vol. 3, No. 2, (Fall, 1973) p. 92.

21. "The Decline of the American National Government" in *Publius*, p. 102. Congressmen have "localized" national powers by increasingly ignoring policy matters and devoting its energies to serving "clients" with economic advantages in the way that was formerly characteristic of state politicians. See Morris P. Fiorina, *Congress, Keystone of the Washington Establishment* (New Haven: Yale University Press, 1977), pp. 41-49 and *passim*.

David Broyles

Alexander Hamilton might have described the new domestication of national politics as an effort to reverse priorities and to give the supervisory role not to a politics of the public good, but to one where citizens are caught up in "attachment and obedience."

The Academic Environment

Their state-of-the-art leaders point the way to the partisanship that motivates the routine studies of federalism which are supposedly neutral and professional. This partisanship is better appraised, however, when it is seen within the academy, where it is possible for these studies to appear professionally neutral. The full significance of these studies can easily be missed because they can be treated separately, although they are parts of a whole and share the bias of their environment. This environment of the academy provides support for obviously political left-liberal activities, and this is clear to anyone who can poll opinions or count votes. But the academy also has its own native bias, one which is better hidden. It is more thoughtful, and might better be called something like "antifederalism" for reasons advanced below.

The life of the academy blinds its citizens to their bias. Thus, most intellectuals unconsciously project on politics a preference for the same "republic of letters" environment that they recommend at school, calling it "culture." Such an environment encourages an uncritical attitude towards all "disciplines" of learning.[22] There can be no critical perspective on the disciplines, because the departments teach contradictory things. Students quickly learn to respond by positioning themselves at an ironic distance from their learning, and professors quickly adapt their instruction to this sensible student posture. The result is a kind of "professionalization" or "bureaucratization" of the spirit among both professors and students. Broad understanding is sacrificed to narrow and illiberal specialties, each of which is pursued without dedication or spirit. Meanwhile

---

22. Uncriticized learning on campus supports a belief in everything and nothing—in nihilism, as Professor Harry Neumann so ably points out. And nihilism breeds fanaticism, as his friendly adversary, Professor Harry Jaffa, responds. See Neumann, "Liberal Education: The Beckmann Retrospective," *Claremont Review*, Vol. IV, No. 2, pp. 16-17. Also, Jaffa, "The Legacy of Leo Strauss," *Claremont Review*, Vol. III, No. 3, p. 14. Today's intellectuals thus recommend the same environment in politics that now sickens the campuses—contradictory behavior alternating between listless drift and partisan frenzy. See Allan Bloom, "Our Listless Universities," *National Review* 34, No. 24 (December 10, 1982): 1537.

a stultifying environment of self-approval is encouraged by those who defend idiosyncrasy as scientific progress, and who are loudest in their claims to defend freedom of expression.

Campus politics is an inevitable byproduct of this teaching environment. It provides an instructive analog of the kind of politics the academy supports extramurally. This politics consists of negotiations among the autonomous sovereignties which are academic departments. Since there is a broad agreement to avoid any real education, these negotiations quickly assume the character of lackluster squabbles over petty perquisites.

The academy obscures its incoherence by forcing attention onto refined pleasures, such as those offered by the fine arts. Aware that there is little controversy over such pleasures in the republic of letters, the academy begins to believe that government might also avoid the use of coercion for punishment or defense. Instead, it supports a "government" which would rule over a new world of culture and would mildly administer non-controversial public goods. This, it believes, would be best in Washington.

Instead of arbitrating competing claims for political legitimacy and authority, such a "government" confines itself to prescribing rules for another realm, a realm which the academy recognizes as culture, but which may also be called privacy or society. As a consequence of honoring another realm as higher, such a "government" is uncertain about its own ends. It abandons the age-old quest for a politics which makes life coherent by ordering its priorities, and it becomes mildly tolerant of all peaceful associative activity. It becomes uncertain about rewarding or punishing any group unless the group causes "a clear and present danger." This determination to ignore any distinguishing characteristics of groups other than their peacefulness is most apparent when groups pursuing bizarre and unnatural activities are honored equally with others so long as they remain peaceful.

Unfortunately, preferential choosing among groups and harsh punishment for those not favored intrude into this otherwise mild and tolerant world. The governing of culture requires not only that all forms of peaceful expression be tolerated, but that individuals and groups be made as autonomous as possible—able to act spontaneously, expressing their unique character. Disadvantaged groups are the inevitable problem created for statesmen who want every individual and group to be free of hindrances to such expression. This is because vanity and selfishness are bound to intrude themselves into the idyllic picture. Ariels turn into Calibans in what had been hypothesized to be a peaceful and innocent world.[23] Harsh authority comes to be needed for extending equal opportunities to its victims, and by extension, also for regulating the selfishness and vanity which caused the problem in the first place.

Political inequality becomes necessary to ensure that the desired equality of self-expression is achieved in all realms except politics. Thus political scientists come to believe that a class of administrators is justified in assuming power, not indeed to perform the traditional function of deciding the merit of various claims, but to perform an entirely new one instead. This new administrative class is to ensure equality of expression for disadvantaged groups by means of affirmative action quotas. So important does this task appear that, according to political science, only the new administrators who facilitate equal self-expression are to be trusted to rule. Only they can be free from a corrupt ambition.

The primary mission of political science's federalism studies now comes to light. It is to defend a new politics of administrative rulemaking and a new class of administrators. This is a difficult assignment, because it requires maintaining the pretense that such rulemaking has no victims. The pretense can be defended only in an environment of thought that exaggerates an artificial contrast between the vanity and selfishness of traditional statesmen on the one hand, and the innocence of administrators and private actors on the other. Because this body of thought is preoccupied with the danger which it supposes to be lurking in some ever-new conspiracy of oppressors, it is inattentive to the difficulties which are inherent in its own program. It is inattentive to the grotesque distortions of ambition which come to be characteristic of its administrative class. It is also inattentive to the possibility that administrative rules might impose an unequal constraint and an unequal privilege on different citizens and groups. It thus generates enemies unawares.

In the real world, however, administrative rules are far from even-handed, in fact. They always single out an oppressor, either private or public. The administrative state of standard rules for everybody is never realized and becomes instead the redistributive state of affirmative action quotas. Evolutionary development towards the administrative state is defended for itself. This phase becomes permanent and its victims do, also.

---

23. Shakespeare's Ariel and Caliban represent two extremes of what an Antifederalist republicanism presumes men to be like. See Paul A. Cantor, "Prospero's Republic: The Politics of Shakespeare's *The Tempest*" in John Alvis and Thomas G. West, eds., *Shakespeare as Political Thinker* (Durham: Carolina Academic Press, 1981), pp. 244-47.

The scholars of federalism make their assignment less difficult, with some success, when they ignore the enemies their politics has created and concentrate instead on supporting a new kind of governing. In the redistributive state, any executive official who is not preoccupied with the effort to aid victims of private or public vanity is labeled perforce as a representative of this oppressor.[24] The practice of chastising such officials can be made quite popular among an envious population. It should be noticed that, in practice, this weakens the best of governments, since it is demanded of administrators that they dedicate themselves to doing battle against whomever has been selected as an oppressor—usually some race, class, or even sex, which history is supposed to have favored.[25] Such statesmen, now turned administrators are confronted with mountains of paperwork, generated by what appears to be an army of professionals, purporting to show how things are mismanaged to the advantage of the oppressor. They have little time to rule in accordance with the Founders' demand for distributive justice and statesmanship.[26]

Furthermore, federalism's defense of its administrative state is complemented by a powerful attack on traditional politics in the name of culture. Its idea of such a culture was born with Hobbes' original liberalism.[27] Today, political science has added a new super-weapon to the arsenal it had previously gathered for the Hobbesian war on politics. It is adopted

---

24. Charles Beard's well known argument to this effect is an outstanding example of a tradition which was guided by this conviction. See *An Economic Interpretation of the Constitution of the United States* (New York: The Free Press, 1913).

25. The religious roots of this kind of hostility to "oppressors" among early Americans are described by Professor Don K. Price: Those who sought to escape the authority of an ecclesiastical hierarchy by appealing to the layman's literal reading of the Bible naturally sought to escape from discretionary political authority by relying on detailed legislation. As an alternative to discretionary authority, it seemed desirable to emphasize the rule of law—emphasis on legislative and judicial process rather than on unified political authority or centralized administrative discipline. See *America's Unwritten Constitution: Science, Religion and Political Responsibility* (Baton Rouge: Louisiana State University Press, 1983), p. 46. "Reverse racism" and other such phenomena attest to the uneven workings of the attempt to avoid political discretion. Nevertheless, the idea perseveres that religion or science (historicism) can make men more uniform and fraternal, and thereby eliminate disagreement over these "neutral" rules. See Price pp. 44-52.

26. Aristotle, *Ethics* 5.3.

27. For a profound analysis of the meaning of "culture," see Carl Schmitt, *The Concept of the Political* (New Brunswick: Rutgers University Press, 1976), especially chap. 8. As to its roots in Hobbes, see Leo Strauss, "Comments on Carl Schmitt's *Der Begriff des Politschen*," ibid.

from German historicist philosophy, and it appeals especially to inexper-ienced youthful audiences of "idealistic" students. A properly constituted "government" over culture, one which has eluded Hobbes' liberals for centuries, is now promised as a future utopia. The future is now under-stood more "scientifically," it is said, as requiring the administration of things and not men. In America, such a future is to be brought into being by a peaceable revolution, rather than by Marx's violent one. It is to develop in the competition of Justice Holmes' "marketplace of ideas."

Professor Samuel Beer traces a version of this utopianism which is of particular use to federalism scholars. Beer supports the widespread opin-ion that America from the Civil War to the New Deal was correctly described by academic "muckrakers," such as Charles Beard. It was a nation of uncharitable competition between the national government and the states. But according to Beer, in the '30s, charitable cooperation displaced this earlier phase, because New Deal legislation introduced a "countervailing power" in government to oppose private greed. This countervailing power, he further argues, later took the form of a benefi-cent technocracy, the rule of the new professionals of federalism.[28] Such a rule is thought to be made possible by the new world of altruistic coopera-tion.

Contemporary Antifederalism

Stripped of its utopianism, the main features of academic bias come to view as having important elements in common with Antifederalist thought which originally opposed the political life advocated by the Founders.[29] This observation explains why the academy is so unremit-tingly hostile to the principal features of the Founders' Constitution: federalism and separated powers. It also makes it possible to defend the Founders' politics, which is still the politics of most Americans, in direct confrontation with the academy.

Suppressed in the name of today's antifederalism bias are important questions of principle which the two original opponents recognized as dividing them. The significance of these questions can be seen in the

28. *Publius*, pp. 69-79.
29. The more likely actual source for this teaching is the less thoughtful egalitarianism and socialism of Eastern academe as expressed in the works of men like Professors Robert Nozick, John Rawls, and Michael Walzer.

debates over ratification. The Antifederalist fight to retain at least the spirit of the Articles of Confederation was not merely a fight over the mechanics of institutional arrangements, but rather over fundamental regime principles. The Antifederalist writer, Agrippa, is a good witness to this.[30] In his 4th letter to the people, Agrippa says that "no extensive empire can be governed upon republican principles," and that "such a government will degenerate to a despotism unless it be made up of a confederacy of smaller states." And it is clear from all his writings that, to Agrippa, the provisions of the Constitution of 1787 did not qualify as a confederacy, and therefore also not as a republic. It was, or would rapidly become a tyranny, he thought. As is well known, the Antifederalist position was that the new government was faulty because it exceeded proper powers and ruled the people directly, rather than as the Articles did, through the intermediation of state "sovereignties" (15-22).

In such ways, the Constitution threatened the regime which Agrippa thought best, the one which he would have called truly republican. This was an idyllic local government of simple unassuming men—yeoman farmers in those days, or perhaps blue-collar workers today. As the opposition was quick to point out, it really did not exist at any level. The states were too large already (9,39), and promising to get larger. But what is more important is that the regime was inherently an artifact of dreamy intellectuals which did not correspond to political experience, or to what this experience taught about natural law and natural right.[31] It really could not exist anywhere unless men were radically denatured. They would have to be stripped of materialism and vanity.

Agrippa's new regime was to be communal in the sense that its citizens would share feelings of pleasure and pain about what another Antifederalist, Brutus, described as "manners, sentiments and interests."[32] Such a

---

30. The Agrippa papers were authored by John Winthrop, whose essays are judged by two editors of Antifederalist writings to be "among the most coherent of all in the Antifederalist literature." This judgment about Winthrop is that of W. B. Allen & Gordon Lloyd, eds, *The Essential Antifederalist* (Lanham: University Press of America, 1985), p. 4. Agrippa's 4th letter was published in the (Boston) Massachusetts Gazette, 3 December, 1787.

31. Publius says that Antifederalist mistakes are "more commonly the fault of the head than of the heart" (1,4). And he accuses them of an "unnatural voice" (14,66) advocating "giving to every citizen the same opinions, the same passions, and the same interests" (10,43). They were "political doctors, whose sagacity disdains the admonitions of experimental instruction" (28,178).

32. Quoted in Herbert J. Storing, *The Complete Anti-Federalist* (Chicago: University of Chicago Press, 1981), Vol I, p. 45. *Cf.* Socrates' healthy city as described in Plato, *Republic* 369b-372c. Such a regime is "virtuous" because it is innocent.

regime would be characterized by shared feelings, but not by sharp exchanges of opinion about merit. Its sociability could not be constructed out of human efforts to accommodate diversity on the basis of justice, but would be guaranteed instead by the fact that peaceful cooperation was agreed upon as obviously necessary for common purposes. (According to many Antifederal thinkers, these purposes were to be made obvious by vigorous church life and disciplinary family/school training.)

So desirable did Agrippa's regime appear to him that he says the reason for confederalism "is obvious." Then he goes on to state this reason in a way characteristic of many writers of his time: it is that climate acting on manners and industry divides men into communities which cannot be united into single republican units.[33] Agrippa regards those elements in human nature which are formed in response to climatic conditions as the most important. They could make republican governments possible. On the other hand, he regards men as being made unfit to live with each other under republicanism by differences originating with climate. But, if climate, why not race also, we might ask, anticipating the opinion of the Southern rebellion? Or, why not any other causes which are plausibly argued to be decisive natural preconditions of republicanism?

It needs to be said that great differences among the population, such as are now described as "ethnic," might make a republic very difficult, even according to the Founders. But the differences between the Founders and the Antifederalists cannot be so easily reconciled by this observation. For Agrippa, what is the very substance of republican self-government, and not just an important precondition, is a common "standard of morals or habits" which arises from climatic determinants and is confirmed by local institutions. Where natural circumstances varied greatly, so would morals and habits. Agrippa assumes that the *necessary preconditions* of republics, common standards of morals or habits, will vary *necessarily* with climate. Universal experience so teaches us, he says. This kind of reasoning leads Agrippa to hint at what was expressed later as Calhoun's firm conviction. Agrippa says:

> The idea of an uncompounded republic, on an average, one thousand miles in length, and eight hundred in breadth, and containing six million white inhabitants all reduced to the same standard of morals or

---

33. Jefferson considered the climatic and geographic causes of politics in his *Notes On Virginia*, as did many others of the day. But Jefferson, unlike his opponents, came to the conclusion that they were not politically decisive. See Harvey Mansfield, Jr., ed., *Thomas Jefferson, Selected Writings* (Arlington Heights: AHM Publishing Corporation, 1979), pp. 18-26.

habits, and of laws, is in itself an absurdity and contrary to the whole experience of mankind.[34]

"Indeed," said Calhoun in a later comment on the effects of climate, "it is difficult to see how two peoples so different and hostile [as North and South] can live together."[35]

Antifederalist reasoning about the effects of climate, and possibly other pre-political determinants, leads to the same result that contemporary academics reach in reasoning about culture. For both, the necessary condition of republicanism, common standards of morals or habits, is determined pre-politically. These "givens" constitute the individuals and groups which it is the task of republican government to encourage in autonomous self-expression. Thus, there is a common problem for the Antifederalists' Confederal governors of states and the contemporary academy's governors of culture. It is the problem of administering to groups who must express their common standards, whether they be specified as those of ethnicity, race, sex, or whatever.

Antifederalist thinkers like Agrippa, who were preoccupied with this problem, worried constantly that the union was too large and the national legislature too small to permit rulers to appreciate sufficient variety. In this, they are joined by today's intellectuals. Both groups also characteristically fear the Founders' statesmanship, which is principled and adjudicates merit. Both are quick to describe such power as a conspiracy of "the wealthy and wellborn" whose aim is to gratify their vanity. And both are quick to associate corruption in government with monopoly wealth.

An antifederal regime can be *imagined* on either a small or a large scale. It was in fact imagined by the Antifederalists, on a small scale for the most part, but on a large scale also, when they entertained the hope that the national union might be sufficiently "corrected." This they thought could be done by weakening its permanent branches[36] and its powers, especially its commercial powers, and also by attaching a Bill of Rights to the main instrument. These were measures which the Constitution makers very properly considered quite dangerous (84,436-39). Contemporary intellectuals entertain the same hope and recommend the same corrections. They seem proper to them for a "government" over culture where a

---

34. *The Essential Antifederalist*, pp. 122-23.

35. Quoted in Gerald M. Capers, *John C. Calhoun: Opportunist* (Gainesville: University of Florida Press, 1960), p. 252.

36. Liberal academics have been known to call for strong Presidents, but only as the heads of a party government which unifies executive and legislative roles.

statesmanship adjudicating merit must be replaced with one promoting self-expression.

A new kind of antifederalism is now so much in favor in the academy that the original Antifederalists are said to be Founding Fathers in spite of the Founders' demonstration that, with the exception of those "honest minds" who were led astray despite their wish for good government, Antifederalists were fundamentally anti-political.[37] The power of the academy's antifederalism is well attested, also, by the proliferation of works putting forth its corrections to the original Constitution. These theories attempt to transform the Constitution into a set of administrative rules by placing the Bill of Rights, not separated powers or federalism, at its heart. A good example is the influential book of Professor George Anastaplo, *The Constitutionalist*.[38] Anastaplo proposes what he considers to be a return to the true spirit of the Constitution, but he is troubled by concerns which are more like the Antifederalists' than the Founders'. He is unusual, for this day, in proposing stronger control by the states over their own internal domestic orders.[39] But, like most contemporaries, he opposes a strong executive, and he wants the First Amendment to be properly understood, *i.e.*, to be understood as an instrument for legislative democracy. Anastaplo fears a government which, *because of its size* enervates men's "character and sense of duty" to the point that they become materialistic: they pursue "the material pleasures that prolonged prosperity furnishes."[40]

---

37. See Storing and Dry, *What the Anti-Federalists Were For*, "Introduction." For an examination of the partisan issues raised by Storing's scholarship, see David B. Broyles, "On Anti-Federalism: A Scholarly Polemic," *The Claremont Review of Books*, Vol. 1, No. 4 (May 1982).

38. *The Constitutionalist: Notes on the First Amendment* (Dallas: Southern Methodist University Press, 1971).

39. But see Daniel J. Elazar, who also favors strength in the states, *American Federalism: A View From The States*, 2nd Edition (New York: Thomas Y. Crowell, 1972). Elazar accepts uncritically the moral superiority of national projects for enforcing the Bill of Rights. He regards states as guardians of the same projects. The national government is necessary only for certain purposes, and in pursuing those purposes is open to undemocratic usurpation. Thus, he says (p. 43): "The central role of federalism in solving a major problem of government [is maintaining] the liberties of the people from vitiation through the consolidation of power into hands far removed from popular control or domination of minorities by an unrestrained majority, while at the same time providing a government with sufficient energy to meet the demands placed upon it."

40. *The Constitutionalist*, p. 199.

Reforming The Contemporary Study of Federalism

Although it is undetected by the largely unconscious bias of the academy, political science's federalism studies remain steadfastly biased, hostile to the national politics of the Constitution. Neither liberal nor conservative leaders can offer any sound approaches to dealing with federalism until the academy's bias is reformed. And such a reform can be achieved only by a revival of the question of federalism as it was understood by the Founders in their original struggle with the Antifederalists. It is necessary to restore the Founders' understanding of the true differences between national and state powers. And it is especially important to clarify their delineation of a set of national powers which, though limited, are critical to achieving purposes supported by natural law and right.

This may not be as difficult as it appears at first. Contemporary intellectual views on national powers differ considerably from those of the Founders. But what is largely overlooked by zealots of the new intellectual elite is that the founding principles remain intact in the hearts of citizens and have not changed in spite of powerful arguments exaggerating the role of history and promising a utopian administrative state. While it is true that a new antifederalism battles against the Founders' democracy, using the Supreme Court as its shock troops, it is also true that it remains an elitist cause. For most Americans, the Civil War's XIVth Amendment, industrialization, and intensified international emergency have changed things, but not all that much.

Furthermore, the academy might well enjoy a special pride in opposing present trends and in leading the way to a revitalization of the Founders' great republican politics. As Leo Strauss once remarked, this politics "is meant to be an aristocracy which has broadened into a universal aristocracy."[41] Such a politics is a great school whose highest aim is, after all, the same as the academy's. It is "taking care and improving the native faculties of the mind in accordance with the nature of the mind."[42]

For the Founders, then, it was not true that peaceful associative activity can be taken as a "given." They did not think such activity was good simply because it was based on pre-political ethnic or other ties which might promote sentimental cooperation and foresight. There are non-factional and factional, good and bad local societies, said the Founders. Constitutional government is intended to encourage man's natural

---

41. "Liberal Education and Mass Democracy" in Robert A. Goldwin, ed., *Higher Education and Modern Democracy* (Chicago: Rand McNally & Company, 1967), p. 75.
42. Goldwin, p. 73.

course, in private as well as in public life, to associate non-factionally, *i.e.* for purposes bringing happiness and dignity. This became feasible, they argued, once men were freed of a tradition dominated by monocratic pretenses—once they came to enjoy a republican environment of natural law and natural right. It was for the purpose of sustaining this natural world that the Constitution promised to maintain the sovereignty of states.

The Founders' aim was higher than the Antifederalists'. Consequently, what they feared most was not that local custom and interest would be overborne, but that government would lose its grounding in principled constitutionalism—would become a direct democracy instead.[43] Power was to be watched carefully, but also to be regarded as capable of great accomplishments. The "gallant" Americans, they argued, could be relied upon to elect officers of sufficient virtue to work for the public good within the framework of the Constitution (55,284).

The Antifederalists seem to have remained oblivious to this possibility. Today's intellectuals also remain oblivious to the actual working of America—improved as it is by a Constitution which encourages citizens to defer to naturally meritorious authority, to Jefferson's "natural aristoi" of statesmen. For both groups, it is impossible for statesmen to distribute public goods in response to true merit. For both, all deference is merely diffidence and all authority merely vanity.

Contrary to what contemporary intellectuals would argue, the Founders were not defensive about federalism when they disputed with the Constitution's opponents. They did not, as is argued by some, try to disguise a distinctly national system.[44] In thinking about the matter at the

43. The instability of such governments is emphasized in *Federalist* 9 and 10, and there it is attributed to the possibility that overbearing factions will emergence. The real problem, however, is government which is bad in a number of ways, not just by being unstable. Publius' argument against the disciples of Montesquieu is intended to lead them to appreciate that good government will come from the people's willingness to accept representatives of high quality, and *Federalist* 51 makes it clear that this means especially representation in the more permanent branches of the separated powers, the executive and judiciary.

44. This is the thesis of Professor Martin Diamond. See his "The Federalist's View of Federalism" in Pietro S. Nivola and David H. Rosenbloom, eds., *Classic Readings in American Politics* (New York: St. Martin's Press, 1986), p. 80. Diamond says, "the great teaching of *The Federalist* is not how to be federal in a better way, but how to be better by being less federal." We argue, instead, that the Founders made national government more effective by incorporating principles that had been understood up to this time as federal or confederal.

Constitutional Convention, they came to believe that federalism has a constructive role to play. They even argued that there would be an advantage to reconstituting it as an element of their new science of politics had it not been present as a historic given. Federalism, they discovered, makes a necessary accommodation to strong affections of blood and propinquity.

As Publius explained, the purpose of federalism is to avoid a "*consolidation* of the States," and establish a Constitution which was a "composition of both" national and federal principles (39,192 & 195). By preserving selected principles of an older federalism (or confederalism) Publius argues further, the Constitution provides a means for the people to associate in various ways at the state level and to take action which is fully effective within their confines. This is because the states retain, concurrently with the national government, their sovereign legislating, taxing, and police powers. Thus the people can be enthusiastic about governing themselves in their own ways, however provincial they may appear to others. They do this, however, in a better way under the Constitution, in such a way as to simultaneously encourage the natural yearning for dignity and happiness in others, even in others whose pursuits differ considerably from their own. This better way is encouraged by the supervision of the national government over the states.

Thus, the great problem for the national government, the Founders made clear, is to encourage the formation of a variety of opinions and tastes of the right kind. When local opinions and tastes are properly influenced by federal policy, the result is a rule of reason. Parochial preferences "ought to be controlled by government," as Publius says. "It is the reason, alone, of the public, that ought to control and regulate government" (49,317). It is thus all important for the national government to develop a desirable environment for public opinion.

The states are too easily captured by their larger economic interests and embroiled in petty conflicts, Publius argues in *Federalist* 9 and 10. As a consequence, they fall victims to tyrannizing elites who impose their own self-interested standards on the whole community for their own advantage. On the other hand, at the national level reason and the common good are aided by the spirited pursuit of honorable objects. Matters of national character and dignity come to the forefront. Also, sufficient steady purpose and military might support the pursuit of objectives which are universally human.

Economic science and its instrument, a vigorous national commerce, are critically important. They make the nation powerful and glorious.

They also show the way to a market which dignifies and rewards all forms of the pursuit of human happiness, whether from the mind of a genius of the *natural aristoi* or the hands of common people. Thus national dignity advances together with individual, both being guided by those high standards which are the likely objects of America's challenging pursuits.

The national power over finance and commerce is crucial to enticing men to higher callings. The connection between commercial life and moral rectitude is often Publius' subject, as in the following passage:

> By multiplying the means of gratification, by promoting the introduction and circulation of the precious metals, those darling objects of human avarice and enterprise, [commerce] serves to vivify and invigorate all the channels of industry and to make them flow with greater activity and copiousness. The assiduous merchant, the laborious husbandman, the active mechanic, and the industrious manufacturer,—all orders of men look forward with eager expectation and growing alacrity to this pleasing reward of their toils (12,91).

The national government is chartered to encourage "avarice" for the sake of "enterprise" and "industry." These necessarily promote such character traits as temperance (in economic terms, deferred gratification) and courage (adventurism or entrepreneurship). Thus Publius, who understands that the national taxing power is a powerful means for controlling economic life, speaks as if it were a power to free the whole range of human activity from oppression. He says:

> The man who understands those principles [of economics] best will be *least likely* to resort to oppressive expedients, or to sacrifice any particular class of citizens to the procurement of revenue (35,216-17; emphasis added).

Here and elsewhere, Publius refuses to concede the Antifederalist claim that monopoly power would defeat free economics.

But economics is only one science which absorbs those "speculative men, who look ... forward to remote consequences" (15,74) and who would be elevated to national government. Military and diplomatic pursuits also require a number of high sciences. And there are others, also.

What powers remain to the states? Publius makes his idea of state powers reasonably clear. He makes it clear that such powers are marked as much by the fact that they are *dearer* to average citizens as that they can be described with such terminology as "police powers." To employ such descriptions is really to make things less clear, rather than more, because they suggest that the powers are confined when in fact they are not. National powers are limited because certain specified powers are crucial to the success of the national project to bring local activities in line with high purposes. Local powers are unlimited, just as any simply "sovereign" powers would be, precisely because they have no such purposes. Publius' best comment on this is worth quoting at length:

> There is one transcendent advantage [over the national power] belonging to the province of the State governments, which alone suffices to place the matter in a clear and satisfactory light,—I mean the ordinary administration of criminal and civil justice. This, of all others, is the most powerful, most universal, and most attractive source of popular obedience and attachment. It is that which, being the immediate and visible guardian of life and property, having its benefits and its terrors in constant activity before the public eye, regulating all those personal interests and familiar concerns to which the sensibility of individuals is more immediately awake, contributes more than any other circumstance to impressing upon the minds of the people, affection, esteem, and reverence towards the government. This great cement of society, which will diffuse itself almost wholly through the channels of the particular governments, independent of all other causes of influence, would insure them so decided an empire over their respective citizens as to render them at all times a complete counterpoise, and, not unfrequently, dangerous rivals to the power of the Union (17,120).

National goals are less attractive to the general public, but of greater dignity. The high aims of national power are more evident when leadership is considered. Publius makes clear his own disdain for state powers and thereby gives the clearest indication of his profound disagreement with men of an antifederal temperament who would gain pleasure from governing states. He says:

> The regulation of the mere domestic police of a State appears to me to hold out slender allurements to ambition (17,80).

Federalism, it seems, is more than a device which sets ambition to counteract ambition. Proper ambition must orchestrate the natural harmony between national and state powers. It must ensure that national powers are concentrated on truly worthy goals.[45]

In the last analysis, Publius' federalism relies on the good character of the people, as modern intellectuals do not. For him, it is much the same when the people approve a certain balance of federal and state powers as it is when they approve a proper balance of the separated national

---

45. The power of the nation's control of commerce would be more evident but for the fact that past mistakes have been made in interpreting it. For example, mistakes seem to have been made when Congress failed in antebellum days to use the commerce power against slavery and when the Supreme Court later failed to understand some of the humanitarian needs of industrialization.

powers. They thereby reveal something about their disposition towards natural law and natural right. The federal balance depends upon the people's disciplined judgment about how well each government is abiding by fundamental constitutional principles. It reveals, in particular, whether the people continue to value the Union as "a general DISCRE-TIONARY SUPERINTENDENCE" (15,71) over the states, even though they are "more devoted in their attachments and obedience to their own particular governments, than to that of the union." Publius refers appropriately to those qualities of good character which must sustain the people when they support a proper federal union: in "preserv[ing] the constitutional equilibrium between the General and the State Governments," [he says,] everything "must be left to the prudence and firmness of the people" (31,151).

American Federalism and American Democracy

John Adams Wettergreen

The papers of the panel on federalism and centralization (here, the essays of this chapter) and the discussion following the papers did not deal with American federalism itself, so much as with contemporary cultural, academic, and political issues which are incidental to federalism. Therefore, a brief introduction to American federalism is useful.

American Federalism

"Federalism" originally referred to the program of the Federalist party, but by the last years of the eighteenth century it was already used as it is today, as a term of art to describe the form of the union of the various states of the United States that resulted from the Constitution of 1787. These two meanings are not inconsistent, because the most important accomplishment of the Federalist party was the establishment under the Constitution of a central government over the union.

Federalist 39 provides the classic description of American federalism: The form of the domestic union of the United States should be partly federal (or confederal) and partly national (or unitary)[1] It would not be simply "unitary," like the Athenian empire at the time of the Pelopponessian war. Under that form, unqualified fidelity to the center is enforced upon all foreign and domestic parts of the empire. Surplus human and material resources tend to be sucked into the center for use or redistribution. This is not American federalism. The clearest example today is the Warsaw Pact, which is enforced by the government and arms of the Soviet Union. American federalism was not intended to be purely "federal" (or "confederal") either.[2] Under the purely federal form, each part lives its own way of life under its own laws and cooperates with the other parts only insofar as it judges cooperation necessary for the defense and pros-

---

1. Hamilton, Madison, and Jay, *The Federalist*, ed. Cooke (Wesleyan University Press: Middletown, 1961), pp. 255-7 (#39).
2. The words were synonymous in the eighteenth-century; see Martin Diamond, *The Founding of the Democratic Republic* (New York: Peacock, 1983), p. 58.

perity of its own way. The alliance that formed around Sparta when it warred against Athens is the classic example of this form; indeed, the Spartans imposed civic freedom upon their allies by arms. Today, the clearest example of this "purely federal" form is the North Atlantic Treaty Organization, which is almost wholly an alliance for military defense. Modern political scientists understand that the American mixture of traditionally unitary with traditionally federal elements was a constitutional imitation of the so-called "unequal league" that constituted the domestic empire of republican Rome.[3] Under this form, the center or head maintains itself by the superiority of its administration of the common affairs of the league.

The Constitution's mixture of purely federal and purely national aspects of union is a perfection of the Roman unequal league in at least two respects. First, the conditions for the league are specified by the Constitution. Second, the peripheral governments or states, including any new states that might be added, are all equally members. Both these perfections are emphatically republican. The first helps insure public, *i.e.*, non-arbitrary, limits upon the powers of the center. The second insures that members consent to be governed by the Union and are not merely forced into the league by older, larger, or more powerful members.

Some of today's difficulties in understanding our constitutional arrangements result from their mixed federal/national character. Consider, for example, the most misunderstood constitutional institution, the Electoral College. In twenty years of teaching "Introduction to American Government," I have yet to begin a class in which more than two or three students understand even the bare mechanics of the constitutional mode of electing the President; rarely does even one know WHY that mode is as it is. A similar ignorance is obvious in the mass media and even in scientific writings.

The character of the basic arrangements is noted in the *Federalist* 39: "The executive power will be derived from a very compound source." The election of the President by the Electoral College is one by "the States in their political characters," says Publius, because each state does cast its electoral votes for itself and because each has the constitutional power to

---

3. See James Harrington, *The Commonwealth of Ocean*, ed. S.B. Liljergren (Carl Winters Universitätsbuchhandlung: Heidelberg, 1924), pp. 185-198; cf. Nicolo Machiavelli, "Discourses on the First Ten Books of Titus Livius," in *Machiavelli, The Prince and the Discourses*, trans. Demold (Modern Library: New York, 1950), pp. 290-296, 344-349, 357-371, 443-448 (II, 4, 19, 23, 24, and III, 10).

determine how it will choose electors. However, the states' electoral votes are not allotted to them in either a purely federal or a purely national manner. Rather, each state has the same number of votes as it does members of Congress. The number of the states' Congressional delegation is "a compound ratio." That number results from considering them "partly as distinct and coequal societies," insofar as each has the equal representation in the Senate which a purely federal union would require. However, it also results from considering them "partly as unequal members of the same society," because each state's delegation to the House is proportionate to its population, as would be the case with a purely unitary form.

This compounding goes further. In the event that the Electoral College cannot choose a President, the election is to be made by the House of Representatives, *i.e.*, "that branch of the legislature which consists of the national representatives," but in electing the President the House assumes a purely federal aspect, because the voting is by state, with each state casting one vote as if the states were "so many distinct and coequal bodies politic." Under a purely national form, the chief magistrate would be elected by a direct, national popular election. Under a purely federal form, the unanimous consent of the states' governments would be necessary to select a commander-in-chief. The mode of election of the President, however, is such a complex concoction of both forms that "it appears to be of a mixed character, presenting at least as many federal as national features."[4]

The reason for this mixed federal/national mode of election is made plain in *Federalist* 68. The President must be elected independent of the Congress; he must have his own majority. Because the President, more than any other officer, must act for the nation as a whole, his majority must be national; that is, by the "requisite qualifications" for the office of President, the Framers meant, above all, "the esteem and confidence of the whole Union," as distinguished from the support of a sector or faction, however numerous. For this reason, the federal aspect of the Electoral College compels Presidents to win votes in several states, with the result that the Presidential majority tends to be *nationally distributed*. For the same reason, Presidents tend to be men of broad appeal, and so of moderate character. One can see then, even from this single example, that the influence of American federalism upon the construction of our institutions was comprehensive, minute, and pervasive.

---

4. *The Federalist* #39, p. 255.

So American federalism is not unprecedented historically and it is not unintelligible theoretically. Nevertheless, federalism may be said to be unique to American constitutional government and difficult for Americans to comprehend. American federalism is unique insofar as it is the irradicable part of the constitutional order. That is, the equal autonomy of the states is the Constitution's sole exception to the Constitution's amending procedures: "no state, without its Consent," says Article V, "shall be deprived of its equal Suffrage in the Senate." Moreover, the same objective cannot, under the Constitution, be achieved by the subterfuge of consolidating or dividing existing states. Separation of powers, the Judiciary, the Congress, the Presidency—to say nothing of the First and Thirteenth Amendments—could each and all be abolished by the ordinary amending procedures, but the constitutional necessities of federalism cannot.

How important are these two hundred year old constitutional necessities today? Are the states still significant, autonomous parts of the American nation? Today, a state's speed limits are set, if not enforced, by the central government. Today, every mile of sewer line laid in a state is approved by a member of Congress. Today, a sizable portion of state and local officials, including even some elected officials, are paid by the central government. Some measure of the gravity of the change may be gathered by considering *Federalist* 45. There Madison explains why, as a practical matter and even leaving aside the niceties of the constitutional forms, the central government cannot dominate the state and local governments:

> The members of the legislative, executive, and judiciary departments of the thirteen and more States, the justices of the peace, officers of militia, ministerial officers of justice, with all the county, corporation, and town officers, for three millions and more people, intermixed, and having acquaintance with every class and circle of people, must exceed, beyond all proportion, both in number and influence, those of every description who will be employed [by the central government].[5]

This description of public employment was accurate until the mid-1960s or early 1970s, when the employees of the central government "of every description" came to equal or exceed State and local employees, and when the distinctions between State and local and Federal employment became obscure. No wonder that today, in the second generation of centralized administration in the United States, some are tempted to dismiss federalism as practically irrelevant.

---

5. *The Federalist*, p. 312 [#45].

To see the practical importance of federalism today, one might reflect upon the political history of the past generation. For example, how different might the history of race relations have been—for better or worse—if Congress had had it in its power to abolish the state of Alabama, or the state of Massachusetts, or to combine into one these states which have been so troubled by racial animosities? How different—for better or worse—if in 1967 President Lyndon Johnson had had it in his power to remove from office the Governor of California, Ronald Reagan, because of his profound political differences with him? Both such powers are characteristic of a unitary republic, as distinguished from the federalist republic created by the Constitution. On the other hand, think how different recent history might have been—again, for better or worse—if Massachusetts had retained the power to raise troops for the army and navy of the United States, and therefore to refuse to raise them—as she tried to do during the Vietnam war. Or imagine if local school boards, which are legally the creatures of the state governments, had the constitutional right to refuse the equal protection of the laws to an unpopular race. Such constitutional powers for the states are characteristic of a purely federal republic, one without the autonomous central government of American federalism. Consider also that, if a national popular election had been in force in 1968, instead of the Electoral College, which compels Presidential candidates to win votes state-by-state, opinion polls indicate a likelihood that George Wallace, the segregationist Democrat from Alabama, not Richard Nixon and certainly not Hubert Humphrey, would have been elected President in 1968.

This catalog of circumstances may be sufficient to indicate the perennial importance of federalism, but it cannot supply that comprehensive evaluation at which the essays of David Broyles and James L. Gibson aim.

The Contemporary Understanding

David Broyles was charged with evaluating the contemporary understanding of federalism. In doing that, he explains how romantic faith in the cathartic effects of political participation, liberal and conservative "mistrust of all political power," and the moral-political obtusity of scientific political science all obscure federalism as an integral part of a republican constitution. What underlies these biased interpretations of American federalism, Broyles argues, is their development in American colleges and universities. The political culture of American higher education—

"The Academic Environment," as Broyles calls it—promotes "the administrative state," *i.e.*, bureaucracy, and not a republic. This environment nurtures and certifies "the administrative class," *i.e.*, bureaucrats, not citizens or democratic republicans, and not federalists.

Seeing that the political life of the American constitutional republic, of which federalism is an institution, is alien to American higher learning, Broyles argues—what might seem to be paradoxical at first glance—that the dominant views of federalism today are "Antifederalist." This terminology caused some confusion at the conference. However, Broyles did not mean that contemporary scholars consciously wish to de-ratify the Constitution and return to the Articles of Confederation. Rather, Broyles' essay contends that the moral and political tastes of contemporary interpreters of American federalism are contrary to the moral and political principles of the Federalists. It is in that sense that they may be said, rightly, to be anti-federalist.

Political positions are defined not so much by one's partisan preferences or interests as by one's opinion of what a good life, led in common with one's fellows, would be. Political institutions, including federalism, are best understood as the props of a particular way of life. According to Broyles, today's intellectual students of federalism are bred in an environment that prizes diffidence and thus prefer a way of life "characterized by shared feelings, but not by sharp exchanges of opinion over merit." This way of life, Broyles indicates, is the same as that preferred by the opponents of the Constitution in 1787-9. Therefore, to reform the study of federalism and to correct contemporary academic moral and political tastes, Broyles concludes his essay by presenting a clear, cogent, and provocative summary of the Framer's understanding of federalism as an institution of the democratic republican way. We shall have to return to this summary for our conclusion.

The conference's discussion threw up two significant objections to Broyles' view of federalism. First, Joshua Miller asserted that, in the final analysis, only the citizens' direct participation in "political power" can educate a civic body capable of democratic governance of a large nation. Miller asserted that Broyles (and the Federalists) favors "civic education by elite statesmen" together with an exclusion of the people from direct participation in government as the essential means of producing a democratic republic on the scale of a nation. This position, he admitted, is the only genuinely democratic alternative to his own avowedly antifederalist views. Accordingly, he tried to make common cause with Broyles against the regnant "welfare-state liberalism," *i.e.*, against bureaucracy. Broyles' reply to this objection was, I think, adequate: civic education by statesmen does not preclude education by direct political participation, but rather builds upon, encourages, and guides the citizens' political experience. In fact, Broyles maintained that American federalism is the case in point, because it is a constitutional guarantee of popular political participation, and so a guarantee of the education favored by Miller, which was secured by the actions of wise statesmen, the Federalists. That wisdom consisted and still consists, as Broyles elaborates in his essay, in the constitutional division of the political authority over "low" matters—which were left to the state governments, if not to local governments and the people themselves—and the political authority over the "high" matters of the national government.

This distinction of "low" from "high" affairs engendered the second significant objection to Broyles' position. M. E. Bradford, in commenting upon Broyles' views, remarked that the affairs left to the states and to the people themselves by the Constitution included not only matters of the "local police," but also matters of civil justice and religion. These, Bradford asserted, are hardly "low" matters. From the audience, Jeremy Rabkin endorsed this view and went on to suggest that the regulation of interstate and foreign commerce, an exclusive concern of the central government, is not a high matter; Rabkin is confident of the standard academic opinion according to which concern with commerce, even government's concern, is vulgar ("low"). Again, Broyles' reply was adequate, but it was not exhaustive. The concern to regulate commerce was "high," he said, in two ways. First, it was and is the absolutely essential power for transforming "the American people into free, opulent, and law-abiding citizens, through the instrumentality of a limited republican government, on the basis of consent, and in the face of powerful vested interests in the status quo."[6] Since socio-economic relations were still partially but pervasively agrarian, aristocratic, and even feudal in 1789, only non-local government would be likely to transform American society, including the American economy, into a fully modern society. Second, Broyles explains, such transformations of the American society and economy—which were initiated by the Federalists, and above all by Secretary of the Treasury Hamilton—would be essential, if the United States were to possess the wealth and military might necessary for it to exercise its rightful influence upon global affairs. In my opinion, Broyles occupies the most advantageous position here: Imagine what the nineteenth and twentieth centuries

---

6. Forrest MacDonald, *Alexander Hamilton* (W. W. Norton: New York, 1979), pp. 235, 3.

would have been, if the United States had become the weak, defensive, confederacy of agrarian, "underdeveloped" peoples' republics, for which the Anti-federalists (and Jefferson) longed.

If these notions of "high" and "low" are sufficiently sharpened, the disagreements among Broyles, Bradford, and Rabkin can be resolved. Surely it is simply true that the proper concerns of the central government are higher-grander or more glorious. Since they are of greater consequence to the nation and to the mankind, national affairs quite naturally win greater honors for those concerned with them. Nor does the fact that national affairs are "higher" than local affairs mean that they are more important for the day-to-day happiness and safety of the American people, nor even that they are intrinsically more important. However, national supremacy certainly does imply that state (and local) governments would be unable to sustain their own ways of life as free societies for long, however safe and happy their citizens might be, in a world filled with super-powerful, globally imperial, modern states, if it were not for the transcendent powers and concerns of the central government.

Federalism and Pluralism

James L. Gibson believes he can fulfill his charge to present the Framers' understanding of federalism by exploring the "enigmatic" relations among freedom, federalism, and pluralism with the tools of "value-free" social science. Gibson takes up the most common evaluation of American federalism, "that democracy is best protected through pluralism," which federalism enhances. Based on his examination of some statistics on state governments' laws regulating Communists in the 1950s, he concludes that this evaluation is sound. Nevertheless, Gibson insists that "the price of federalism may [sic] be measured in terms of freedom lost," because he believes that the states violated "the rights" of Communists. In other words, federalism perfects democracy, insofar as it helps to establish a large, diverse, and so more tolerant society, but it also undermines democracy, insofar as it secures the states as smaller, less diverse societies which are intolerant of an "unpopular political minority," as Gibson is pleased to call the Communists. Presumably (for this was clearer at the conference than it is in his essay), if the states did not exist or if they could be consolidated into larger, more pluralistic states, "the rights" of Communists could be still better protected. So Gibson is in what he himself characterizes as a "perverse" agreement with the Framers' federalism. Relative to confederacy, American federalism is useful, but considered in itself it "limits freedom and endangers democracy." Indeed, in the course of the conference's discussion of his paper, Gibson declared flatly, "Federalism is the greatest enemy of freedom."

The bulk of the discussion during this session concerned two significant objections to Gibson's paper. The first came from Jeffrey Wallin and Dennis Mahoney in the audience. Gibson's first premise is untrue, they noted, because legislation against Communists is not intolerance, Communists being the enemies of the United States and of political freedom. Bradford's comments made a similar point:

> Gibson's . . . illustrative instance, from the "Red Scare" following World War II . . . does not prove up his point. Or even quite apply to it. Or to the issue of the founders' views or their value for today. Since . . . no regime can be expected to agree to its own destruction or to tolerate speech which threatens not just the party in power but the existence of an established political system not separable from the being of the nation which it governs.

Gibson flatly refused to answer this objection: "I will not debate Communism." However, this did not prevent him from making favorable references to Allende's Communist regime in Chile—members of the audience were quick to point out that these references were insensitive to Allende's anti-democratic, anti-American, and pro-Soviet actions and intentions.

Secondly, several scholars questioned Gibson's claim that local majorities are bigoted. Bradford pointed out that, according to Gibson's own data, only about one half the states acted "intolerantly," but most of these followed the lead of the central government: it would seem that the larger, "pluralistic," national majority was more hostile to Communists than the states. With this in mind, I asked Gibson and Miller whether the American people were so bigoted as to be incapable of self-government. Gibson claimed that overwhelming empirical evidence demonstrated popular ignorance and prejudice so great as to render the people incapable of self-government. In fact, the opinion surveys which he cites purport to prove that "elites" are more enlightened than the "masses." Miller, the other leftist on the panel, agreed that the common people are more bigoted than the "elites," and that the opinion surveys proved this, but only disagreed by contending that the people's bigotry was due to a lack of the enlightening experience of exercising power. There are, however, grave defects of method and substance in the studies cited by Gibson, because they are invariably based upon a theory of the structure of public opinion which posits not only that popular opinion is inferior to the opinion of "elites," but also that it is derivative of the opinion of "elites." Furthermore, even if the methods of these studies were sound, they do not support Gibson's contention that the mass is bigoted, much less that the common people is incapable of self-government. They might show that the mass is more hostile toward Communism, Nazism, and other forms of modern tyranny than the elites; however, if that hostility is enlightened, as many in the audience contended, then Gibson's own evidence would show that the common people is more enlightened that the elites.[7] Once again, Gibson's argument is undone by his merely subjective commitment to tolerance for the partisans of modern tyrannies.[8] Such tolerance of tyranny is characteristic of the anti-democratic attitude of "objective, value-free political science," which Gibson claimed to represent at the conference.

Federalism and Democracy

Both Broyles and Gibson (however half-heartedly) contend that federalism protects democracy. To judge the merits of this proposition, the distinction of federalism—the existence of the states—from *"enlargement of the orbit"*—the multiplicity of interests and opinions consequent to a large republic—needs to be elaborated, because the central issue of the whole conference was the security to the democratic way afforded by the constitutional institutions. Such a task requires an understanding of democracy and, even more, of the problems typical to democracy.

James Gibson rightly contended that he was the only participant in the conference even to offer a definition of democracy; the rest of operated on intuition. However, Gibson's definition—equal political opportunity —does not accord with reality, with the historical record, or even with the public ideals of any self-proclaimed democracy which has ever existed. That is why, very quickly, Gibson's essay abandons its definition in order to distinguish between democracy "as a system of majority rule" and democracy "as a system of equal opportunity to compete for political power." Which kind of system is protected by American federalism?

---

7. The anti-democratic methods and conclusions of survey research are explained in my "The American Voter and Its Surveyors," *Political Science Reviewer*, Vol. VII (1977).

8. In *Civil Liberties and Nazis: The Skokie Free-Speech Controversy* (New York: Praeger, 1985), he decries "intolerance" of Nazis.

Unfortunately Gibson is too much concerned to protect the rights of those who favor socialistic tyrannies to take account of the importance of federalism for democracy "as a system of majority rule." Like most contemporary academic leftists, he ignores or denies the majority's right to rule, as if it were easily established, but agonizes about the protection of minorities—even brutal, anti-democratic, racist, imperialistic, and anti-American ones—as if that were were the really difficult thing to accomplish under constitutional government. As Broyles would have us know, this understanding of the problems of democracy is contrary to that of the Framers. They knew that throughout human history regimes of discrete minorities—which protect their own rights without respect for right of the governed to consent—had been the rule and democracies the exception. In other words, non-democratic regimes, like the Communist and National Socialist ones whose partisans Gibson is so anxious to protect, are so much more common than democracies that the Framers devoted their considerable political talents to discovering the means of perfecting democracy *as a system of majority rule.* That is, they wished to perfect the rule of the common people. Protection of the rights of members of the minor party is one, and only one such perfection. Another is the effective government and administration of the nation's affairs.

Federalism, like other constitutional institutions such as separation of powers, an independent judiciary, and bicameralism, was not designed to frustrate majority rule or to advance the anti-democratic cause, as Gibson seems to suppose. Rather, as Broyles makes clear, federalism encourages the common people to govern themselves effectively. At the state level the Framers were primarily concerned that local majorities follow their own ways, however parochial they might appear to some, without allowing these ways to infect the national government or its policies. At the national level, federalism was intended to implement the rule of *articulated* national majorities, majorities which were not mere collections of individuals but assemblages of local majorities. Surely Broyles is correct to insist that an enlightened central government might be able to refine local prejudices to some extent. However, such is not the central government's purpose, whereas the purpose of the state governments within American federalism is to make, as Broyles puts it, "a necessary accommodation to strong affections of blood and propinquity" so that such affections can be transcended at the national level. Thus, Gibson is almost exactly wrong in his practical judgment that a union with fewer, larger states or no states at all would be more pluralistic, and hence more tolerant, than a nation of more and smaller states. To repeat: he confuses the multiplicity of political authorities, which is sustained by federalism, with the multiplicity of interests and opinions, and so of factions, which is the consequence of "*enlargement* of the *orbit.*"

Consider: if there were no states, if we lived in a unitary republic, natural diversity would probably be as great as it is today, but that diversity could only find authoritative expression, if indeed it could, at one center. Consequently, under such a unitary form local or parochial interests, however narrow or bigoted, would be compelled to enter into the deliberations of the national government in order to be heard at all. For example, suppose the citizens of North Hollywood wish to replace Christmas with Halloween on their list of civic holidays: without federalism, the approval of the whole nation would, in principle, be necessary; with federalism, only the people of California need acquiesce. One does not have to have a prejudice for Halloween in order to see that the nation would not be well governed if such essentially local issues had to be decided at the center.

Just this kind of bad government, of course, has started to develop here over the past two decades as administration has been centralized. Increasingly, members of Congress and even Presidents must neglect the national interest in order to solve the problems of their local constituents. Usually, these are problems caused by the central bureaucracy. American federalism could only slow, it could not stop a central government bent on bureaucratization, especially when many of the states themselves prefer bureaucracy.[9] Thus, as Broyles remarks, federalism can be an important part of sound, *i.e.* non-bureaucratic, administration, but only because it

---

9. On the states' (winning) fight against centralization of administration, see *Amending the Social Security Act* ... , Hearing before a Subcommittee of the Committee on Finance, U.S. Senate, 75th Cong., 3rd sess. (February 15, 1938), pp. 1-5, 27; see also *Social Security Act Amendments*, Hearings before the Committee on Finance, U.S. Senate, 76th Cong., 1st sess. (June 12, 13, 14, 15, 26, 29, 1939), pp. 26-27, 31, 32, 34-5, 137, 140, 290-1. On their capitulation to bureaucracy, see *Intergovernmental Personnel Act of 1967* ... , Hearings before the Subcommittee on Intergovernmental Relations of the Committee on Government Operations, 90th Cong., 1st sess. (Apr. 26, 27, 28, 1967) , pp. 128-138; *Intergovernmental Personnel Act of 1966*, Hearings before the Subcommittee on Intergovernmental Relations of the Committee on Government Operations, U.S. Senate, 89th. Cong., 2nd sess. (Aug. 16, 17, 18, 1966), pp. 2, 5; and *Intergovernmental Cooperation Act of 1965*, Hearings before the Subcommittee on Intergovernmental Relations of the Committee on Government Operations, 89th Cong., 1st.sess. (Mar. 29, 30, 31; Apr. 1, 2, 1965), p. 199. The demise of the Hatch Acts was also important; see *Federal Employees Political Activities Act of 1977*, Hearings before the Subcommittee on Civil Service of the Committee on Post Office and Civil Service, U.S. House of Representatives, 95th Cong., 1st sess. (Feb. 23, 24, 1977), p. 138.

authorizes the central government to ignore many pressing local needs for the sake of the national interest.

Because of the remarkable success of American federalism in sustaining democracy on the scale of a nation, contemporary political scientists commonly suppose, as Gibson does, that "social pluralism creates more tolerant individuals, just as it creates a more tolerant polity." Clearly, this is incorrect: free institutions, not natural diversity, secure the democratic way of life, including democracy's much vaunted tolerance. The Soviet Union, for example, has far greater social diversity than even the United States, but it could hardly be said to have as tolerant a polity as, *e.g.* Iceland, an extraordinarily homogeneous society. The famous *Federalist* 10 notices just this decisive importance of democratic political institutions for liberty. Whereas social diversity is rooted in human nature and, therefore, must be present to some extent everywhere and always, only a democratic republic—especially a large one—can take full advantage of that natural diversity. A small republic and all the more the brutal oligarchies preferred by Nazis and Communists will be disrupted and threatened by natural diversity because they are not built to the standards of human nature. Generally speaking, failures of government can be traced to failures to understand human nature, for government is "the greatest of all reflections on human nature."

Contemporary social scientists, of whom Gibson is representative, do not accept the standard of nature for politics. Like most contemporary intellectuals, they would have us believe that democracy ought to be as tolerant of unnatural diversity as it is of natural or healthy diversity.[10] This is contrary to the original spirit of the Constitution. As Broyles puts it, the Framers fully expected "to encourage the formation of a variety of opinions and tastes *of the right kind*" by the "*enlargement* of the *orbit*" of republican government and by federalism. Only moral obtuseness prevents contemporary social scientists from seeing that, since there do exist evil-doers with opinions and tastes *of the wrong kind* in whose hands no citizen's rights can be safe, there are moral and political limits to pluralism and tolerance. Consider: a society which protects "the rights" of cannibals (and there have been and are such societies) would be more diverse with respect to diet—at least for a while—than a society that represses cannibalism, but its individual members and its government would in fact be intolerant of civilization. Certainly the central government has the consti-

10. See "John Adams Wettergreen Replies," *Claremont Review of Books*, Vol. IV, No. 4 (Winter, 1985), 27-31 for the prevalence of this view in contemporary politics.

tutional power to encourage the healthy diversity which is natural to a large nation; by the same token, it has the power to discourage barbarism.

Although natural diversity best finds expression through American federalism, we can now see that the main constitutional purpose of federalism is not the discouragement of factions of the wrong kind, but the insulation of the central government from the influence of parochial interests. During the period of centralization of administration in which we now find ourselves, it is important to understand that many of the failures of the central government, whether in foreign or domestic policy, are due its failure to take advantage of this insulation.

Contributors

Larry Berman is Professor of Political Science at the University of California, Davis. He is the author of *Planning a Tragedy: The Americanization of the War in Vietnam* and *The New American Presidency*.

David Broyles is Associate Professor of Political Science at Wake Forest University. Among his numerous articles, his latest is "Southern and American Conservatism." He is currently working on a book on *The Federalist Papers*.

Anne M. Cohler is Lecturer in Continuing Education at the University of Chicago. She is the author of *Rousseau and Nationalism*. Her most recent works are a translation of Montesquieu's *The Spirit of the Laws* (forthcoming from Cambridge) and *Spirit and Moderation: Montesquieu and the Constitution* (forthcoming from Kansas).

Richard H. Cox is Professor of Political Science at the State University of New York at Buffalo. He has written articles on a variety of subjects ranging from Shakespeare to international relations. He is also the author of *Locke on War and Peace*.

Louis Fisher is a Specialist in American National Government for the Congressional Research Service of the Library of Congress. He is the author of *Constitutional Conflicts between Congress and the President*. His most recent work is *Constitutional Dialogues* (forthcoming in 1988).

James L. Gibson is Associate Professor of Political Science at the University of Houston. He is co-author of *Party Organizations and American Politics* and *Civil Liberties and Nazis: The Skokie Free-Speech Controversy*.

Lino A. Graglia is the Rex G. Baker and Edna Heflin Baker Professor in Constitutional Law at the University of Texas School of Law. He has extensive experience in the law profession in both practice and education. He is the author of *Disaster by Decree — The Supreme Court Decisions on Race and the Schools* and *The Supreme Court's Busing Decisions: A Study in Government by the Judiciary*.

Dennis Mahoney is Assistant Professor of Political Science at California State University, San Bernadino. He is co-editor of *The Constitution: A History of Its Framing and Ratification*, and a contributor to *Reflection and Choice, Essays on the Federalist*.

Jane Mansbridge is Associate Professor of Political Science at Northwestern University. She is the author of *Why We Lost the ERA* and *Beyond Adversary Democracy*.

John Marini is a special assistant to Clarence Thomas of the U.S. Equal Employment Opportunity Commission. He is the author of numerous articles on public administration. His most recent work (in progress) is *The Politics of Budget Control: President, Congress, and the Administrative Process*.

Ken Masugi is the former Director of the Bicentennial Project at the Claremont Insitute and currently a special assistant to Clarence Thomas of the U.S. Equal Employment Opportunity Commission. He is the author of numerous articles and is currently working on a book titled *Ethnicity and Politics*.

Gary L. McDowell is the Associate Director of the Office of Public Affairs of the U.S. Department of Justice. His most recent books are *Curbing the Courts: The Constitution and the Limits of Judicial Power* and *Friends of the Constitution: Writings of the Federalists, 1787-1788*.

Grant B. Mindle is Assistant Professor of Political Science at North Texas State University. He has published essays on Machiavelli, and is currently working on an article titled "Religion, Politics, and the Supreme Court's Definition of Religion."

Robert Scigliano is Professor of Political Science at Boston College. He is the author of *The Supreme Court and the Presidency* and *South Vietnam: Nation Under Stress*. His most recent work is *Citizenship*, co-authored with Harvey Mansfield, Jr.

Glen E. Thurow is Associate Professor of Politics at the University of Dallas. He is the author of *Abraham Lincoln and American Political Religion* and co-editor of *Rhetoric and American Statesmanship*. He is currently completing a book on the Supreme Court.

Sarah Baumgartner Thurow (editor) is the Associate Director of the University of Dallas Bicentennial Project, "Constitutionalism in America." She has written on Plato, Shakespeare, and contemporary political issues.

John Adams Wettergreen is Professor of Political Science at San Jose State University. He is the author of articles on subjects ranging from the bureaucracy to political philosophy. His most recent publication is an essay titled "Demography of 1984's National Majority," in *The Election of 1984*.

Michael Zuckert is the Dorothy and Edward Congden Professor of Political Science at Carleton College. He is the author of plays, book reviews and numerous articles in political science. The two books he is currently working on are *The Natural Law Tradition* and *Locke, Filmer, and the Struggle for Protestant Politics*.